A Curriculum of Agape

Stacy C. Johnson

A Curriculum of Agape

Reimagining Love in the Classroom

New York · Berlin · Bruxelles · Chennai · Lausanne · Oxford

Library of Congress Cataloging-in-Publication Data

Names: Johnson, Stacy C., author.
Title: A curriculum of agape : reimagining love in the classroom / Stacy C.
Johnson.
Description: New York : Peter Lang, 2024. | Includes bibliographical
references and index.
Identifiers: LCCN 2023041929 (print) | LCCN 2023041930 (ebook) |
ISBN 9781636673578 (paperback) | ISBN 9781636673592 (epub) |
ISBN 9781636673585 (pdf)
Subjects: LCSH: Teaching—Psychological aspects. | Teacher-student
relationships. | Motivation in education. | Social justice and
education. | Agape.
Classification: LCC LB1027 .J564 2024 (print) | LCC LB1027 (ebook) |
DDC 371.102/3—dc23/eng/20231012
LC record available at https://lccn.loc.gov/2023041929
LC ebook record available at https://lccn.loc.gov/2023041930
DOI 10.3726/b21317

Bibliographic information published by the Deutsche Nationalbibliothek.
The German National Library lists this publication in the German
National Bibliography; detailed bibliographic data is available
on the Internet at http://dnb.d-nb.de.

Cover design by Peter Lang Group AG

ISBN 9781636673578 (paperback)
ISBN 9781636673585 (ebook)
ISBN 9781636673592 (epub)
DOI 10.3726/b21317

© 2024 Peter Lang Group AG, Lausanne
Published by Peter Lang Publishing Inc., New York, USA
info@peterlang.com - www.peterlang.com

This publication has been peer reviewed.

This book is dedicated first to all *wakanyeja*—little sacred ones—
past, present and future. I am because you are. Finally, to my
ancestors—I see you! We are still here!
Some of the names have been changed to protect the privacy of
my students.

CONTENTS

Part III. Meet Them Where They Are

Part IV. Forgive and Forget

FOREWORD

These are troubling times in the history of school curriculum in the United States and around the world. As Apple reminded us, classroom curriculum does not exist within a socio-political vacuum.[1] It is always connected to the current socio-political climate of any given society. The murder of George Floyd by Minneapolis police officer, Derek Chauvin, in 2020 and most recently the beating to death of Tyre Nichols by Memphis police, sparked a renewed call for a deeper dialogue about issues of institutional inequities and oppression in the United States. Schools are one of the avenues to enable such a dialogue. In this volume, Stacy Johnson demonstrates various ways in which schools can help ameliorate these institutional inequities. The volume calls for dialogues through school curriculum. For many years, progressive scholars advocated for school curriculum that can bring increasing awareness of the troubling history of racial discrimination and the oppression of minoritized communities in the U.S. Yet, this effort also brought an increased opposition of classroom curriculum that is inclusive and critical to humanize all students.

Specifically, attempts by progressive curriculum scholars to introduce classroom textbooks that recognize and represent all identities, histories, including current social struggles, have been fiercely opposed by a segment of neo-conservative legislators, governors, and their constituencies. For instance,

Governor Ron DeSantis of Florida has outlawed the teaching of Critical Race Theory in classrooms; Governor, Sarah Huckabee of Arkansas, has outlawed the use of the *Latinx* identity in classroom curriculum. Brain Lopez reports that Texas (the state in which I live) has banned more books than any other state, specifically targeting those that represent the LGBTQ+ and Black and Brown communities.[2] For these neo-conservative critics, a curriculum that represents all different groups is indoctrination. What is even more troubling is not simply the banning of inclusive curriculum textbooks, but the denial to acknowledge the long overdue curriculum of love, which Stacy Johnson eloquently discusses in this volume.

A Curriculum of Agape: Reimaging Love in the Classroom couldn't have appeared at better time when our classroom curriculum is overly focused on standards and testing. The notions of love as curriculum that are discussed in this volume represent ideas beyond standards and testing and beyond the traditional Eurocentric curriculum that the gatekeepers fight to retain. This volume makes a renewed call for equity, diversity, and inclusion in classroom curriculum. The book is a critical attempt to remind teachers and those involved in our public schools to actively humanize all students, and, much more importantly, to include their identities in the curriculum.

In many ways, *A Curriculum of Agape* reinforces the call for inclusive curriculum and teaching for the common good. Curriculum for the common good, as I have argued elsewhere, promotes democratic goals and seeks to empower all citizens who participate in it.[3] Teaching for the common good is exemplified by dedicated teachers who provide students with learning experiences that promote a democratic way of life.[4] Similarly, Stacy Johnson's volume has demonstrated beyond a doubt that teachers who are afforded a space to teach curriculum characterized by love can in fact teach for the common good. In such a curriculum, there is a great potential for all diverse students to learn about their communities, the roles they play in their communities, and to think about ways in which they could engage with one another for the purpose of communal growth, which fosters co-existence with others.

This volume must be read by all teachers and education stakeholders who are committed to transforming our curriculum. It offers critical and potential solutions for humanizing curriculum so that all students in classrooms will be valued and respected as human beings. The volume helps the reader understand the significance of curriculum that is not devoid of love. It is also a vivid reminder of the struggles faced by minoritized communities who have been otherized by our social institutions, as we have witnessed in the banning of books that represent all students' identities in the curriculum, including the teaching of truth about the history of inequities. One of the important questions this volume pushes the reader to wrestle with is: How can we incorporate and use critical curriculum, a loving curriculum, to rethink the notions of equity and diversity in US classrooms? I believe the reader will agree with me that this volume brings a glimmer of hope as curriculum must take a leadership role in building stronger, democratic communities.

Bekisizwe S. Ndimande
The University of Texas San Antonio

Notes

1 Apple, M. W. (2004). *Ideology and curriculum* (3rd ed.). New York: RoutledgeFalmer.
2 Lopez, B. (September, 19, 2022). Texas has banned more books than any other state, new report shows. Texastrubnue.org, https://www.texastribune.org/2022/09/19/texas-book-bans/ accessed January 28, 2023.
3 Ndimande, B. S. (2018). The struggles against Fundamental Pedagogics in South Africa: Toward the pedagogy of common good. In N. Hobbel & B. Bales (Eds.), *Navigating the common good in teacher education policy: Critical and international perspectives* (pp. 128–145). New York: Routledge.
4 Apple, M. W., & Beane, J. (2007). *Democratic schools* (2nd ed.). Alexandra, VA: Association for Supervision and Curriculum Development.

   Johnston-Parsons, M., Wilson, M., & The Teachers at Park Street Elementary (2007). *Success stories from failing school: Teachers living under the shadow of NCLB.* Charlotte, NC: Information Age.

   Westheimer, J. (2015). *What kind of a citizen: Educating our children for the common good.* New York: Teachers College.

PREFACE

"... [I]f they can learn to hate, they can be taught to love, for love comes more naturally to the human heart than its opposite." (Nelson Mandela, *Long Walk to Freedom*)

Reportedly, among Buddha's final words to society was the charge to be our own light—to use our intelligence and life experiences to awaken to truth and mediate our path.[1] How is it that a society which professes to value academic preparation also under-prepares, under-resources, and under-pays its primary assets—educators? The depth of disrespect for the role of education and educators is captured in the long standing phrase, popularized by George Bernard Shaw in his 1903 play, *Man and Superman*, "Those who can, do; those who can't, teach."[2] Educators are the load bearing beams of society, more appropriately characterized by Aristotle: "Those who know, do. Those that understand, teach." The COVID-19 pandemic has brought an already stretched U.S. educational infrastructure to its knees and has provided an unavoidable moment of critical reflection, encouraging us all to reimagine our understanding of today's student and our social persistence on lovelessness as it impacts the role of education and educators.

This trauma upon the American educational system is further complicated by political jockeying, laying bare the caste system that has traditionally abandoned Black, brown and impoverished students to marginalization through inequitable academic preparation. Our current condition, as several U.S. states are on the precipice of outlawing antiracist, anticolonial classroom dialogues within public spaces, is an autobiographical one in which the future of education hangs in the balance of a historical curricular identity of censorship that remains prevalent on both the sociopolitical left and the right.[3] Race is censored, spiritual identity is separated, critical thought is excised, culture is canceled, and love is circumvented. In this darkness we grope for effectual resolutions to poor learning outcomes for marginalized student populations through novel approaches—Culturally Responsive Pedagogy, Multicultural Education, Growth Mindset, Social Emotional Learning (SEL)—avoiding one key dialogue that ought to enlighten them all, reimagining a curriculum that is centered in love—unconditional love.[4]

The word *agape* is the Greek description of unconditional love—a love that is purely altruistic in nature and is often associated with Christianity's view of God and the goal for which our human nature strives. I endeavor to share a theoretical and practical self-reflection upon my experiences employing a curriculum of agape over my near 30 year teaching career. My intention is to lend an understanding of the salience of love in the classroom, particularly as it pertains to critical pedagogies and the drive to humanize both curriculum and pedagogy through the disruption of exclusively colonial and imperialistic western onto-epistemologies in U.S. education.[5] With ontology referring to ways of being or becoming and epistemology meaning how one knows or builds knowledge, the aim of this book is to assist the pre-service or in-service educator in shaping an engaging and motivational instructional design that appropriately meets the inherent ontological and epistemological needs of a diverse student body.

Teaching is a sacrifice and, in my opinion, an arduous one that is worth every moment. I am honored to say that I have had a remarkable career, having received in love and personal maturity many times over what I feel I gave. My largest concern as I have moved into teacher education is that my practice of agape education—an umbrella term describing my approach to an instructional design that is rooted in what I call *a curriculum of agape*—was an accidental one. It evolved over the years and, unfortunately, was born not out of my pre-service education, but out of my personal trauma as a young student. The problem is that many teacher preparation programs provide an imbalanced emphasis on theory and academic work, over practice.[6] Once in the field, it is not unusual for teachers to find themselves isolated, simply surviving the year on instinct more than proficiency. My colleagues and students share a familiar frustration over the want to engage in effective and transformative pedagogies that meet the diverse needs of their students while lacking the mentorship and exercise that converts theory to understanding and action.[7]

In 2018, I conducted a small unpublished study in which I surveyed a graduate class of in-service and pre-service teachers regarding their sense of readiness to apply the transformative pedagogies they were learning in their programs; eight of these students were the subjects of a semester long case study to determine the same.[8] Of the 18 students who chose to respond to the survey, only five were confident in their preparedness to apply what they had learned. The eight case study participants unanimously voiced concerns about understanding, accepting, and affirming the need to apply their knowledge in their own practice while not feeling confident to do so. In every case, the participants desired opportunities to practice their skills before experimenting on their students in their classrooms. To illustrate this sentiment, one participant said, "I understand the theory, but I still do not know how to go about it." Another expanded upon this concern, " I need to see it and experience it applied in a relevant way . . . Without the application arm . . ., I'm not likely to apply [it] quickly."

To simply theorize unconditional love in the classroom would be to perpetuate an already existing frustration that leaves educators with a practical hesitancy while they struggle over the question of "how?" In a social climate of narcissistic divisiveness and rudeness, where we kill on screen for entertainment and in real-time out of mental exhaustion and a lack of regard for life, justice requires that we establish in one another an actionable guide to developing empathy and mutual respect that reconnects us all.[9] Home is, of course, the central ecological space where unconditional love ought to develop, but, considering that a school age child spends more time in a classroom than he or she does at home, teachers are not simply disseminators of all things academic; they are also the next closest line of defense for shaping the heart of an American citizen. The 21st century U. S. educational system is suffering from an existential crisis that ought not lean on accidental pedagogical or curricular revelations but rather consider a deliberate instruction towards unconditional love—inclusive of staff members, parents, and children—to hasten the positive changes in teacher retention and student learning outcomes to which the field of education aspires.[10] It is in this spirit that I theorize unconditional love while situating that theory in research and storytelling to give educators an opportunity that they seldom have—real-time examples of implementation intended to bridge the gap between concept and execution.

Before I begin this curricular journey, it is essential to stay rooted in the notion of agape love as I identify myself and the various groups of students in this theoretical and practical discussion. Essentialism—the assumption that biological or cultural traits are universally applicable to a group—can be a dangerous trap as educators and scholars seek to know and understand people.[11] The following referents such as Native American, African American, Latino(a), Black, Muslim, Christian, Western, Non-Western, and the like, are carefully applied in this book, acknowledging the diversity of expression and experience that makes up the intersectional identities of individuals within cultural communities.[12] The singlemindedness with which we often attempt to understand ideologies like Western versus non-Western, rarely exists.[13] Instead, individuals and groups often experience a convergence of multiple understandings that define them at any one moment in time.[14] I honor this bouquet of multiple identities, even as I theorize or apply broad racial-ethnic-cultural or religious terminology; Native Americans, Africans, Latinos, etc., are not one people but many distinct nations; members of religious groups are often diverse in individual beliefs and practices. I am simultaneously Western and Non-Western in knowing and being because my ancestral onto-epistemes have been imparted amid a Eurocentric acculturation.[15] Agape love does not support the imposition of one's own assumptions upon others, so wherever I use group terminology, I attempt to do so in keeping with the way members of that group have identified themselves to me, either in scholarly writing or in person. Although I recognize that sometimes a distinction might be preferable between the identifiers Black and African American, I use them interchangeably, not intending to cause offense but to express what I know through who I am as a historical and current member of the Black community.[16]

Notes

1 Grubin, D. (2010). *Death & legacy, part 2 | The Buddha.* PBS. Retrieved October 27, 2023, from https://www.youtube.com/watch?v=XW_JmF7OF-Y.

2 Shaw, B. (1922). *Man and superman: A comedy and a philosophy.* Brentano's.

3 Dutton, J. (2021, June 11). Critical race theory is banned in these states. Newsweek. Retrieved January 12, 2022, from https://www.newsweek.com/critical-race-theory-banned-these-states-1599712.

Zou, I. (2021). *Texas Senate bill seeks to strip required lessons on people of color and women from "Critical race theory" law*. The Texas Tribune. Retrieved November 11, 2021, from https://www.texastribune.org/2021/07/09/texas-critical-race-theory-schools-legislation/.

4 Au, W. (2017). When multicultural education is not enough. *Multicultural Perspectives, 19*(3), 147–150. https://doi.org/10.1080/15210960.2017.1331741.

Gay, G. (2018). *Culturally responsive teaching: Theory, research, and practice*. Teachers College Press.

Ladson-Billings, G. (2014). Culturally relevant pedagogy 2.0: aka the remix. *Harvard Educational Review, 84*(1), 74–84.

Weissberg, R. P., Durlak, J. A., Domitrovich, C. E., & Gullotta, T. P. (2015). Social and emotional learning: Past, present, and future. In J. A. Durlak, C. E. Domitrovich, R. P. Weissberg, & T. P. Gullotta (Eds.), *Handbook of social and emotional learning: Research and practice* (pp. 3–19). The Guilford Press.

Yeager, D. S., & Dweck, C. S. (2020). What can be learned from growth mindset controversies?. *American Psychologist, 75*(9), 1269.

5 Baker, M. (2012). Modernity/coloniality and Eurocentric education: Towards a post-Occidental self-understanding of the present. *Policy Futures in Education, 10*(1), 4–22. https://doi.org/10.2304/pfie.2012.10.1.4.

6 Clark, C. (2002). Effective multicultural curriculum transformation accross disciplines. *Multicultural Perspectives, 4*(3), 37–46.

7 Ibid.

8 This mixed-methods study analyzed data collected from surveys, ethnographic field notes as I observed the students' responses to the course content, and interviews of the eight graduate students who were not yet certified teachers.

9 Cox, J. W., & Rich, S. (2022, January 2). *'please help me': Kids with guns fueled a record number of school shootings in 2021*. The Washington Post. Retrieved January 5, 2022, from https://www.washingtonpost.com/dc-md-va/2021/12/31/2021-school-shootings-record/?campaign_id=9&emc=edit_nn_20220104&instance_id=49344&nl=the-morning%C2%AEi_id=86340798&segment_id=78602&te=1&user_id=d88a92611aab0bb98a785ee5af35f796.

Fromm, E. (2000). *The art of loving: The centennial edition*. A&C Black.

Pinar, W. (2004). *What is curriculum theory?*. Routledge.

10 Dove, M. K. (2004). Teacher attrition: A critical American and International education issue. *Delta Kappa Gamma Bulletin, 71*(1).

Edelman, M. W. (2009). The cradle to prison pipeline: America's new apartheid. *Harvard Journal of African American Public Policy, 15*(Summer Issue), 67–68.

Ladson-Billings, G. (2006). From the achievement gap to the education debt: Understanding achievement in U.S. schools. *Educational Researcher, 35*(7), 3–12.

Logan, J., & Burdick-Will, J. (2016). School segregation, charter schools, and access to quality education. *Journal of Urban Affairs, 38*(3), 323–343. https://doi.org/10.1111/juaf.12246.

Miron, G., & Applegate, B. (2007). *Teacher attrition in charter schools*. East Lansing, MI: Great Lakes Center for Education Research and Practice.

Op. Cit., Pinar (2004).

Sass, D. A., Flores, B. B., Claeys, L., & Pérez, B. (2012). Identifying personal and contextual factors that contribute to attrition rates for Texas public school teachers. *Education Policy Analysis Archives/Archivos Analíticos de Políticas Educativas, 20,* 1–26.

11 Hall, S. (2018). *Essential essays, volume 1: Foundations of cultural studies.* Duke University Press.

Malott, C. (2007). *A call to action: An introduction to education, philosophy, and Native North America* (Vol. 324). Peter Lang.

May, S., & Sleeter, C. E. (2010). *Critical multiculturalism: Theory and praxis.* Routledge.

12 Ibid.

13 Op. Cit., Malott (2007).

14 Arredondo, P., Gallardo-Cooper, M., Delgado-Romero, E. A., & Zapata, A. L. (2015). Latino worldviews and cultural values. *Culturally Responsive Counseling with Latinas/os, 15*–30.

Op. Cit., Hall (2018).

Op. Cit., Malott (2008).

Op. Cit., May & Sleeter (2010).

Montero-Sieburth, M., & Villaruel, F. (2003). *Making invisible Latino adolescents visible: A critical approach to Latino diversity.* Routledge.

15 Op. Cit., Hall (2018).

Op. Cit., Malott (2007).

Op. Cit., May & Sleeter (2010).

16 Adams, C. (2020). *Not all black people are African American: Here's the difference.* CBS News. Retrieved November 11, 2021, from https://www.cbsnews.com/news/not-all-black-people-are-african-american-what-is-the-difference/.

ACKNOWLEDGMENTS

I would like to thank my students for their impact on my growth as an educator as well as a human being. I would also like to thank my administrators and co-workers who have entrusted me with the education and welfare of many classes of children and young adults. It was your confidence in me that gave me the opportunity to expand my knowledge and practice to meet the diverse needs of our students. To Lauren Dones, who reminded me that a fresh pair of eyes, although new, are full of insight. To my husband and my sons, you are my center of gravity and my constant source of inspiration. Finally, I thank my mother, Marilyn Fountain, who has patiently encouraged me and shaped me as a writer, bringing my knowledge and experience into written form.

INTRODUCTION-HOW I ARRIVED AT AGAPE

"In educating the minds of our youth we must not forget to educate their hearts."
(Dalai Lama)

I believe that teaching, particularly at the primary through secondary levels, is a profession that one enters by way of a calling. It is not for the faint of heart. Teaching is an innate craft, an art form, that seeks expression. It may find its beckoning within the DNA, but only finds its fullness after years of skill-building, self-reflection, collaboration, mentorship, and practice. The profession itself may draw a person into the field of teaching, yet it is the calling that will keep him or her there.

Except for my childhood ventures into make-believe which I imposed on my siblings and all of my stuffed animals, forcing them to be the students in my imaginary school, I never gave a thought to becoming a teacher. What's more, I remember only two separate occasions when it was recommended that I consider teaching. "You would make a wonderful teacher," Mrs. Haas, my freshman high school English teacher, told me after I delivered a required presentation. The other poor soul who made a similar observation was my mother. I say "poor soul" because my indignant reaction would have made one think that each had insulted my intelligence. I saw no money or prestige in the art or craft of teaching, so their suggestions were more reflective of an insult in my mind instead of the compliment they were intended to be. I was going to become an electrical engineer with an MBA like my dad and make "big money", or so I thought.

I entered The University of Pittsburgh (Pitt) as an electrical engineering student and, after three years and an internship with General Electric Aerospace—Re-entry Division, I realized I did not enjoy what I was doing. I turned my attentions to Pitt's undergraduate business program and continued my education as a dual major. The undergraduate business program was run by the Graduate School of Business which only required enough courses to be completed in two years. Any undergraduate student had to choose a second major to amass the credits needed to graduate with a four-year bachelor's degree. With the requirement to declare a dual major in college, second to business, I chose Spanish Language and Culture.

In high school, I loved Spanish as much as I had learned to love math and science. It was as if the language had always belonged to me; I just needed the exposure to unlock my natural affinity for linguistics. My Spanish teachers in general were warm and engaging; one, Sandy Betegh, was colorful beyond words. There wasn't a student of high school Spanish who did not want to be in her class to enjoy the loud, energetic family that was Señora Betegh's pedagogical sanctuary. Her classroom was packed with adoring students whether class was in session or not.

Unfortunately, I had to enjoy Señora Betegh only vicariously through the noise and laughter pouring into the hallway. The Spanish Department had to start skipping levels for me. Between my Puerto Rican and Costa Rican friends and my formal world language classes, I was learning so fast and with such ease that the lower level courses were becoming pointless. I skipped right over Sandy Betegh's course, yet still, she knew me enough to yell my name out in the hallway—"Hola, Fountain!"—and the impact of who she was remained with me. The choice to major in Spanish Language and Culture wasn't a great departure from my plan to become a wealthy business mogul. With the change in my major, I also transferred my internship from General Electric to CIGNA Corporation and set my sights on the Worldwide Division in Madrid, Spain. I had every intention of pursuing this course, but I still felt stifled—I was not happy.

Three months away from graduation, I received a request from the Black Action Society at the University of Pittsburgh to tutor inner city high school students who were struggling with math. My life was abruptly and forever altered by my work with those high school students. For the first time, I experienced a deep and overwhelming sense of purpose and joy. It was life-giving to co-labor with the students who initially sat deflated before me, too uncomfortable to make eye contact with me, because they very quickly found confidence in their success and ended our brief relationship looking directly at me, smiling. I had found my reason for being—I was a teacher after all and, thus, immediately applied to my university's Master of Arts in Teaching (MAT) program. I suppose I owed Mrs. Haas and my mother a very humble apology for being so short sighted.

The Apprenticeship of Observation explains the concept of the teacher candidate who infuses his or her own internal biases around what it means to be a teacher into the content of the teacher preparation program.[1] As teachers, we are highly influenced by our experiences as students, something that is unique about the field of teaching.[2] It's an unusual career path that allows us to apprentice by observation for 17 years before we become practitioners. Equally, educators are members of the greater society and are not immune to the effects of the American ecosystem in which they live. Sociocultural biases can remain hidden under the surface of our American being and contribute to what Brown calls a dysconsciousness in which limited and distorted understandings about inequity and cultural diversity make it difficult for teachers to act in favor of equitable education.[3]

> Pre-service and in-service teachers are generally unconscious to the racist ideologies that have founded and permeated every aspect of American culture, to include the school system, and the ways in which it has been used to inform how [marginalized groups of] students are understood and treated in schools on a daily basis.[4]

My Apprenticeship of Observation that lived under the surface of my pedagogical practice, quickly evolved into a pursuit of agape education—an instructional design that is situated in a curriculum of unconditional love.

My education, therefore my Apprenticeship of Observation, occurred within multiple contexts—public, private, and suburban. The funding and physical locations varied, but I was consistently educated by White teachers whose curricular and pedagogical practice was shaped often by geographies of privilege—spatial boarders drawn by wealth that are supportive of racist and sexist, albeit partially dysconcious, points of view.[5] I enjoyed the advantage of racially, ethnically, and culturally diverse classmates only until I was moved to wealthier schools and advanced courses.

My Apprenticeship of Observation was distorted by White classmates whom I could never date or know as true friends, lest they endure the scorn of their families, and for whom belittling Black people was endemic, despite my presence. "Oh no, Stacy, we're not talking about you. You're different." Those glossy words that were meant to elevate me to some false status of acceptability were nothing more than microaggressions, separating me from my own identity. If I wasn't Black, if I truly was "different," then what did that leave me with? I certainly wasn't White, so basically I was reduced to "nothing." I felt that I belonged to no one. I was further challenged by teaching staff who could not see past their low expectations of women or Black and brown students to the point that they worked tirelessly to dissuade me from specific academic programs.[6]

In middle school, all students were required to take cooking, sewing, fine arts, metal shop and wood shop. The wood shop and metal shop teachers were close colleagues and shared the doorway between the two classrooms. My wood shop teacher embodied the type of toxic masculinity that has enriched academic scholarship as much as Hollywood. He wore a crew cut as if recently retired from the Marines and, up until then, I never understood the origins of the term "red-neck." His skin was quite red underneath, indeed. Our introduction to the shop course was a monologue of rules, regulations, course expectations and a strong exercise in demeaning female participation. "Girls! Make sure your POOONYTAILS don't get caught in the lathe!" "Girls, we don't want you to break a NAIL in the machines."

The loathsome demoralization with which our teacher regarded a female's capacity to accomplish the tasks of shop class was contrary to my home life—I stuck my hands in any construction projects that brought my male relatives together. I was rarely turned away except when there was a concern my personal safety. I made it my business to become the walking, breathing counter narrative to my shop teacher's prejudice and handled those machines until I won his favor—For my final project, I made a shelving system that put his misogynistic imaginations to shame. By the time I had to rotate to metal shop, I was a welcomed guest and the source of a paradigm shift on behalf of the "girls." However, my apparent success story did not mean that I felt good about being a female or had gained an equitable sense of belonging in the world.

My guidance counselor at Lower Merion High School, a majority White wealthy school outside of Philadelphia, Pennsylvania, attempted to prevent me from both enrolling in honors classes and from graduating early to attend Pitt. His rationale was that the students who attended those classes were accustomed to a level of rigor that I might not survive.[7] He was determined enough to prevent me from committing academic suicide that he sought the help of an English teacher. Between the two of them, I was convinced of certain doom, but my mother was not as easily swayed, and I was enrolled in the honors course. As it turns out, the sophomore English course was the least rigorous course of my high school career. When it became clear by the end of my junior year that I was culturally suffocating in my high school, I wanted to leave by early admittance to The University of Pittsburgh's School of Engineering. The same guidance counselor in his exasperation cautioned my mother, "We have had only three students ever to leave this early and they did not do well, and they were White. To be frank, I don't know any Black people who are electrical engineers." His observation was myopic and irrelevant to my personal experience since my own father was a highly successful electrical engineer.

The shameful displays of racial bias and oppression between my guidance counselor and my English teacher were matched only by the silence at my high school commencement when my accomplishment, the only student in the history of the school to successfully complete the requirements of early admittance—a successful freshman year in college—went ignored. They did, however, honor a White student who recovered from a broken arm and was able to return to her participation as a flautist in the orchestra.

By this point in my life, the racism I endured within educational spaces had skewed my sense of belonging and who I was in my identity—a Black female; one with European American, African American, Native American, and Cuban ancestry. My ability to cope in my educational places and spaces was by no means a manifestation of freedom.[8] Regardless of the outcomes of these stories or the love and encouragement showered upon me by my inner circle of relatives and close friends, my experiences left me questioning whether I was truly intelligent or acceptable in society.

I was a tortured human being, suffering through what is termed, *cognitive dissonance*—a persistent internal conflict resulting from systemic ecological inconsistencies of normative beliefs, expectations, and experiences.[9] I was overwhelmed by doubt, amassed through experiences dispelling distortions, myths, and misperceptions that invalidated who I was, often at the hand of educators and my own peers.[10] Finding myself caught between races and genders, attempting to navigate the double consciousness that W.E.B. DuBois spoke of, these experiences only reified my subordinated status and the expectation that I would have to fight for a modicum of physical, emotional, and intellectual legitimacy beyond a marginalized stereotype or corporate affirmative action statistic.[11]

When I entered college, I was seventeen years old and worn down by the racial tension in my high school. I was accustomed to a learning space in which

I must maintain a constant juggling act. As in the poem, *We Wear the Mask*, by Paul Lawrence Dunbar that inspired Maya Angelou's own stirring and similarly titled rendition, I wore many masks designed to appeal to my peers, my teachers, and myself. My college instructors, both undergraduate and graduate, were still predominantly White, but I was once again exposed to Spanish instructors who made me feel like I was among family.

Rosario Camineras, a professor of Cuban descent in the Spanish department, taught Latin American and Spanish history. I disliked history, but I adored her. Like Sandy Betegh, she was engaging, personal, loud, and exciting. Her door had to remain closed when she taught if other professors hoped to teach a class on the same floor. Another professor, whose name escapes me, was also Cuban and, although his personality was like a gentle breeze, he exuded an effusive warmth and familiarity that was consistent with my home life—my cultural capital—and my experiences with Señora Betegh and Dr. Camineras. He called me, "Nena" or "Cariña," which in English means "baby" or "my love." Until this professor, I had only experienced one teacher who addressed me in such loving terms—my middle school math teacher, Allan Koch. He was not sexist or predatory in his familiarity; like Mr. Koch and Dr. Camineras, he was a warm demander whose cultural competence in many ways aligned with my own and provided me a sense of safety, value, and self-determination.[12] It was my university professors who were the first to introduce the concept of racism and social justice into my learning.

When I was in college, Critical Theory and its social justice lens, through which we now interrogate relations of power and privilege within curricular and pedagogical practice, was not a mainstreamed part of the academic discourse in teacher preparation courses.[13] My instructors taught from a positionality of well-established best practices that few would have challenged as racially, ethnically, or culturally biased. Fortunately, the proficiency movement was in full swing in the late 80s, which meant a close adherence to the American Council on the Teaching of Foreign Languages (ACTFL) standards of communicative ability.[14] My Foreign Language teacher preparation courses led me to a profound understanding of the beneficial impact on cognition when students could make meaningful connections between curriculum and the personal utility of language.[15] The reciprocal relationship between language and culture also required students to embrace the nuances of one in order to successfully understand the other.[16]

It was in this dynamic, culturally exploratory space that a synergy emerged between the ideas of cognition, meaning making, and my Apprenticeship of

Observation. This space was my precursor to a critical consciousness and the necessity to embrace the curricular and pedagogical inclusion of what we now call a student's cultural capital.[17] I viewed my life experiences as a student to be a pool from which I drew my pedagogy and, in many ways, my curriculum. Mine was an environment of high expectations, creativity, interconnectedness, empathy, courage, and resiliency. When asked to teach math, English or even study skills, my evolving pedagogy still applied. It was my explicit intention to never leave my students to endure in silence the same miseries I had suffered. My personal and professional mission was to imbue a sense of value, agency, and self-determination into the learning space and not to abandon a student to voicelessness or discomfort. From this standpoint, I began to consider the loveless environment that is often the American classroom, and the antithetical way in which it disrupts the very learning theories upon which pre-service and in-service teacher training is based.

Social Learning Theory, Social Constructivism Theory, Situated Learning Theory, and Ecological Systems Theory all acknowledge the connection between a healthy social environment and proper cognition and are foundational theories upon which we learn to teach.[18] John Dewey, probably the most closely studied learning theorist, espoused learning to be socially motivated, necessitating the centering of children, not the curriculum, in teaching and learning goals.[19] In this social ecosystem we call school, be it a K-12 or adult space, my instinct to induce a sense of safety and cognitive freedom was to embody the familial pedagogy of Mr. Koch and my Spanish teachers. In my own classrooms, we have been a family of diverse identities dedicated to moving through our learning environment as one supportive, empowering and interdependent body.[20] Allan Koch, Sandy Betegh, and my two Cuban professors inadvertently gave me permission to reconsider curriculum and pedagogy as emancipatory in nature and experience—making authentic meaningful connections between the classroom and society—both as a source of love that did not sacrifice professionalism.[21]

Curriculum is any body of knowledge that frames our understanding of ourselves in relationship to the world and its many phenomena. It is a complicated, symbolic exchange that is socially constructed and deeply subjective through which "reality is produced, maintained, repaired, and transformed."[22] Curriculum is not simply a thing but it is also an action. It is a social practice that answers William Pinar's question regarding what knowledge is valued and is of most worth, and for whom it is most beneficial.[23] Curriculum includes all processes through which students acquire knowledge and skills and are assessed to determine success in learning.[24] It is both explicit and implicit, often hiding in the shadows of subconscious cognition, shaping our thinking, our being, and our value system—for good or for bad.[25] Pedagogy is the vehicle through which curriculum is actuated and supported. Pedagogy is "[a]ny interaction between the teacher and the student that is meant to facilitate learning: the philosophy of teaching, the methods used to instruct, the physical and relational environment in which instruction takes place or is supported."[26]

Today, the first concept my students explore in any course is that of unconditional love. It is the foundational knowledge that undergirds our class rules, policies, and procedures and becomes our learning culture. Unconditional love is part of my pedagogy, but it is also an explicit and implicit curriculum that is actionable and measurable. It is a socially constructed exchange between my students and myself that shapes our thinking, our being, and our value system within the community that is my classroom—a transformative reality of altruistic love that, together, we produce, maintain and repair as needed.

I want my students to know they can rely on me to be patient with them socially, emotionally and cognitively, never losing hope for their success. I want to create an intentional culture of kindness, centered in humility. I want to put them first, and deliberately forgive them their shortcomings, as I hope they will forgive mine. It is paramount that they can depend on me to support them, encourage them, trust and protect them, as I work to encourage them to exercise an in-kind response with one another. It never has seemed to matter whether these tenets emanated from 1 Corinthians 13 of the Christian Bible, Ubuntu, Buddhism, or Native American philosophies—no one has asked about their origins in all my years of teaching. The priority has been to experience a demonstratively safe classroom where the students' identities are welcomed, celebrated and cultivated as an integral part of the knowledge that we construct and enjoy.

My teaching career has included suburban, rural, and urban populations of students across several states, from kindergarten to adult education within public, private, and charter schools. I have had the privilege of teaching students from diverse backgrounds, and the joy of being invited to know who they are in their private, cultural spaces. The evolution of my classroom, influenced by my Apprenticeship of Observation, has been one of openness and vulnerability, of thinking and being, one in which I have found myself growing exponentially alongside my students. With each year, I have become more self-reflective, more attuned to global issues of social justice and the need for my students to share a safe space for their own self-reflection.[27]

Equally, I have found a deeper understanding of the importance of love as curriculum and how that love contributes to cognition and a culture of justice, humanity, and democracy. When I speak of democracy, I am referring to a society that rests on the ideals of community, the sovereignty of the people, particularly in political participation, and equality of all citizens under the law such that social, political, economic and environmental justice prevails.[28] To quote Dr. Cornel West, "Justice is what love looks like in public," most specifically in public education. Within this curriculum of agape, all students find justice—an equitable place of belonging, encouragement and engagement in which they can grow alongside their teachers academically and socially as citizens of America and as human beings.

Explore, Think, Act

The Introduction explored the idea of an Apprenticeship of Observation and the way that it affected my understanding of the role of an educator as well as my approach to pedagogy through a curriculum of agape. Take a moment to explore your own Apprenticeship of Observation.

(A) Think about your experiences as a primary and secondary student.
1. What did you learn about who you are?
2. Were you able to see yourself, your gender, race, ethnicity, etc., in the curriculum? Was that representation positive? How did your curriculum make you feel about yourself?
3. What did you learn about who you are as an American? Did your school preparation make you feel like you had an equal voice in determining the social, political or economic future of America?
4. Did your academic preparation cause you to feel socially, intellectually and spiritually valuable?
5. What knowledge was most valuable according to your primary and secondary preparation?
6. In what ways did you feel that this knowledge was (not) meant to benefit you?
7. Did you feel unconditionally loved by your teachers, administrators, and support staff?
8. What did you learn, through your own experience as a student, is the role of a teacher? What about the role of a student?

(B) Now, answer these same questions as they pertain to your undergraduate and graduate preparation.

1. How do you think your Apprenticeship of Observation (answers to the preceding questions) has informed or shaped who you are in your relationship with your students and the content to which you choose to expose your students?

Notes

1 Boyd, A., Gorham, J. J., Justice, J. E., & Anderson, J. L. (2013). Examining the apprenticeship of observation with preservice teachers: The practice of blogging to facilitate autobiographical reflection and critique. *Teacher Education Quarterly, 40*(3), 27–49.

2 Ibid.

3 Brown, K. D. (2013). Trouble on my mind: Toward a framework of humanizing critical sociocultural knowledge for teaching and teacher education. *Race Ethnicity and Education, 16*(3), 316–338.

4 Johnson, S.C. (2019). U.S. education and the persistence of slavery. *Journal of Curriculum and Pedagogy*, 1–20. https://doi.org/10.1080/15505170.2019.1618757.

5 Op. Cit., Brown (2013).
   Helfenbein, R. J. (2021). *Critical geographies of education: Space, place, and curriculum inquiry*. Routledge.
   King, J. E. (1991). Dysconscious racism: Ideology, identity, and the miseducation of teachers. *The Journal of Negro Education, 60*(2), 133–146. https://doi.org/10.2307/2295605.

6 Ibid.

7 Delpit, L. (2013). *"Multiplication Is for White people": Raising expectations for other people's children*. New York, USA: The New Press.
   Op. Cit., Helfenbein (2021).
   Op. Cit., Johnson (2019).
   Taylor, K. B., & Reynolds, D. J. (2019). Dissonance. In rethinking college student development theory using critical frameworks. *Journal of College and Character, 21*(3), 234–236.

8 Op. Cit., Helfenbein (2021).
   Op. Cit., Taylor & Reynolds (2019).

9 Op. Cit., Taylor & Reynolds (2019).

10 Ibid.

11 Du Bois, W. E. B. (2009). *Souls of Black folk*: MobileReference.com.
    Ibid.

12 Kleinfeld, J. (1975). Effective teachers of Eskimo and Indian students. *The School Review, 83*(2), 301–344.

13 Brayboy. (2005). Toward a tribal critical race theory in education. *The Urban Review, 37*(5), 425–446. https://doi.org/10.1007/s11256-005-0018-y.
    Op. Cit., Helfenbein (2021).
    Op. Cit., Taylor & Reynolds (2019).

14 Liskin-Gasparro, J. E. (1984). *The ACTFL proficiency guidelines: A historical perspective*.

15 Stainton, R. J. (1998). Quantifier phrases, meaningfulness "in isolation", and ellipsis. *Linguistics and Philosophy*, 311–340.

  Stephens, J. M., Rubie-Davies, C. M., & Watson, P. (2015). The role of meaning systems in the development of motivation. In *Routledge international handbook of social psychology of the classroom* (pp. 95–108). Routledge.

16 Op. Cit., Liskin-Gasparro (1984).

17 Hammond, Z. (2014). *Culturally responsive teaching and the brain: Promoting authentic engagement and rigor among culturally and linguistically diverse students.* Corwin Press.

  Smith-Maddox, R. (1999). The social networks and resources of African American eighth graders: Evidence from the National Education Longitudinal Study of 1988. *Adolescence, 34*(133), 169–170.

18 Belgrave, F. Z., & Brevard, J. K. (2015). *African American boys: identity, culture, and development* (2015 ed.). New York, NY: Springer.

  Guy-Evans, O. (2020). *Bronfenbrenner's ecological systems theory.* Bronfenbrenner's Ecological Systems Theory | Simply Psychology. Retrieved November 10, 2021, from https://www.simplypsychology.org/Bronfenbrenner.html.

  Lave, J., & Wenger, E. (1991). *Situated learning: Legitimate peripheral participation.* Cambridge, UK: Cambridge University Press. Reading Chapters 1 and 2.

  Mcleod, S. (2016). *Albert Bandura's social learning theory.* Albert Bandura's Social Learning Theory | Simply Psychology. Retrieved November 10, 2021, from https://www.simplypsychology.org/bandura.html.

  Vygotsky, L. (1997). Interaction between learning and development. In N. Gauvain & M. Cole (Eds.), *Readings on the development of children* (pp. 29–36). New York, NY: W.H. Freeman and Company.

  Vygotsky, L. S., & Cole, M. (1978). *Mind in society: The development of higher psychological processes.* Cambridge: Harvard University Press.

19 Flinders, D., & Thornton, S. (2013). *The curriculum studies reader* (4th ed.). New York: Routledge.

  Public Broadcasting Service. (n.d.). *PBS online: Only a teacher: Schoolhouse pioneers.* PBS. Retrieved November 10, 2021, from https://www.pbs.org/onlyateacher/john.html.

20 Arredondo, P., Gallardo-Cooper, M., Delgado-Romero, E. A., & Zapata, A. L. (2015). Latino worldviews and cultural values. *Culturally Responsive Counseling with Latinas/os*, 15–30.

  Delpit, L. (1995). *Other people's children: Cultural conflict in the classroom.* New York: New Press.

  Grossman, P. L., Smagorinsky, P., & Valencia, S. (1999). Appropriating tools for teaching English: A theoretical framework for research on learning to teach. *American Journal of Education, 108*(1), 1–29.

  Lee, C. D., & Smagorinsky, P. (2000). *Vygotskian perspectives on literacy research: Constructing meaning through collaborative inquiry.* New York: Cambridge University Press.

  Montero-Sieburth, M., & Villaruel, F. (2003). *Making invisible Latino adolescents visible: A critical approach to Latino diversity.* Routledge.

  Murrell Jr., P. C. (2002). *African-centered pedagogy: Developing schools of achievement for African American children.* SUNY Press.

  Vygotsky, L. S., & Cole, M. (1978). *Mind in society: The development of higher psychological processes.* Cambridge: Harvard University Press.

21 Freire, P. (2005). *Teachers as cultural workers: Letters to those who dare teach with new commentary by Peter McLaren, Joe L. Kincheloe.* Westview Press.

Freire, P. (1993). *Pedagogy of the oppressed* (New Rev 20th-Anniversary ed.). New York: Continuum.

22 Pinar, W. (2004). *What is curriculum theory?* (p. 1). Routledge.

23 Kridel, C. (2010). Currere. In *Encyclopedia of curriculum studies* (Vol. 1, pp. 178–178). SAGE Publications, Inc., https://www.doi.org/10.4135/9781412958806.n102.

Pinar, W. (2004). *What is curriculum theory?*. Routledge.

24 Johnson, S. (2020). *Afrocentricity: Student voices on African American identity in multicultural education reform.* The University of Texas at San Antonio.

25 Brown, K. D., Brown, A. L., & Grant, C. A. (2015). *Black intellectual thought in education*: Routledge.

Op. Cit., Pinar (2004).

26 Op. Cit., Johnson (2020).

27 Op. Cit., Freire (1993).

28 Price, J. M. (2007). Democracy: A critical red ideal. *Journal of Thought, 42*(1/2), 9–25.

Part I
THEORIZING LOVE

"A good teacher is like a candle—it consumes itself to light the way for others."[1]

Think Ahead—Define Love

1. How do you personally define *love*?
2. Do you feel that *love*, as you define it, has any relationship to the practice of teaching?
3. Is there any benefit to entering the word *love* into the current discourse over teaching practice, student learning experience, curriculum, or pedagogy?
4. Can you define the word *agape*? If you can define it, how might it apply to your experience with your students, the content that you teach, and the way in which you teach that content to your students?

· 1 ·

AGAPE LOVE IN THEORY

The notion of an unconditional, sacrificial love might be the highest form of love as expressed through many sacred texts and secularized ancient philosophies alike.[1] Yet, the frequency with which society applies the signifier, love, to describe everything from McDonald's to a Subaru diffuses its more ambitious and noble meaning. It invites a correction upon the flaccidity of the conventional word, love, as it clouds the emotions, attitudes, intentions, and actions of our humanity.

So abused is love as a construct that a human confession of undying commitment to another stands equally in expression as a leave taking, a sarcastic frustration, or a deep affinity for food, a place, or an activity. The fracture in authenticity of the word love is catastrophic within common discourse, as it is rendered empty, lacking in its intended transformative nature.[2] Contemporary "love" in contemplation and in action is reduced to an "alienated and alienating blah"—"idle chatter" equating to meaningless "verbalism".[3] It does matter how society attaches meaning to the word "love."

Paulo Freire said, "Human existence cannot be silenced, nor can it be nourished by false words, but only by true words, with which men and women transform the world."[4] No greater example could emerge out of the lifelessness within the common linguistic and textual discourse of *love*, and the imperative of a reconceptualization, than the following: I witnessed a pre-service student in a curriculum and instruction course ask a famed visiting scholar whether he or she felt it problematic that so many pre-service teachers might enter the field of education without truly loving the students they were about to serve. The scholar replied by saying, "fu—love", because even pedophiles profess love for their victims.

My shock and horror over such a suffocating and futile assessment of love in K-12 education inspired me to contemplate the impact of a curriculum of lovelessness on teacher education, specifically when enough scholarship has dedicated itself to validating the direct connection between non-cognitive factors in academic spaces and learning outcomes.[5]

To investigate the current state of love in practice within the K-12 learning space, I conducted a small qualitative study in which 85 pre-service teachers, ranging from 18 to 37 years old, and 19 in-service teachers, between 23 and 48 years old, were invited to participate in a questionnaire to define love and its role in education.[6] The only parameter for in-service teacher recruitment was that the participant be in public school service beyond the statistical attrition rate of five years. This was done to ensure that the in-service teachers experienced comparable preparation programs to the pre-service participants, and that they remained in the field of teaching beyond the typical 3–5 year attrition rate.[7] 69 pre-service teachers and 17 in-service teachers across diverse intersectionalities completed and returned questionnaires which I analyzed to develop a theoretical understanding regarding how teachers define love and how their concept of love informs their approach to teaching and learning.[8]

Participants were asked to respond in their own handwriting to the following open ended questions: How do you personally define *love*? Do you feel that *love*, as you define it, has any relationship to the practice of teaching? Is there any benefit to entering the word *love* into the current discourse over teaching practice, student learning experience, curriculum, or pedagogy? Can you define the word *agape*? If you can define it, how might it apply to your experience with your students, the content that you teach, and the way in which you teach that content to your students? An analysis of responses was conducted by each service group, pre-service separately from in-service. The two important variables to correlate were *definition of love* and *application of love in a classroom*.

Findings showed that, across both groups, definitions lacked concreteness, were highly discrepant, and, at times, self-conflicting since they were predominantly expressed in terms of "a feeling" or "caring". Further, participants often attributed these responses to non-human objects or beings in equal measure to people. Very few, 26, defined love in actionable, intentional, and measurable terms while only 28 participants defined love in terms of an unconditional, selfless, sacrificial construct, even when their religious practice or familiarity with ancient Greek definitions of love allowed them to successfully identify and define the word, agape. While there was ample evidence that participants understood a link between positive learning outcomes and a curriculum of love, approximately one-third of all participants conveyed only self-serving outcomes such as "enjoying your job", being "impassioned", being "happy" in the job.

The relevance of these findings is that they suggest a pervasive lack of understanding about what love is as well as its importance to the overall welfare of students and their learning outcomes, which opens an opportunity for critical reflection and dialogue. Regarding *love*, Thich Nhat Hanh is quoted as saying, "Words sometimes get sick and we have to heal them."[9] The findings of the study speak to a theoretical and practical concern as to the impact of a hidden curriculum of anti-love, the by-product of a capitalistic society which places its value on the commodification of all things, including teachers and students.[10]

Certainly, statistics around school failure, dropout rates, teen suicide, low teacher retention, and the dependency on high stakes testing and standardization are somewhat attributable to the onto-epistemological abyss of separateness into which our students and educators have fallen.[11] "We must dare so to never dichotomize cognition and emotion."[12] Consequently, it becomes important to theoretically reframe what love ought to be relative to education, with the goal being that any pattern of anti-love becomes exposed and disrupted for the sake of advancing transformative learning spaces where, particularly, marginalized students experience freedom in education.[13]

Whether contextualized by a recognition of "God" or a secular point of view, an examination of several predominant philosophical worldviews helps us to concretely define unconditional love as being pertinent to student growth, empowerment, and overall well-being. Second only to a devoted love for God, the highest mandate from Christian thought is to "love your neighbor as yourself."[14] More impactful is that beyond loving a neighbor, the higher imperative is to love an enemy.[15] Ubuntu, a popular African moral theory, and Buddhism are similarly oriented. Black Elk, a Lakota medicine man, said, "The first thing an Indian learns is to love each other . . ."[16] Love, according to Wivestad, Eric Fromm and Paulo Freire, is the answer to all problems concerning human existence because it is what defines us.[17] The quest to resolve the issues of existence, positive educational outcomes included, remains a futility as society loses itself in the grasp of capitalism, imperialism, and the narcissism that closely follows the former two.[18] Only in the "interpersonal union . . . of love" can society arrive at what it seeks.[19]

Ubuntu comes from the Zulu and Xhola languages and is often interpreted through the expression, "A person is a person through other persons." In other words, a person's existence is eternally connected and defined by the existence of others. It is a pervasive way of knowing and being that is shared predominantly by Africans of Bantu origin. Ubuntu has at its onto-epistemological core a concept of self-less love that extends beyond human interactions and is a state of being relative to all of the creation—"I am because you [we] are" is reminiscent of an outward concern for welfare, without boundaries or limitations of any kind, and is shared by Native American and Buddhist metaphysical worldviews.[20] It may also be relevant to the Hindu philosophy of Maitri [compassion] and Bhakti [love for God].[21]

Central to Ubuntu are consensus building and dialogue, a similar acculturation of listening and understanding that is also pertinent to Native American and Buddhist worldviews.[22] Ubuntu values community respect, love, caring, trust, compassion, dignity, humanity, integrity, justice, responsibility, and mutuality.[23] Like Christianity's urging to love a neighbor as much as self, for Ubuntu, communal proximity or familiarity is not the basis for selflessly preserving harmony through the well-being others. It is the belief that we are connected to one another in spirit and in matter that drives Ubuntu to altruism.[24]

Buddhist and Hindu philosophical perspectives also approach love through a lens of interconnectedness, implying that suffering and joy are co-experienced.[25] What happens to one happens to another—when one suffers, all suffer. As with Ubuntu, love proactively identifies and understands the suffering of another with the intention of relieving that suffering.[26] Jalaluddin Rumi, possibly the most celebrated 13th century Persian poet in the Islamic world, stressed the importance of "madhhab al-'ishq," the path of love [and justice], through the relief of suffering:

> . . . These are the brave ones:
> Who tend to the lament of the oppressed
> Whenever they hear
> the heart's anguish of those oppressed
> They come running
> Like God's mercy

These are the ones who hold up the world
Healing diseases of the heart
They are:
Pure love
Justice
Mercy
Someone asked the brave soul
Why did you come running
When everyone ran away?
He said:
I came
because
I heard his cry
And saw his sorrow
Wherever there is pain
The remedy runs towards it
Wherever there is lowliness
The water flows towards it . . .[27]

This makes it impossible for love to seek self-interest. From the perspective of Buddhism, love exists in mutual freedom without selfish attachment, discrimination or prejudice. Love is not oppressive. Bell Hooks said, "The moment we choose to love we begin to move against domination, against oppression. The moment we choose to love we begin to move towards freedom, to act in ways that liberate ourselves and others."[28] Other philosophical worldviews, such as the Chinese philosophy of Jên—the foundational principal of Confucianism, share a similar ethos at their foundation and may further strengthen the theoretical concept of unconditional love.[29] Regardless of the philosophical approach, it follows that love is intended to be unconditional—altruistic.[30] It is in the sacrificial giving with no expectation of reciprocity that it finds its theoretical center.[31] Further, and pertinent to the educator, the giving is not of material things but of self—that which is alive in one for the sake of another.[32]

Love in this context would not be defined as a passive feeling but an active pursuit towards deliberateness—a humble, others-centered concern for "the life and growth" of another.[33] According to Fromm, four basic elements are common to love: care, responsibility, respect, and knowledge.[34] Responsibility concerns itself with responding to the expressed or unexpressed needs of the other person; where respect values a person as is, according to his or her uniqueness, without exploitation[35] None of which is possible if the teacher makes little or no effort to know the student. Agape, as Missler and Missler would describe it, is a curriculum of patience and kindness, without envy, boastfulness or pride;

love does not seek its own self-gratification or anger easily—it forgives all, seeks out truth, always protects, trusts, hopes and endures.[36]

From a critical standpoint and supportive of Buddhism and Ubuntu, Freire and Fromm agree that love takes courage—it cannot exist in fear.[37] It forces us, as James Baldwin so eloquently put it, to "take off the masks that we fear we cannot live without and know we cannot live within." As curriculum, love is a dialogical commitment to students, to their cause towards freedom; it is an act of bravery on behalf of the teacher to disrupt social, political and economic inequities that exploit, manipulate and dehumanize students.[38] Learning being social, relational from both a curricular and pedagogical point of view, may be perfected through an act of unconditional love.[39]

Ironically, within this theoretical framework is the notion that self-love—the demonstration of an educator's love of being, not doing—is inconsistent with unconditional love and is only achievable through the love of other beings.[40] Freire states, "If I do not love the world—if I do not love life—if I do not love people—I cannot enter into the dialogue [liberatory knowledge construction or teaching]" because profound love rests at the core of freedom, not domination, and therefore proper knowledge construction.[41]

The problem with love is not a theoretical one; it is a matter of practice. Poor attempts at implementation are responsible for the moral and ethical hypocrisy that contradicts love where its purity has been tainted by deliberate socioeconomic and political manipulation as well as ideological shifts due to globalization and ill-conceived radicalizations. The notion that love can be compartmentalized—negotiable within socio-politically normalized contexts like patriarchy, caste systems, manifest destiny, or the commodification of classrooms—results in a failure to love altogether, across all contexts, including those we hold dear.[42] This failure incites what Fromm calls separateness, which is the gateway to anxiety—one of the most pervasive and disturbing trends evidenced across all U.S. educational contexts.[43]

Although articulated in their own unique ways, theoretically, many of the world's major philosophical schools of thought concur with Fromm's warning.[44] Further, the mature love that resolves the contemporary, existential crisis within social justice discourses ought not be conflated with more immature forms of love.[45] From an onto-epistemological and axiological[46] standpoint, Agape love describes the former and is not simply a way of feeling or being.[47] It extends beyond pedagogy, beyond acting upon the world around us (our students). Agape is, in itself, a type of content. It is curriculum, and one that is sorely lacking in society and in education.

Explore, Think, Act

Chapter 1 explored the notion of unconditional love in order to define it relative to a curriculum of agape. For educators, metrics is an inescapable tool that lets us know whether our students have satisfied the learning objective. An exploration of love that allows us to define it also allows us to measure its successful application in the classroom. Take a moment to explore your own ideas about love and its utility in learning and teaching.

(A) Think about the current climate in which you live. List any socio-cultural, political, economic, spiritual or environmental evidence of anti-love that you observe.
  1. How do these anti-loving cultural practices affect what or how your students learn?
  2. How do they affect the way you teach?
  3. Can you trace any of these anti-loving practices to historical events?
  4. In what ways do you believe these anti-loving practices will impact your future as an educator? What about the future of your students?
(B) Think about the way you responded to the pre-quiz questions at the beginning of the chapter.
  1. In what ways has theorizing unconditional love changed or supported your perception of love in the classroom—its value in educating your students?
  2. Have you identified any curricular practices that you would like to change in light of this chapter? If so, list them.
  3. Have you identified any pedagogical practices that you would like to change in light of this chapter? If so, list them.

Notes

Part I

1 Leavy, A. M., McSorley, F. A., & Boté, L. A. (2007). An examination of what metaphor construction reveals about the evolution of preservice teachers' beliefs about teaching and learning. *Teaching and teacher education*, 23(7), (p. 1226).

Chapter 1

1 Missler, C., & Missler, N. (2014). *The way of agape*. King's High Way Ministries.
  Templeton, J. (1999). *Agape love: A tradition found in eight world religions*.

2   Freire, P. (1993). *Pedagogy of the oppressed* (New Rev 20th-Anniversary ed.). New York: Continuum.

Safi, O. (Ed.). (2018). *Radical love: Teachings from the Islamic mystical tradition*. Yale University Press.

3   Ibid. p. 87.

4   Ibid. p. 88.

5   Haynes, N. M., Emmons, C., & Ben-Avie, M. (1997). School climate as a factor in student adjustment and achievement. *Journal of Educational and Psychological Consultation, 8*(3), 321–329.

Stajkovic, A. D., & Luthans, F. (1998). Social cognitive theory and self-efficacy: Goin beyond traditional motivational and behavioral approaches. *Organizational dynamics, 26*(4), 62–74.

Thapa, A., Cohen, J., Guffey, S., & Higgins-D'Alessandro, A. (2013). A review of school climate research. *Review of educational research, 83*(3), 357–385.

6   Corbin, J., & Strauss, A. (2008). *Basics of qualitative research (3rd ed.): Techniques and procedures for developing grounded theory*. Thousand Oaks: SAGE Publications, Inc.

7   NCES-National Center for Education Statistics. (2021). *Analyzing teacher mobility and retention: Guidance and considerations report 1–2*. Retrieved May 28, 2021, from https://nces. ed.gov/pubsearch/index.asp?HasSearched=1&searchcat2=subjectindex&L1=49&L2=19.

8   Amidon, J. (2013). Teaching mathematics as agape: Responding to oppression with unconditional love. *Journal of urban mathematics education, 6*(1), 19–27.

Op. Cit., Corbin & Strauss (2008).

Op. Cit., Freire (1993).

Fromm, E. (2000). *The art of loving: The centennial edition*. A&C Black.

Saldaña, J. (2016). *The coding manual for qualitative researchers* (3rd ed.). Los Angeles: SAGE.

Wivestad, S. M. (2008). The educational challenges of agape and phronesis. *Journal of Philosophy of Education, 42*(2), 307–324. https://doi.org/10.1111/j.1467-9752.2008.00626.x.

9   Robinson-Morris, D. W. (2018). *Ubuntu and Buddhism in higher education: An ontological (re) thinking* (p. 72). Routledge.

10 Apple, M. W., & Beane, J. A. (2007). *Democratic schools: Lessons in powerful education*: Heinemann.

Darder, A. (2017). *Reinventing Paulo Freire: A pedagogy of love*. Taylor & Francis.

Op. Cit., Fromm (2000).

Giroux, H. A., & Giroux, S. S. (2006). Challenging neoliberalism's new world order: The promise of critical pedagogy. *Cultural Studies ↔ Critical Methodologies, 6*(1), 21–32. https://doi.org/10.1177/1532708605282810.

11 Centers for Disease Control and Prevention. (2021). *Facts about suicide*. Centers for Disease Control and Prevention. Retrieved November 10, 2021, from https://www.cdc.gov/suicide/facts/index.html.

Dove, M. K. (2004). Teacher attrition: A critical American and international education issue. *Delta Kappa Gamma Bulletin, 71*(1).

Edelman, M. W. (2009). The cradle to prison pipeline: America's new apartheid. *Harvard Journal of African American Public Policy, 15*(Summer Issue), 67–68.

Flannery, M. E. (2019). *The epidemic of anxiety among today's students*. NEA. Retrieved November 11, 2021, from https://www.nea.org/nea-today/all-news-articles/epidemic-anxiety-among-todays-students.

Horowitz, J. M., & Graf, N. (2020, May 30). *Most U.S. teens see anxiety, depression as major problems*. Pew Research Center's Social & Demographic Trends Project. Retrieved November 11, 2021, from https://www.pewresearch.org/social-trends/2019/02/20/most-u-s-teens-see-anxiety-and-depression-as-a-major-problem-among-their-peers/.

Johnson, S. C. (2019). U.S. education and the persistence of slavery. *Journal of Curriculum and Pedagogy*, 1–20. https://doi.org/10.1080/15505170.2019.1618757.

Ladson-Billings, G. (2006). From the achievement gap to the education debt: Understanding achievement in U.S. schools. *Educational Researcher, 35*(7), 3–12.

McCarter, S. (2017). The school-to-prison pipeline: A primer for social workers. *Social Work, 62*(1), 53–61. https://doi.org/10.1093/sw/sww078.

National Dropout Prevention Center. (2018). *Economic impacts of dropouts*. Retrieved from https://dropoutprevention.org/resources/statistics/quick-facts/economic-impacts-of-dropouts/.

Sass, D. A., Flores, B. B., Claeys, L., & Pérez, B. (2012). Identifying personal and contextual factors that contribute to attrition rates for Texas public school teachers. *Education Policy Analysis Archives/Archivos Analíticos de Políticas Educativas, 20*, 1–26.

Yard, E. (2021, June 17). *Emergency department visits for suspected suicide attempts among persons aged 12–25 years before and during the COVID-19 pandemic— United States, January 2019–May 2021*. Centers for Disease Control and Prevention. Retrieved January 5, 2022, from https://www.cdc.gov/mmwr/volumes/70/wr/mm7024e1.htm?campaign_id=9&emc=edit_nn_20220104&instance_id=49344&nl=the-morning&i_id=86340798&segment_id=78602&te=1&user_id=d88a92611aab0bb98a785ee5af35f796.

12 Freire, P. (2005). *Teachers as cultural workers: Letters to those who dare teach with new commentary by Peter McLaren, Joe L. Kincheloe* (p. 5). Westview Press.

13 Op. Cit., Apple & Beane (2007).
     Op. Cit., Darder (2017).
     Op. Cit., Fromm (2000).
     Op. Cit., Giroux & Giroux (2006).

14 *New International Version*. (2021). Mt. 22:38–39.

15 Ibid. Mt. 5:43–44.

16 Forbes, J. D. (2001). Indigenous Americans: Spirituality and ecos. *Daedalus: Journal of the American Academy of Arts & Sciences*. Retrieved May 26, 2021, from www.amacad.org/publication/indigenous-americans-spirituality-and-ecos.

17 Op. Cit., Freire (1993, 2005).
     Op. Cit., Fromm (2000).
     Op. Cit., Wivestad (2008).

18 Darder, A. (2011). Chapter 9: Teaching as an act of love: Reflections on Paulo Freire and his contributions to our lives and our work. *Counterpoints, 418*, 179–194.
     Op. Cit., Fromm (2000).
     Op. Cit., Giroux & Giroux (2006).

19 Op. Cit., Fromm (2000), p. 17.
20 Nhat Hanh, T., DeAntonis, J. (2014). *How to love*. USA: Parallax Press.
  Op. Cit., Robinson-Morris (2018).
21 Op. Cit., Forbes (2001).
  Lipner, J. (1998). Capturing gods: The god of love and the love of god in Christian and Hindu tradition. *Boardman Lectureship in Christian Ethics, 3*. Retrieved May 26, 2021, from http://repository.upenn.edu/boardman/3.
  Tshivhase, M. (2018). Love as the foundation of Ubuntu. *Synthesis Philosophica,* 65(1/2018), 197–208. https://doi.org/10.21464/sp33112.
22 Price, J. M. (2007). Democracy: A critical red ideal. *Journal of Thought, 42*(1/2), 9–25.
  Op. Cit., Robinson-Morris (2018).
23 *Chapter four: The African Ubuntu philosophy.* (n.d.). Retrieved January 4, 2022, from https://repository.up.ac.za/bitstream/handle/2263/28706/04chapter4.pdf?sequence=5.
  Mayaka, B., & Truell, R. (2021). Ubuntu and its potential impact on the international social work profession. *International Social Work, 64*(5), 649–662.
  Op. Cit., Robinson-Morris (2018).
24 Ibid.
25 Op. Cit., Lipner (1998).
  Op. Cit., Nhat & DeAntonis (2014).
26 Op. Cit., Nhat & DeAntonis (2014).
27 Op. Cit., Safi (2018).
  Safi, O. (2020). *"god commands you to justice and Love": Islamic spirituality* . —IIIT. Retrieved June 6, 2022, from https://iiit.org/wp-content/uploads/Omid-Safi-Final.pdf
28 Hooks, B. (2006). *Outlaw culture: Resisting representations.* Routledge.
29 Op. Cit., Robinson-Morris (2018).
30 Op. Cit., Amidon (2013).
  Op. Cit., Freire (1993).
  Op. Cit., Fromm (2000).
  Op. Cit., Lipner (1998).
  Op. Cit., Nhat & DeAntonis (2014).
  Op. Cit., Tshivhase (2018).
  Op. Cit., Wivestad (2008).
31 Ibid.
32 Op. Cit., Fromm (2000).
33 Op. Cit., Amidon (2013).
  Op. Cit., Freire (1993).
  Op. Cit., Fromm (2000).
  Op. Cit., Lipner (1998).
  Op. Cit., Nhat & DeAntonis (2014).
  Op. Cit., Tshivhase (2018).
  Op. Cit., Wivestad (2008).
34 Op. Cit., Fromm (2000).
35 Ibid.
36 Op. Cit., Missler & Missler (2014).
37 Op. Cit., Freire (1993).

Op. Cit., Fromm (2000).

38 Op. Cit., Darder (2011, 2017).
    Op. Cit., Freire (1993, 2005).

39 Op. Cit., Amidon (2013).
    Vygotsky, L. S., & Cole, M. (1978). *Mind in society: The development of higher psychological processes*. Cambridge: Harvard University Press.

40 Op. Cit., Forbes (2001).
    Op. Cit., Lipner (1998).
    Op. Cit., Missler & Missler (2014).
    Op. Cit., Nhat & DeAntonis (2014).
    Op. Cit., Templeton (1999).
    Op. Cit., Tshivhase (2018).

41 Op. Cit., Freire (1993), p. 90.

42 Op. Cit., Fromm (2000).

43 Ibid.
    The state of mental health in America. Mental Health America. (2022). Retrieved January 22, 2022, from https://www.mhanational.org/issues/state-mental-health-america.

44 Op. Cit., Forbes (2001).
    Op. Cit., Lipner (1998).
    Op. Cit., Missler & Missler (2014).
    Op. Cit., Templeton (1999).
    Op. Cit., Tshivhase (2018).

45 Op. Cit., Fromm (2000).

46 Value system.

47 Op. Cit., Fromm (2000).
    Op. Cit., Wivestad (2008).

· 2 ·

LOVE IS NOT IMMATURE

"Getting too close to our students, we've often been told, violates professional standards and the distance needed to maintain control in the classroom."[1] This reminds me of a saying my husband used when referring to the brand new trainees who were interspersed on the military installation among fully seasoned soldiers, many of whom were older and carried considerable leverage via the authority conferred on them by their service rank. "Don't touch the puppies," my husband would advise his staff members. It was fundamental that commissioned and non-commissioned officers alike understood the vulnerability of an 18 year old trainee who, in most cases, was far from home and impressionable. These seasoned personnel were entrusted to support, care for and develop trainees as soldiers and not confuse this others-centered role with an inappropriate and self-serving one.

In 2015, roughly 3.5 million students surveyed in grades 8 through 11 reported having had physical, sexual contact from an adult.[2] Most prevalent was an abuse by a teacher or coach, ranging from unwanted touching of their body to sexual intercourse.[3] When other types of abuses are considered—being shown pornography or subjected to sexually explicit language or exhibitionism for example—the results increased to approximately 4.5 million children.[4] The nonprofit organization, Stop Educator Sexual Abuse Misconduct &

Exploitation (SESAME), reports that one out of 10 children between kindergarten and 12th grade are victimized by educator sexual misconduct.[5] Of all reported abuses, 40% are perpetrated by female staff members who "attribute their misconduct to romantic love."[6]

Readdressing the misguided notion that love and pedophilia can occupy the same discursive space, the imperative here is to know the difference between what Fromm called mature and immature love.[7] Immature love, according to the definition in chapter 1, does not meet the demands of the referent, *love*, because it seeks its own satisfaction and is driven by lust and an equally immature set of emotions. Mature love, the brand that is worthy of its name, is altruistic— it is giving without need of return. Mature love does not take advantage of the inequitable power dynamic that exists between a student and a teacher or mentor. A curriculum of agape is in no way to be confused with the type of emotional and mental immaturity that recontextualizes the protective role of a loving teacher to that of an abusive sexual predator.

Certainly, even in a mature love, circumstances arise in which we have to use our good sense and good intentions to protect our students and ourselves from drifting into unwise interactions. Although, to insist on maintaining a teacher-student distance in the name of "professionalism" is to deprive students of the opportunity to know their teachers and to form those deep agape relationships that we will learn are so closely connected to engagement and motivation.[8] Getting "close" to our students does not imply that we lose sight of or abandon a sense of boundaries that ought to be a natural outflow of the age-rank and authority of an adult teacher with respect to a student. In my experience, those boundaries are both implicitly and explicitly shaped by a professional bearing, and the way in which a class culture of community is established from the first day of any class. Part of establishing the relationship between teacher and student is the formation of loving and responsible boundaries. Nothing is more pertinent to establishing boundaries than classroom management.[9]

I ran a loving but tight ship, bell to bell, and rarely went to work in jeans and a T-shirt.[10] My professional office-style dress sent a subtle but clear signal that I occupied the learning space for business purposes, and it established a visible boundary between teacher and student.[11] My students would periodically comment on my unusually formal attire, "Miss. J, do you own jeans?" "You're on fleek, Mama J." "How big is your closet!? You never repeat." Young people seem to observe everything and miss nothing—except the fact that on my teacher's salary, my closet was limited, and I was simply a master at re-combining my wardrobe. I had no idea what "on fleek" or "repeat" meant, but it was amusing to allow them to educate me, and it gave me an opportunity to return the appreciation by sharing my intentions behind my work fashion— "You all are V.I.P.s, and so I dress in a way that honors how important you are." Funny enough, my students would react as if Armageddon were upon us whenever I did shake the dust off my jeans for a "dress-down day." Their interactions towards me would meet the informality as well and would require a reminder that the teacher in the suit was the very same teacher who was now in the jeans. Students often interpret professional dress as a sign of caring, especially among minority students.[12]

It has also been my observation that students do not want their teachers to be their BFFs, or their lovers for that matter. As a high school or adult educator, my students want to know that they can come to me with anything, no matter how grave or inconvenient, but they do not want me to insert myself into their "business." My male students, particularly at the high school level, have made many flirtatious displays of admiration intended to draw my attention toward them. None, however, have expected a response in-kind but simply a warm, affectionate redirection to their work. When students "push the [boundary] envelope," they fully expect the teacher to protect them and guide them back within the boundaries where they are safe.[13] To do otherwise is to skew a student's natural development towards a type of cognitive dissonance that leaves the student ambivalent, conflicted over the appropriateness of their circumstance, and is further contrary to academic engagement, motivation and proper cognition.[14]

I remember one of my young men, whom I believe thought he was to attempt a 4.0 in flirtation as much as in AP Spanish. As was the case with my students in general, he was acutely aware of my dedication to ballet. As he and his classmates swarmed into my room, I was finishing some notes on the board at the front of the classroom. He grinned at me, getting my attention, winked and nodded his head towards the runway of space between the board and the back of the classroom, and my confusion gave way to clarity that this student, as he was removing his sneakers, was challenging me to a leap! ANYTHING to win my attentions. I laughed, nodded back to accept his challenge, hand signaled our combination, and with a 5-6-7-8 we took off: tombé, pas de bourrée, glissade, saut de chat. It was a well synchronized landing with shock and cheering from the class. We both laughed hysterically and exchanged high-fives as I walked directly to my podium and said, "Your warm-up is on the board: 10 minutes everyone!" I have always viewed *play*, when appropriate, as part of the normal human dynamic and a healthy addition to relationship building in the classroom. In this case, the play was welcomed, but, at the same time, the well-established boundaries remained in place in the midst of my student's flirtatious silliness.

The longer I taught, the more concrete the rules became that under no circumstances do you touch your students.[15] America, having become the most litigious society, influenced education more heavily with each passing year as students and their parents levied legal threats against educators who mistakenly, as well as intentionally, exchanged an unwelcomed touch.[16] In an effort to mitigate the disruptive optics as well as the financial strain that comes with a suit against a school, it has become less risky to erase the grey area between "good touch" and "bad touch" in exchange for the safety of "no touch".[17] Admittedly, I do not have a concrete, mathematical solution to bring into balance a student's need for a "good touch" within the reasonable parameters of agape love and the risk an educator takes in extending that "good touch." I can only attest to the role that a high five, a fist bump or, at times, a hug plays in human development and the role it has played in my classroom.

What was concrete for me, whether addressing a student through a term of endearment or touching a student, was that establishing my professional bearing and our classroom culture always precipitated these overtures, and always within public view. Agape is an action that must carry wisdom alongside it, and it is well established wisdom among educators to maintain a public view when working with students: talk in the hallway, in the library, leave the door open, interact quietly while in full view of the class, etc. This being said, only from the two standpoints of human development theory and my own experience can I argue that, within a curriculum of agape, students sometimes need a loving touch.[18] The touch I am referring to supports agape in that it may have wisdom but, certainly, no fear, expectation of reciprocity, self-interest or need of its own. It is an altruistic giving of self to inspire, celebrate, or comfort young people whose good emotional development relies on the warmth of their teachers. In its absence lies that separateness that leads to anxiety.[19]

I am reminded of several occasions when I found myself caught between my professional programming to not touch and the pull on my heart to not abandon my students' need for the compassion of a hug. On fairly regular occasions, my middle school and high school girls would either enter my class or take their leave with a surprise hug and an "I love you." Side hugs were my rule, but on these occasions, the hugs were directionally impossible to gauge because the girls had a way of taking the opportunity when I was engaged with another student or an administrative task. I would simply feel the thud of a body upon any available plane of my own with arms soon to follow, wrapped around me lovingly and seeking my attention. As quickly as they came, they moved on to their seats or out of the door. Middle and high school boys were less apt to invade my personal space, but it did happen. On these occasions, wisdom welcomed a side hug. This was the custom with my boys—mostly due to their comfort level for which I was grateful—except for one very publicly, shocking moment when I was hoisted up front-facing and spun around at the joy of my arrival to a graduation.

I had taught a young man whom I will call Rico. He was my high school student for my last year at this school, at a time when I was involved with his class as a faculty advisor. He made me promise that I would return for his class's graduation. It was my agape policy to always honor my word, especially to a student, so I assured him that I would do my best. I was greeted on commencement day by many of my former underclassmen students, but the graduates were nowhere in sight. At least I could say I had come as expected and moved on to enter the gym where the commencement would take place. There were the seniors lined up in full regalia, ready to enter the graduation ceremony with staff members, friends, and family flooding the lobby of the gym. I waved as I moved towards the gym doors in the direction of the excited whispers of my name—the seniors knew that I had come to celebrate them—but then I spun around in a fright to the shrieking of my name, "SEÑORA!" Suddenly, without full comprehension or sight, I was lifted off my feet and spun 360 degrees about the axis of my student. Rico's display of joy stopped all the lobby traffic and dismayed the two staff members whose job it was to maintain good commencement order for the procession. Everyone, including me, was simultaneously stunned, tickled, and taken aback by the effusiveness of that hug. It was definitely intrusive but innocently done and fully situated in Rico's experience with a curriculum of agape.

Similarly, in my short time teaching kindergarteners, hugs became a daily norm irrespective of gender, and more intrusive was the height challenge of a five or six year old with respect to my adult stature. Still, those little arms wrapped around me as far as their reach would allow, but unlike the waist high hug of a middle or high schooler, a kindergartener's reach was only on level with my derrière. The self-talk that was needed to convince myself to enjoy the loving overture was emotionally challenging, as it is counterintuitive to freely accept even the innocent touch of little paws on one's backside.

Hugs are probably not unusual to any K-12 educator who has been in the field for a few years. Where they are more unexpected is at the adult level of education. Any wariness that I may have felt at the elementary and second-ary levels was exacerbated many times over within my adult courses. There is an even stronger caution to use wisdom when an adult is teaching his or her peers. Not unlike education at the lower levels, I have found that safe and loving boundaries are established in professional presence, classroom cul-ture and public visibility, and they provide a sense of trust and freedom when moments for those hugs are upon me. One such case involved an adult student whom I will name, Erwin. Erwin had joined a Wounded Warrior Basic Skills class and took his learning opportunities seriously. It was a complicated matter to prioritize education in the environment of equally prioritized needs within the battalion to which Wounded Warriors were assigned. Yes, they were stu-dents, and their duty station was my classroom, but they were also soldiers, sailors and airmen, accountable to their assigned company. The fear of the unknown and the desperation for hope and self-confidence sometimes collided with the commander's view of what was best for the servicemember.

Erwin relied heavily on the encouragement and strength he drew from the Basic Skills Course, and when an error of judgment invited a stiff response from his company that would withdraw him from his academic sanctuary, he became overwrought with frustration. I agreed with him that the punishment did not seem to fit the crime, but my role was not to judge a situation for which I had limited insight. My role was compassion, to simply be there to love on, support and reassure Erwin in his hour of deep distress. Erwin's emotions grew demonstratively, so I escorted him into the hallway outside of my classroom to preserve his dignity among his classmates, but also to allow him the safety of a meltdown if that was what he needed, and melt down he did. I have endured terrible heartbreak by loving so many students over the years—it is an inevi-tability of interconnectedness. The heartbreak that I felt as Erwin broke down into profound, soul-crushing sobs of grief overcame any resistance I might have felt as he, standing at about six feet in height and enormous in girth, slumped onto my shoulder and, ultimately, into me, having lost all composure. To touch or not to touch?[20] Even though I was publicly visible to my office colleagues, I still did not know what to do. I could not just stand there. I felt compelled out of compassion for my student to pat him gently on the shoulders, "It's okay, Erwin, I'm here. I've got you."

Andrew was also a student in the Basic Skills Course who's health condi-tion and management caused his hands to shake violently. When he attempted to write, either to practice his math problems, complete a short writing assign-ment or take a practice standardized test, Andrew's pencil would hover over the paper, violently trembling. He could not touch his pencil down without creat-ing a mess of random scribbles. Once he began to write, the shaking ceased and he was able to legibly complete his written tasks. He just needed help getting started. The only way to help him was to place my hand on his to guide the pencil smoothly to the paper. What would my alternative have been to help my student succeed except to touch him? I always asked Andrew for permission to touch his hand to maintain safety, trust, and professionalism, and always in public view of the rest of the class. Once I had permission, I put my hand on his and got his writing started. If I had held fast to the mainstreamed "no touch" policy, Andrew would have suffered constant frustration and anxiety that may have hindered his academic confidence and overall progress.

A curriculum of agape would have been disrupted had I manipulated a "touch" or pursued those hugs to satisfy self. However, reflecting upon the interconnectedness that underpins the theoretical framework for a curriculum of agape, were I to neglect those moments, I would have also neglected my students' humanity, and my own, erasing unconditional love altogether. Love in education, as it is enacted unconditionally, emulates care, responsibility, respect and knowledge. It takes nothing but gives everything, freely, justly and without need of reciprocity. It aims to inspire liberated, life-long learners who are empowered to participate well in their own agency and self-determination to the betterment of society as a whole.

Explore, Think, Act

Chapter 2 expands our theoretical lens through which we explore the term, *love*, as it is relevant to the classroom, by addressing the profound difference between mature and immature forms of love. It considers the appropriateness of mature relational closeness with our students to include questions of *touch*. Explore your own ideas about the difference between mature and immature love as they impact learning and teaching.

(A) Think about the activities of a mature and immature love.
  1. What types of activities demonstrate a mature love for your stu-dents? Make a list.
  2. What types of activities demonstrate an immature love for your students? List them.

3. Since any of us is capable of succumbing to immature forms of love, particularly when teaching at the high school and adult levels, what safeguards do you observe that allow you to draw "close" to your students without sacrificing mature love?

(B) Talk to your students about unconditional love and the difference between mature love and immature love.

1. Ask your students to list the types of teacher and classmate activities that demonstrate a mature love?

2. Ask your students to list the types of teacher and classmate activities that they would perceive to be immature, uncomfortable forms of love?

Based on the responses to parts A and B, construct a set of community guidelines for your class that foster a close community of mature, unconditional love. Be sure to reinforce these guidelines together as the school year progresses.

Notes

1 Nieto, S. (2013). *Finding joy in teaching students of diverse backgrounds: Culturally responsive and socially just practices in U.S. classrooms* (p. 33). Heinemann.

2 Shakeshaft, C. (2013). Know the warning signs of educator sexual misconduct. *Phi Delta Kappan*, 94(5), 8–13. https://doi.org/10.1177/003172171309400503.

3 Ibid.

4 Ibid.

5 *Stop educator sexual abuse misconduct and exploitation* [SESAME]. (n.d.). Retrieved November 10, 2021, from https://www.sesamenet.org/.

6 Op. Cit., Shakeshaft (2013), p. 10.

7 Fromm, E. (2000). *The art of loving: The centennial edition*. A&C Black.

8 Bluestein, J. (2008). *The win-win classroom: A fresh and positive look at classroom management*. Corwin Press.

   Irvine, J. J. (2003). *Educating teachers for diversity: Seeing with a cultural eye*. New York: Teachers College Press.

   Nieto, S. (2013). *Finding joy in teaching students of diverse backgrounds: Culturally responsive and socially just practices in U.S. classrooms*. Heinemann.

   Vygotsky, L. S., & Cole, M. (1978). *Mind in society: The development of higher psychological processes*. Cambridge: Harvard University Press.

   Ware, F. (2006). Warm demander pedagogy: Culturally responsive teaching that supports a culture of achievement for African American students. *Urban Education*, 41(4), 427–456.

9 Op. Cit., Bluestein (2008).

Morris, Z. A. (2015). Contemporary professional boundaries and their relationship with teacher and student well-being. In *Routledge international handbook of social psychology of the classroom* (pp. 400–410). Routledge.

10 Cheng, Y. C. (1996). Relation between teachers' professionalism and job attitudes, educational outcomes, and organizational factors. *The Journal of Educational Research, 89*(3), 163–171. https://doi.org/10.1080/00220671.1996.9941322.

Rojas, L., & Liou, D. D. (2017). Social justice teaching through the sympathetic touch of caring and high expectations for students of color. *Journal of Teacher Education, 68*(1), 28–40.

11 Op. Cit., Cheng (1996).

12 Ladson-Billings, G. (2009). *The dreamkeepers: Successful teachers of African American children*. Somerset, USA: Wiley.

13 Op. Cit., Cheng (1996).

Montuoro, P., & Lewis, R. (2014). Student perceptions of misbehavior and classroom management. In *Handbook of classroom management* (pp. 354–372). Routledge.

14 Hernandez, F., McPhetres, J., & Hughes, J. (2021). Using adolescent perceptions of misconduct to help educational leaders identify and respond to sexual misconduct. *SAGE Open, 57*(4). https://doi.org/10.1177/2158244021997419.

Jaffe, P., Straatman, A., Harris, B., Georges, A., Vink, K., & Reif, K. (2013). Emerging trends in teacher sexual misconduct in Ontario 2007–2012. *Education & Law Journal, 23*(1), 19–39.

Martin, A. J., & Collie, R. J. (2019). Teacher–student relationships and students' engagement in high school: Does the number of negative and positive relationships with teachers matter?. *Journal of Educational Psychology, 111*(5), 861.

Taylor, K. B., & Reynolds, D. J. (2019). Dissonance. In rethinking college student development theory using critical frameworks. *Journal of College and Character, 21*(3), 234–236.

15 Owen, P. M., & Gillentine, J. (2011). Please touch the children: Appropriate touch in the primary classroom. *Early Child Development and Care, 181*(6), 857–868.

Vars, G. F. (1981). To touch or not to touch? That is the question!. *Middle School Journal, 12*(3), 14–17.

Zirkel, P. A. (2000). Don't touch!. *NASSP Bulletin, 84*(614), 84–87.

16 Ibid.

17 Ibid.

18 Ibid.

19 Op. Cit., Fromm (2000).

20 Op. Cit., Vars (1981).

Part II
To Know Them Is to Love Them

"Children learn more from what you are, than what you teach." (Du Bois)[1]

· 3 ·

AND HOW ARE THE CHILDREN?

As the field of education leans forward through a veil of school failures termed teacher attrition, achievement/learning gaps, student anxiety, cradle to prison pipelines and more, it may benefit our professional community to extract some wisdom from the Massai tribe of Kenya and Tanzania and ask ourselves, *Kasserian Ingera*—And how are the children?[1] I find myself ruminating on this question regularly. In light of our national struggle to safely and equitably educate all of America's children, a struggle that has been exacerbated by the global COVID-19 pandemic, it has become an essential question, sparking much dialogue within my graduate and undergraduate courses.[2]

The Massai understand that the safety, well-being and prosperity of the children directly impacts the destiny of the tribe—as one goes, so goes the other.[3] Ubuntu guides the community to consider children as an equal part of society, including giving them access to decision making processes. As in many traditional Native American communities where children are considered to be *wakanyeja*, little sacred ones, not just to the immediate family but to the whole tribe, children are so deeply loved and valued by our African neighbors that their welfare is prioritized by the whole community and guides even the most common salutation, regardless of whether those engaged have children of their own or not.[4] This communal high regard for children is evident in Latino(a) and Middle Eastern cultures as well.[5] "Ubuntu imparts to us that we see our neighbor's child as our own, and their success is our success too."[6] The coveted response for the Massai is, "All of the children are well."[7]

How might we answer this question in 21st century America? Some of the children are well; some of them are alcoholics, drug addicted or killing themselves; many of them are under-funded, under-educated, under-resourced and dropping out; many are disenfranchised from the curriculum and the overall learning environment and still more of them require mental health services and anti-anxiety medication in their teens.[8] Were we to view an honest and self-reflective response to this question through the onto-epistemological and axiological lens of the Massai, or perhaps many of the First Nations of America, the result would be a well-earned sense of community shame and alarm. Could it be that in our misapplication of love, educators have de-centralized students for love of career or other self-serving pursuits, reducing the students to commodities that are measured in profits and losses, test scores and gaps? Imagine an educational system in America where educators at every level greeted each other by asking the most substantive question levied in any teacher preparation course, in-service, or board meeting, not, "And how are the test scores?" but, "And how are the children?"[9]

Archbishop Tutu said, "You might have much of the world's riches, and you might hold a portion of authority, but if you have no ubuntu, you do not amount to much." His remarks find similarity in the biblical introduction to the definition of love in that both present an indictment towards the certain failure of a loveless enterprise and speak directly to Freire's premise that the dialogue of emancipatory pedagogy within education is mute without it:

> If I speak in the tongues of men or of angels, but do not have love, I am only a resounding gong or a clanging cymbal. If I have the gift of prophecy and can fathom all mysteries and all knowledge, and if I have a faith that can move mountains, but do not have love, I am nothing. If I give all I possess to the poor and give over my body to hardship that I may boast, but do not have love, I gain nothing.[10]

The normative educational outcomes that all educators pursue—engagement, motivation, and the resulting academic achievement—are perhaps reduced to white noise in the absence of an ethos of unconditional love.[11] It then follows that without this love to undergird what is explicitly and implicitly taught and modeled through such curricular and pedagogical movements as Culturally Relevant or Responsive Pedagogies, Social Emotional Learning and Growth Mindset or federal acts of reform such as the No Child Left Behind

Act or Race to the Top, students, having become accustomed to a curriculum of anti-love, may widely suffer disconnections from their learning spaces that may also attribute to lower academic outcomes.[12] Sentiments of disconnection from the learning environment were found to be prevalent among high school students who struggled with lacking several integral aspects of a curriculum of agape: value in who they are, a sense of community, interconnectedness and belongingness.[13] Comments during student interviews like the following are a stark example of the type of alienation that results from lovelessness, "Modern man is alienated from himself, from his fellow men, and from nature."[14]

On the Topic of Lacking Close Relationships with Teachers

"I want a mentorship relationship with most of my teachers. They're adults and they've been through life experiences. They've been around longer than we have. And I feel like their input would be valuable to somebody that is still trying to figure out what they want to do with their life and where they want to go and how they handle things."[15]

". . . [I]t would probably help if some of the teachers and staff would take the time, like really break it down for those who just may not get it. I feel like . . . there are still a bunch of teachers who just aren't doing that at all. They are just teaching the material . . ."[16]

On Erasure

"So, walking into those type[s] of classes, you are seen as the minority, and there isn't a lot of people that look like you when you are 'advanced,' as they say. So, just coming in, you're bombarded with that type of, like, exclusion of 'Where are your folks?' 'Where's your culture?' 'Where's your people that look like you?' So, you kind of begin those type[s] of things, kind of, like, isolation . . ."[17]

"I can connect to my personality to math because math is, like, numbers and stuff. I like numbers a lot . . . But, like, the way that I look and the color of my skin and where I come from doesn't really connect to math."[18]

". . . [W]e're looked at as not as academically strong or, lazy, not hardworking. And, I'm a straight A/B honors student, for the most part. So, it's kind of disappointing that that's how most people look at African Americans . . .

Basically, I feel like the history book is written by, like, White people to teach to the kids, and they don't really tell the truth about how some of these Black people, like African Americans, actually invented these inventions and don't get credit for it . . . I don't really feel represented at all—there's nothing that connects. [In] English, we talk about, like, poems that has nothing to do with my identity whatsoever. It's mostly about old English stuff, you know? . . . [A]nd, it's more negative, now that I think about it; we're being taught negative things. Like, they're not going on a positive—like, African Americans' inventions."[19]

"[I]t's just so crazy to me how they say America is like a tossed salad or a melting pot. But how are we a melting pot when you don't even teach people about they ancestors and stuff? . . . [W]hy try to downplay the things that we went through and the things that we still go through, but then when it comes to something like 911, or anything else, it's so terrible and we still got to honor it? But then, you still got people walking around talking about how slavery, 'Oh, we shouldn't talk about it no more.' Like, that's very disrespectful. It's very disrespectful."[20]

On the Importance of Belonging, Cohesiveness and Collaboration

"It makes you feel like you have somebody there that like is helping you or guiding you or making you feel . . . like . . . you can do it and then that gives you motivation to actually do it. But when you have no classmates helping you out . . . you're not going to have motivation to do anything."[21]

[expressing deep frustration]—"Your competition or your competitors [should not be] the person who's sitting next to you."[22]

For these students, teachers who embody some form of a "Fu-- love" approach to teaching and learning, and/or a misplaced concept of what love is as it relates to the educational experience, in many respects, have left them feeling isolated, undervalued, and unsure of the contribution U. S. education makes towards their future.

The environment of curricular anti-love has fostered a discursive sliding signifier we call "school reform," evidenced by the way our national discussions exude care, concern, and action while, simultaneously, veiling media driven political posturing that exacerbates the status quo of a banking style of education. It is a natural outgrowth of a capitalistic agenda that marginalizes specific demographics through dehumanization and under resourcing.[23] Love, like education, has become a commodity, also a sliding signifier, that has lost its intended value and meaning via opportunistic discursive manipulation. On the surface it may appear that a discussion of love is incongruent with that of education reform, yet from the standpoint of critical pedagogy in which learning occurs along the social paradigm of justice, one does not exist without the other.[24] It follows, then, that a culturally relevant teacher, one who maximizes the social-emotional health of students, and who grows the mindset of those whose high expectations of themselves are militated by poor socioeconomic access and stereotypical dehumanizing imagery, will never reach the fullness of his or her pedagogical liberatory capacity because the current curriculum of anti-love prevents it.

An example of a culturally relevant educator who overcame the curriculum of anti-love and did exude the fullness of liberatory capacity of which I speak was a guidance counselor in one of our nation's larger, urban, Title I schools. I will call her Ms. Davis for the sake of this story. I came to meet Ms. Davis as a result of some volunteer work I was engaged in with her district. Her school was unusual in that it was a combined middle and high school, and she was deeply motivated to introduce mentorship programs that might close the opportunity gaps for her students and increase their learning outcomes. Very quickly after our initial meeting, our long term working relationship began. I returned to Ms. Davis' school several times over a few years to work with her middle and high school students and, on one occasion, the teaching staff.

Ms. Davis was a relational educator who was acquainted with the statistical likelihood that her students would not thrive well in academics or in life. She dedicated herself to knowing, understanding and loving her students, affording them every opportunity to widen their scope of possibilities. She knew so many students by name, which was incredible for a population that large. Her office was a rotating door of students coming to visit for official purposes as often as unofficial excuses to simply be with her and share their lives. I was stunned by the effortless way Ms. Davis could simultaneously counsel a student who had been referred to her for disciplinary infractions, host a student committee meeting, and allow place of repose for a student who just needed a time-out from the day. She could fuss at a student in private or in the hallway in a way that only a parent or close relative could get away with because she wasn't simply doing her job—she loved the students and they loved her. She believed in them. "Now, I know you can do better than this!" More often than not, the student whom she assessed to be out of order would agree with her and return to class apologetically and in a better state of mind to learn.

I had occasion to be in the building when the students were working on school-wide tryouts for the drill team. Ms. Davis was the faculty supervisor for the student led drill team and oversaw the practices, demonstrations, and voting. The drill team committee as well as the student hopefuls respected Ms. Davis and her leadership to the point that they could be released to the hallways with full confidence that they could carry out an unsupervised practice. I walked through the hallways admiring the professionalism with which the committee members executed their administrative duties, a clear result of Ms. Davis' mentorship program. There was none of the adversarial behavior that typifies young people at this age. The bullying epidemic within our nation's schools attests to this fact.[25] To my amazement, there was no teasing, arguing, or fighting. The students were patient, supportive, and encouraging of one another, knowing that all were not equally skilled and would not make the team. Younger students leaned on older students, enveloped by their loving arms, while the older students stroked their hair and watched each other learn the choreography.

This scene epitomized the goal of a learning community that is situated in a curriculum of agape and the investment that Ms. Davis made in building it. When it came time to eliminate those students whose execution of the choreography did not meet the necessary standards of the drill team, the committee displayed the same loving humility, patience, and supportiveness that I had observed in the hallway during practice and demonstration. I recall the discussion over one student who had to re-start her demonstration several times. I was certain she would not make the team, but the committee agreed that she was terribly nervous. They were willing to give her a spot on the team and work with her. Ms. Davis' influence on her students was remarkable. When she retired, I was saddened for every student who would not know the unconditional love that informed her pedagogy.

As was demonstrated by Ms. Davis' impact on her students, love, returned to its intended unconditional context, onto-epistemologically speaking, imparts a sense of humanity, dignity and value within each student that disrupts the marketization of the mind and the body and liberates the learner.[26] What may be missing at the higher discussion tables of education reforms is a moral and ethical decision to elevate the notion of unconditional, altruistic love as pertinent to justice in education and the improvement of learning outcomes, and to voice a concern that this is the love for which pre-service and in-service teachers lack understanding and practice. Further, as agape is not passive in nature, it would be antithetical to find satisfaction in the theoretical alone. Educational justice, like love, would require an active pursuit, a deliberate enactment of curricular and pedagogical agape.[27]

Either innately or due to impartation resulting from my own experiences with teachers who exuded unconditional curricular and pedagogical love—or some combination thereof—as a novice teacher, I knew I was in the classroom for the sake of the students, not for my own good. As much as I loved the various subjects I taught and longed to excite new minds to fall in love with them, I knew that the joy of my career was inextricably tied to the degree with which I loved each one of the students who came through my door and were entrusted to my care. At the beginning of my teaching career, I was unaware of the traditional Massai greeting that asks, "And how are the children?" I did, though, find it essential to discover, "Who are the children?" In other words, the well-being of our students has to begin with relationship.[28] Relationship, according to African tradition, involves discovering who a child is, not what he or she is—the labels society has used to identify him or her—acknowledging the child to be a divine and unique contributor to the amalgam that is a community.[29] According to Lisa Delpit, "This means developing relationships with our students and understanding their political, cultural and intellectual legacy."[30] Increasingly, with each year, I emphasized that, like the Lakota, my classes needed to begin by learning to love one another—and since it is impossible to love another whom we do not know, whom we do not understand, thus began the very intentional work of love and the evolution of my teaching praxis.[31]

Explore, Think, Act

Part II assumes that educators must first know their students if they aim to love them. Chapter 3 explores the current condition of our students in a loveless social system as many of them struggle to connect with educators, and education in general. Explore the well-being of your own students. How well do you know them?

(A) Think about each one of your students.
1. How are the children? What do you know about your students' well-being emotionally, spiritually, financially, socially with their peers and family, etc.?

2. Do you feel that you truly know your students? To help you process this question, open your class roster. Think about two things you know about each student personally/culturally that, if introduced into the learning space as curriculum or pedagogy, might stimulate their interest.

3. In your opinion, how does agape relate to educational justice?

4. In what ways can you improve upon your curriculum of agape in the following areas?
   - Initiating a close relationship with your students that includes mentorship
   - Creating an environment that culturally, socially and intellectually centers your students
   - Establishing belonging, cohesiveness and collaboration

Notes

Part II

1 Beachum, & Gullo, G. L. (2020). School leadership: Implicit bias and social justice. In *Handbook on promoting social justice in education* (p. 431). Springer International Publishing. https://doi.org/10.1007/978-3-030-14625-2_66

Chapter 3

1 Cajete, G. (1994). *Look to the mountain: An ecology of indigenous education.* ERIC.

Degruy-Leary, J. (2017). *Post-traumatic slave syndrome: America's legacy of enduring injury.* Portland, OR: Joy DeGruy Publications Inc.

Dove, M. K. (2004). Teacher attrition: A critical American and international education issue. *Delta Kappa Gamma Bulletin, 71*(1).

Edelman, M. W. (2009). The cradle to prison pipeline: America's new apartheid. *Harvard Journal of African American Public Policy, 15*(Summer Issue), 67–68.

Flannery, M. E. (2019). *The epidemic of anxiety among today's students.* NEA. Retrieved November 11, 2021, from https://www.nea.org/nea-today/all-news-articles/epidemic-anxiety-among-todays-students.

Horowitz, J. M., & Graf, N. (2020, May 30). *Most U.S. teens see anxiety, depression as major problems.* Pew Research Center's Social & Demographic Trends Project. Retrieved November 11, 2021, from https://www.pewresearch.org/social-trends/2019/02/20/most-u-s-teens-see-anxiety-and-depression-as-a-major-problem-among-their-peers/.

Johnson, S. C. (2019). U.S. Education and the persistence of slavery. *Journal of Curriculum and Pedagogy,* 1–20. https://doi.org/10.1080/15505170.2019.1618757.

Ladson-Billings, G. (2006). From the achievement gap to the education debt: Understanding achievement in U.S. schools. *Educational Researcher, 35*(7), 3–12.

Sass, D. A., Flores, B. B., Claeys, L., & Pérez, B. (2012). Identifying personal and contextual factors that contribute to attrition rates for Texas public school teachers. *Education Policy Analysis Archives/Archivos Analíticos de Políticas Educativas*, 20, 1–26.

2 Dorn, E., Hancock, B., Sarakatsannis, J., & Viruleg, E. (2020). COVID-19 and student learning in the United States: The hurt could last a lifetime. *McKinsey & Company, 1.*

Op. Cit., Ladson-Billings (2006).

3 Op. Cit., Degruy-Leary (2017).

4 Op. Cit., Degruy-Leary (2017).

Red Shirt, D. (2015). *The Lakota children are called wakanyeja 'little sacred ones'.* Native American Times. Retrieved November 11, 2021, from https://nativetimes.com/index.php/life/commentary/11125-the-lakota-children-are-called-wakanyeja-little-sacred-ones.

United Tribes says every child sacred. Tribal College Journal of American Indian Higher Education (2012, March 26). Retrieved November 11, 2021, from https://tribalcollegejournal.org/united-tribes-child-sacred/.

5 *Arabic customs and traditions.* Arab Academy (2017, May 15). Retrieved February 9, 2022, from https://www.arabacademy.com/arabic-customs-traditions/.

Montero-Sieburth, M., & Villaruel, F. (2003). *Making invisible Latino adolescents visible: A critical approach to Latino diversity.* Routledge.

6 Mayaka, B., & Truell, R. (2021). Ubuntu and its potential impact on the international social work profession. *International Social Work*, 64(5), 649–662, p. 3.

7 Op. Cit., Degruy-Leary (2017).

Op. Cit., Red Shirt (2015).

Op. Cit., *United Tribes says every child sacred* (2012).

8 *Aap-AACAP-Cha declaration of a national emergency in child and adolescent mental health.* American Academy of Pediatrics (2021, October 19). Retrieved January 5, 2022, from https://www.aap.org/en/advocacy/child-and-adolescent-healthy-mental-development/aap-aacap-cha-declaration-of-a-national-emergency-in-child-and-adolescent-mental-health/?campaign_id=9&emc=edit_nn_20220104&instance_id=49344&nl=the-morning®i_id=86340798&segment_id=78602&te=1&user_id=d88a92611aab0bb98a785ee5af35f796.

Centers for Disease Control and Prevention. (2021). *Facts about suicide.* Centers for Disease Control and Prevention. Retrieved November 10, 2021, from https://www.cdc.gov/suicide/facts/index.html.

Contrera, J. (2018). *A boy tried to kill himself by jumping from a highway bridge: He killed someone else instead.* The Washington Post. Retrieved November 10, 2021, from https://www.washingtonpost.com/news/local/wp/2018/12/13/feature/the-boy-on-the-bridge/.

Op. Cit., Edelman (2009).

Op. Cit., Flannery (2019).

Gill, J. H. (2002). *Native American worldviews an introduction.*

Op. Cit., Horowitz & Graf (2020).

Hurst, M. (2021). *'my baby told me he was tired': First-grader who killed himself may have been bullied to death, parents say.* kens5.com. Retrieved November 11, 2021, from https://www.kens5.com/article/news/community/first-grader-death/273-bf2203fa-e368-4bfe-8f84-c2770fc49a9d.

Op. Cit., Johnson (2019).

Op. Cit., Ladson-Billings (2006).

Malott, C. (2007). *A call to action: An introduction to education, philosophy, and Native North America* (Vol. 324): Peter Lang.

McCarter, S. (2017). The school-to-prison pipeline: A primer for social workers. *Social Work, 62*(1), 53–61. https://doi.org/10.1093/sw/sww078.

National Dropout Prevention Center. (2018). *Economic impacts of dropouts.* Retrieved from https://dropoutprevention.org/resources/statistics/quick-facts/economic-impacts-of-dropouts/.

Yard, E. (2021, June 17). *Emergency department visits for suspected suicide attempts among persons aged 12–25 years before and during the COVID-19 pandemic—United States, January 2019–May 2021.* Centers for Disease Control and Prevention. Retrieved January 5, 2022, from https://www.cdc.gov/mmwr/volumes/70/wr/mm7024e1.htm?campaign_id=9&emc=edit_nn_20220104&instance_id=49344&nl=the-morning®i_id=86340798&segment_id=78602&te=1&user_id=d88a92611aab0bb98a785ee5af35f796.

9   Op. Cit., Degruy-Leary (2017).

10   *New International Version.* (2021). 1 Corinthians 13:1–3.

11   Op. Cit., Montero-Sieburth & Villaruel (2003).

12   Ali, S. (2019). A second-class workforce: How neoliberal policies and reforms undermined the educational profession. *Journal of Curriculum and Teaching, 8*(3), 102–110.

Apple, M. W. (2017). *Cultural and economic reproduction in education: Essays on class, ideology and the state* (Vol. 53). Routledge.

Apple, M. W., & Beane, J. A. (2007). *Democratic schools: Lessons in powerful education.* Heinemann.

Beane, J. A. (2005). *A reason to teach: Creating classrooms of dignity and hope: The power of the democratic way.* Heinemann Educational Books.

Darder, A. (2015). *Culture and power in the classroom: Educational foundations for the schooling of bicultural students.* Routledge.

Gay, G. (2018). *Culturally responsive teaching: Theory, research, and practice.* Teachers College Press.

Ladson-Billings, G. (2014). Culturally relevant pedagogy 2.0: aka the remix. *Harvard Educational Review, 84*(1), 74–84.

Montero-Sieburth, M., & Villaruel, F. (2003). *Making invisible Latino adolescents visible: A critical approach to Latino diversity.* Routledge.

Weissberg, R. P., Durlak, J. A., Domitrovich, C. E., & Gullotta, T. P. (2015). Social and emotional learning: Past, present, and future. In J. A. Durlak, C. E. Domitrovich, R. P. Weissberg, & T. P. Gullotta (Eds.), *Handbook of social and emotional learning: Research and practice* (pp. 3–19). The Guilford Press.

Yeager, D. S., & Dweck, C. S. (2020). What can be learned from growth mindset controversies?. *American Psychologist, 75*(9), 1269.

13   Johnson, S. (2020). *Afrocentricity: Student voices on African American identity in multicultural education reform.* The University of Texas at San Antonio.

14   Fromm, E. (2000). *The art of loving: The centennial edition* (p. 79). A&C Black.

15 Op. Cit., Johnson (2020), unpublished interview data.

16 Ibid., p. 114.

17 Ibid., p. 196.

18 Ibid., p. 200.

19 Ibid., p. 208.

20 Ibid., p. 222.

21 Ibid., unpublished interview data.

22 Ibid., p. 106.

23 Freire, P. (1993). *Pedagogy of the oppressed* (New Rev 20th-Anniversary ed.). New York: Continuum.

   Hall, S. (2017). *The fateful triangle: Race, ethnicity, nation.* Harvard University Press.

   Pinar, W. (2004). *What is curriculum theory?.* Routledge.

24 Op. Cit., Freire (1993).

25 Polanin, M., & Vera, E. (2013). Bullying prevention and social justice. *Theory into Practice, 52*(4), 303–310.

26 Op. Cit., Freire (1993).

27 Op. Cit., Freire (1993, 2005).

   Op. Cit., Fromm (2000).

28 Nieto, S. (2013). *Finding joy in teaching students of diverse backgrounds: Culturally responsive and socially just practices in U.S. classrooms* (pp. 33–34). Heinemann.

29 Delpit, L. (2013). *"Multiplication Is for White people": Raising expectations for other people's children.* New York, USA: The New Press.

30 Ibid., p. 38.

31 Robinson-Morris, D. W. (2018). *Ubuntu and Buddhism in higher education: An ontological (re) thinking.* Routledge.

· 4 ·

TERMS OF ENDEARMENT

In western society, the beginning of knowing anyone new almost always includes the introduction of a name. We *know* by connecting people to their primary identifiers—or given names. Sometimes, names are less formal and people are introduced by hypocoristic names—diminutive forms of given names. Regardless, just as babies born to parents in western culture are particularized by their names, students' names are the primary introduction to who they are and the beginning of loving them. *Naming* children in any culture is a deliberate celebration of who the children are, often seeing their destiny through the life of their spiritual or earthly ancestry.[1] To be named is an honor and quite possibly a multigenerational one.[2] *Naming* is a complex mechanism through which children develop a sense of self, therefore, I began to know and love my students through a communion of name exchange.[3]

My name was Miss Fountain to my first class, middle schoolers, and wound up having almost as many conjugations as any regular verb by the end of the first quarter—Miss, Miss Fou-an, Miss Fou'n, etc. I didn't mind. I suppose I viewed it then as I would today—a growth of cultural competence of a fashion. My students were addressing me correctly through the uniqueness of their own voices, their own inner beings. As the years moved on and many classes of my beloved students came and went, so did the terms of endearment that began as my *name*. Eventually married, my last name changed to Johnson. My students called me Ms. J, Professor, Profe, Señora and, eventually Dr. J or Dr. Johnson. One year, one of my high school classes was "acting up" and I smiled and spoke gently to them in a manner that only Maya Angelou could better. I asked them if they had ever seen a barracuda. Most had not, so I projected a picture on the screen of a beautiful barracuda gliding through the Caribbean blue. I told them that I was very much like this fish—serene and perceptibly innocuous when undisturbed. Then I cast a picture of a barracuda on the attack—mouth full of ominous teeth—and I assured my class that when exasperated, I also had nothing but teeth and, further, like the fish, I might bite. We all got a laugh, as well as my point, and from that day forward, every year, some sibling or close associate of the prior class made sure we added "barracuda" to the list of aliases to which I might respond. When my smile turned upside down, it was a guarantee to hear someone across the class call out, "Hey ya'll . . . here comes la barracuda . . . cut it out!".

The coup d'état of pet names became Mama J for which I have no recollection of its beginnings, but it took off like a wildfire. It became the all-time favorite name and one by which I am deeply moved as it bespeaks a level of trust, joy, and interdependence that is reminiscent of the depth of love between the Massai and their children. Yes, I would tell my middle and high school students regularly, "You are my children for 50 minutes each day. I love you; I am responsible for your welfare and I am completely invested in you. When it's wrong with you, it's wrong with me, and when you leap for joy, I am at peace." "Mama J" was my students' way of letting me know how loved they felt, and with that level of endearment we accomplished a lot in Spanish class, in English, and in Math.[4]

I came to understand the level of emotional connection that exists in a name through my students' use of Mama J, and how that emotionality is uniquely relative to each student. Case in point was a set of twins in my ninth grade Spanish class whom I will call Steve and Robert. Steve's face lit up with excitement matched only by his motion in his seat when he realized that "Mama J" was an acceptable name by which he could call me. Robert looked at me strangely, and then with utter disgust at his brother. He wasted no time in bringing correction to what he perceived to be his brother's over-familiarity, expecting that his scorn might correct his brother's embarrassing behavior. Steve was resolved and Robert let me know in no uncertain terms that he would call me "Mrs. J" because "Mama J" was too informal. At the risk of losing my composure to utter laughter, I acknowledged the value and acceptability of both of their choices and reinforced the importance of mutual respect regarding the individual freedom in choosing what they might call me.

By that point in my career, I had learned to give my students curricular and pedagogical choices, including the name by which they would address me. Just as a parent, without hesitation or scorn, allows for a spectrum of references—mom or mommy, da-da or daddy—it occurred to me to widen my aperture regarding the modes of inclusiveness that support student identity and consider the idea that an act of unconditional love in this area could come in the shape of *naming*.

Drawing upon Native American onto-epistemes, largely counter intuitive to western thought which names a child at birth permanently and without alteration, *naming* is a dynamic process as a person's life defines their character and is subject to community involvement.[5] It is not automatic but a function of readiness—a person may go years before a name is selected.[6] As a person's character shapes and re-shapes, so does that person's name until it more accurately reflects who they are in that moment.[7] Allowing my students to name me as they saw me, provided it was respectful of the teacher-student or mentor-student relationship, drew on their cultural capital and gave each student his or her own individualized foundation upon which we began to know and love each other.

Cultural erasure is a horrible thing. Personally, my life as an American has left me bereft of the profundity and celebration of many of the ethnic cultures that have constituted my bloodline. Instead, like so many in America, I have been forced to navigate my way through mainstreamed erasures and marginalizations that are a direct result of colonial imperialism and White dominance, limiting my access to my White and Brown ancestry alike.[8] Surviving racism in America cost my family the full expression of its multiethnic belonging. Any European or Native American identity was swallowed up by the "one-drop rule" that legally and/or normatively defined Black identity.[9] My soul suffered a persistent emptiness and melancholy, having regretted the lost honor of receiving my Blackfoot or Seminole name.

Towards the end of my career, one of my adult students, whom I'll call Ron, gifted me with a name that was not only our special bond with one another but a spiritual restoration of a sort to my lost Native American ancestry and the most profound and unforgettable privilege. Ron was a student in a basic skills course that was uniquely designed to meet the diversified needs of Wounded Warriors, also termed Warriors in Transition, whose medical conditions predisposed them to medical retirement from their branch of service. The Wounded

Warrior Basic Skills Course satisfied the need for an academic refresher course that would improve their military entrance exam scores and the possibility to remain in the armed services or maximize their competence and survivability to enter college as a civilian.

Ron suffered a traumatic event that compromised his relational skills and in his desire to connect with me, he began to text me using military radio communications. "Lone Wolf this is Screaming Eagle; how copy? Over." I stared at that text— "Lone Wolf . . ." How he could have chosen a more appropriate name for me, only heaven knows, but given my life experience, he saw right through me and named me for exactly who I was—a lone wolf. Wolves are, by nature, highly social and resilient pack members.[10] A wolf without a pack is a survivor, ever searching for that illusive community from which it was severed, enjoying membership by adoption within many a welcoming pack but never ceasing the search for its own.[11] In a total loss of composure, I responded to my student, "Screaming Eagle, this is Lone Wolf. That's a good copy. Over." And, so became my most precious name, birthed out of a relationship of trust via a curriculum of agape and bestowed upon me by a student.

Ron's choice of name for me was a loving, transcendental gesture, reflective of who I was currently as a function of my historical identity. His classmate, whose pseudonym is Richard, named me for precisely who I was to him in the present moment: "Hero." Richard began to sporadically call me "Hero," which unnerved and confounded me. There were Wounded Warriors by the dozens in my classes for whom that title was far more appropriately befitting. I never rejected the nickname, but I could not understand why he felt the need to see me in that light. I wasn't a hero. I was a teacher. I never caught a bullet meant for someone else, or as in the case of one of my students, a rocket propelled grenade (RPG). I never left friends, family or country to defend our nation or our allies.

I finally came to understand the intention behind "hero" when I confided in a classmate over my confusion. He explained to me that "hero" is a common identifier between soldiers that honors the sacrificial bond they share, and understandably so since they may not always like each other but are committed to love each other in the most profound and heroic way—they lay their lives down in battle for country and one another. Calling me "hero" was Richard's way of acknowledging the unique educational experience that an agape curriculum inspires by letting me share a sacred bond typically reserved for his fellow soldiers. This was an Ubuntu moment in which he identified the interconnectedness he shared with his teacher—that which was alive in me for his sake.[12]

Theoretically, the concept of a curriculum of unconditional love can appear difficult to measure. I would argue that learning outcomes centered in a framework of love can be not only observable but measurable, as is the case with Richard.

Ron named me as he saw me through a historic lens, Richard named me in my current state of being and Byron, also an adult classmate of them both, as if with some inspirational prophetic knowing, projected upon my present self an image of who I ought to be—not that I had contemplated or accomplished his vision at that point. Byron insisted upon calling me "Professor." His mischievous grin would widen the more perturbed I became in response to a title that people traditionally aspire to at great expense. I understood that he meant it as a compliment out of reverence and honor for a teacher he esteemed, but I was mortified that someone who had earned the crown of Ph.D. might hear him calling me professor and think me a thief. As it turns out, what Byron did, as I have done many times with my students, was to call forth something unseen as if it were fact. He was returning a favor by planting a seed in me, something for me to awaken to which would catapult me into my destiny.

Nicknaming, which includes the use of pet names, carries with it a deep social significance that can rival the importance of a given or first name.[13] It is never a neutral assignment and is a powerful device for affecting behavior, in this case through reinforcing value and a positive sense of identity, along multiple intersectionalities, in who a student is historically and currently.[14] Well intentioned and mutually negotiated, it serves to plant that good seed in our students, calling them forth into their destiny while they are still too blinded by inaccurate and self-destructive social messages to know their own brilliance.[15] This is a deliberate act of unconditional love that sees beyond the unrefined project that is a student's current humanity and into the promise of future possibility. Lisa Delpit observed the measurable, positive academic outcomes of this aspect of curricular agape in recounting an experience in her book, "*Multiplication Is for White people*": *Raising Expectations for Other People's Children*, while visiting the classroom of a teacher who engaged her students as if they were "scholars." The teacher identified the students according to her expectation, and their very real capacities, and this group of youngsters rose to the occasion.[16]

As our own identities—our worldviews set by experiences, biases, and values—tend to enter our classrooms with us, my determination to create an identity-supportive agape learning environment meant that I, like the teacher in Delpit's book, intentionally addressed my class of students as "beautiful", "brilliant," and the like.[17] It was years later, after I had retired as a K-12 teacher, when I discovered through my research that names, not usually being arbitrary, carry with them cultural knowledge that guides the recipient in choosing courses of action.[18]

Reflective of this idea is my memory of one particular class of high school students struggling with several demanding classes in one semester, including my own. They were beginning to disconnect, and I became concerned. It occurred to me to purchase faux diamond gems from the arts and craft store and some black clay. I stuffed 30 gems into 30 balls of black modeling clay and took them to school in individual Ziploc bags. I distributed them to each student with the explanation that we all experience overwhelming pressures and stressors along life's pursuits. Sometimes, what seems to be a ceaseless source of suffering causes us to want to give up. I assured the class that the dark moments represented in the clay were not what defined them—that wasn't who they were. "Dig a little deeper," I told them. It was fun to watch them tearing open the clay to reveal the diamonds. Of course, I reminded them that heat and pressure are simply the catalysts that bring to fruition who they really are—diamonds.

The message that their teacher did not see their failures as anything other than a refiner of diamonds, and that they were to keep those diamonds in clay with them to the end of the school year in case they needed a reminder of their true identities, did manage to lift their spirits. I observed a much more resilient class of students after that. As is the case with all of humanity, they were diamonds in the rough.

My students tended to name and re-name me throughout the year, but I only named them once our relationship was established.[19] One act of anti-love that has historically plagued our classrooms with cultural injustice and erasure has been the deliberate mispronunciation of names.[20] In its extreme form, teachers have been guilty of renaming those students whose names fell outside of Euro dominant social norms.[21] This level of disrespect in the form of subtle but daily microaggression is an insult that upholds the notion of ethnic and cultural stratification.[22] To disrupt a student's name is to disrupt his or her identity and, therefore, a sense of safety and belonging in the learning space. The outcome of this risks academic achievement.[23] Refusal to learn a student's name is an act of selfish love, loving self over others, instigating a separateness as Fromm described between the teacher and the students.[24] This separateness doesn't just affect the targeted student but threatens the entirety of the learning community.[25] It repositions the question from "And how are the children?"

to "And how is the teacher?" A curriculum of agape is sacrificial and deliberately outward, seeking the good of others above self—exampled by learning a student's name even though it is difficult.

Having properly learned my students' given names, it was not unusual for me to openly assign pet names to them in return. Amor, Cielo, Cariño(a),[26] my love, rock star, super star were among the many terms of endearment that I playfully lavished upon my students as a reminder of their brilliance and value in the world and in my classroom. Although De Klerk and Bosch found that young children, more than adolescents, tend to gravitate towards terms of endearment that relay affection or familial roles, my experience seemed to demonstrate tremendous fluidity between an adolescent's preference for a more contextualized pet name and one that exhibits affection or familial ties.[27] I found it more appropriate to assign terms of endearment for my adult students that reflected those contextualized pet names: friend, champ, superstar, etc.

It amazed me to observe my primary and secondary students' response to correction when a genuine term of endearment, based upon our relationship of unconditional love, preceded the word of caution. "Mi amor, you may want to re-think the choice you are making right now." This usually tempered the behavior into a warm smile and a more appropriate choice almost instantly. Prefacing discipline with a confirmation of unconditional love prioritized and affirmed how much I cherished them, regardless of their wrongdoing, and seemed to call them to their own internal higher ground.

If I were ever unsure of the profound impact a term of endearment had on my students, "Mariquita's" story was my confirmation. By some soulish impulse, I wound up calling one high school student "Mariquita" now and again until one day she asked, "What does mariquita mean?" I told her it meant "ladybug." Her entire countenance tendered as she replied, "I love that." Mariquita's response was reminiscent of my own heart melting under the feeling of validation that my Cuban professor's "Cariña" evoked in me. I was failing his class but he loved me anyway and that love inspired me to pull my grade up. "Ladybug", like "Cariña", was a simple signifier that could have been widely interpreted, yet this student, without prompting or explanation, drew the appropriate meaning out of it as I had intended, from one heart to another. She understood in the symbolism that I was affirming her identity as a welcomed blessing, a lovely source of happiness. She would often say, "I hate Spanish—it's hard—but I love your class." Only love can consistently draw students into a class that they "hate." I dare say Spanish was not Mariquita's favorite course of study but, despite that, in class, she was one child for whom the question of "how are the children" could be answered by saying, "Mariquita was well."

Explore, Think, Act

Continuing with the idea that educators must first know their students if they aim to love them, Chapter 4 begins the *knowing* process with the introduction of names. We explored the importance of names and *naming* to the identities of my students and the ways in which they identified me in relation to them. Explore your own relationship with your students and the ways in which names and *naming* impact your classroom environment.

(A) Think about the names you use to address your students.
1. Are they nicknames or, exclusively, their given names?
2. How do your students feel about the way you address them? How do they feel about the way they address you?
3. What does your *naming* practice tell you about your relationship with your students?
4. What message are your students giving you about their relationship with you through the name(s) they call you?
5. What message are you giving your students by the way you address them?

(B) Think about the way you responded to the questions in section A.
1. How might you restore or improve your relationship with your students through your *naming* practices?
2. Regarding your answer to 1B, what input have your students given you that will guide you in restoring or improving your relationship in this way?

Notes

1   De Mente, B. L. (2016). *Etiquette guide to China: Know the rules that make the difference!*. Tuttle Publishing.

   Kohli, R., & Solórzano, D. G. (2012). Teachers, please learn our names!: Racial microaggressions and the K-12 classroom. *Race Ethnicity and Education, 15*(4), 441–462.

   Montero-Sieburth, M., & Villaruel, F. (2003). *Making invisible Latino adolescents visible: A critical approach to Latino diversity.* Routledge.

Nanticoke Lenni-Lenape Tribal Nation. (2019). *Native American naming ceremonies: We are still here!* Retrieved November 11, 2021, from https://nlltribe.com/native-american-naming-ceremonies/.

Noel, J. (2002). Education toward cultural shame: A century of Native American education. *The Journal of Educational Foundations, 16*(1), 19.

2   Ibid.

3   Seeman, M. (1976). The psychopathology of everyday names. *Psychology and Psychotherapy: Theory Research and Practice, 49,* 89–95. https://doi.org/10.1111/j.2044-8341.1976.tb02356.x.

4   Crozier, W. R. (2004). Recollections of schoolteachers' nicknames. *Names, 52*(2), 83–99.

5   Gill, J. H. (2002). *Native American worldviews an introduction.*

Op. Cit., Nanticoke Lenni-Lenape Tribal Nation (2019).

Op. Cit., Noel (2002).

6   Ibid.

7   Ibid.

8   Arredondo, P., Gallardo-Cooper, M., Delgado-Romero, E. A., & Zapata, A. L. (2015). Latino worldviews and cultural values. *Culturally Responsive Counseling with Latinas/os,* 15–30.

Darder, A. (2015). *Culture and power in the classroom: Educational foundations for the schooling of bicultural students.* Routledge.

Darder, A. (2017). *Reinventing Paulo Freire: A pedagogy of love.* Taylor & Francis.

Delpit, L. (2013). *"Multiplication Is for White people": Raising expectations for other people's children.* New York, USA: The New Press.

Gatto, J. T. (2010). *Weapons of mass instruction: A schoolteacher's journey through the dark world of compulsory schooling.* New Society Publishers.

Gatto, J. T. (2017). *Dumbing us down: The hidden curriculum of compulsory schooling.* New Society Publishers.

Khanna, N. (2010). "If you're half Black, you're just Black": Reflected appraisals and the persistence of the one-drop rule. *The Sociological Quarterly, 51*(1), 96–121.

Ladson-Billings, G. (2006). From the achievement gap to the education debt: Understanding achievement in U.S. schools. *Educational Researcher, 35*(7), 3–12.

Op. Cit., Arredondo et al. (2015).

Ogbu, J. U. (1978). *Minority education and caste: The American system in cross-cultural perspective.* New York: Academic Press.

9   Op Cit., Khanna, N. (2010).

10 *The social wolf.* Living with Wolves. (2021, August 2). Retrieved January 22, 2022, from https://www.livingwithwolves.org/about-wolves/social-wolf/.

11 Ibid.

12 Fromm, E. (2000). *The art of loving: The centennial edition.* A&C Black.

13 De Klerk, V., & Bosch, B. (1999). *Nicknames as evidence of verbal playfulness.*

Leslie, P. L., & Skipper, J. K. (1990). Toward a theory of nicknames: A case for socio-onomastics. *Names, 38*(4), 273–282.

Op. Cit., Seeman (1976).

14 Op. Cit., De Mente (2016).

Op. Cit., De Klerk & Bosch (1999).

Op. Cit., Leslie & Skipper (1990).

Op. Cit., Seeman (1976).

15 Ibid.

16 Op. Cit., Delpit (2013).

17 Brown, K. D. (2013). Trouble on my mind: Toward a framework of humanizing critical sociocultural knowledge for teaching and teacher education. *Race Ethnicity and Education*, 16(3), 316–338.

King, J. E. (1991). Dysconscious racism: Ideology, identity, and the miseducation of teachers. *The Journal of Negro Education*, 60(2), 133–146. https://doi.org/10.2307/2295605.

18 Op. Cit., Leslie & Skipper (1990).

Op. Cit., Seeman (1976).

19 Op. Cit., De Mente (2016).

20 Op. Cit., Kohli & Solórzano (2012).

Op. Cit., Noel (2002).

21 Ibid.

22 Op. Cit., Kohli & Solórzano (2012).

Op. Cit., Noel (2002).

Payne, K. E., Philyaw, Z., Rabow, J., & Yazdanfar, S. (2018). Names: A new dimension of transformation. *Race Ethnicity and Education*, 21(4), 564–571.

Torres-Mackie, N. (2019). *Understanding name-based microaggressions*. Psychology Today. Retrieved November 11, 2021, from https://www.psychologytoday.com/intl/blog/underdog-psychology/201909/understanding-name-based-microaggressions.

23 Dee, T. S. (2004). Teachers, race, and student achievement in a randomized experiment. *The Review of Economics and Statistics*, 86(1), 195–210. https://doi.org/10.1162/003465304323023750.

Op. Cit., Delpit (2013).

Op. Cit., Kohli & Solórzano (2012).

Op. Cit., Noel (2002).

24 Op. Cit., Fromm (2000).

25 Ibid.

26 Translation: my love.

27 Op. Cit., De Klerk & Bosch (1999).

ONE KNEE DOESN'T BRING UP A CHILD

Naming was one aspect of beginning to know and learning to love one another. The second was the establishment of our common being—a loving community, to the best of my ability, bonded by unity. Within the first two days of a new class, knowing and loving began with who I was, who the students were, and who we were together, which is still my modus operandi to this day. Of course, our common way of being in education is often attributed to establishing classroom rules and procedures at the beginning of a school year. As teacher-facilitators, the burden is fully ours to establish and maintain a good foundation for our class culture, to set the tone for the learning community in a way that is inclusive of and meaningful to our students.

I introduced many sets of rules and classroom policies over the years, eventually conceptualizing a curriculum of agape that incorporated diverse philosophies and became the emergent framework for building a classroom culture of love. My class rules, appropriated mostly from Native American worldview as well as Christian and Ubuntu philosophies on unconditional love, are still as follows:

- This is a safe place
- We support and encourage each other

- We respect each other's thoughts, person, belongings
- We are kind and considerate, not rude
- We are humble at all times
- We do not compete with one another
- We stand by and protect each other
- We are patient with one another
- We rely on and trust each other
- We resolve our anger . . . we don't hold on to it
- We are "others centered"
- We persevere together

The end of my classroom teaching career brought with it a focus and a culmination of sorts regarding the imperative to establish a culture of unconditional love in the learning space. Establishing the rules was closely followed by an investigation of the term *agape*. This was meant to help the students understand the rules and to further solidify what was to be our class culture. We dissected the Greek words *agape* (unconditional love), *phileo* (brotherly love) and *eros* (romantic love); constructed examples of each and questioned which signifier best described our rules and our goals as a learning community.[1] From this foundational goal of maintaining an environment of unconditional love, we built every aspect of our class: academic resilience, personal interactions and classroom management. The signifier, *agape*, became such a part of our being that it emerged as part of the middle and high school students' regular lexicon. "We agape you!" was as likely a pronouncement as "We love you!" *Agape* introduced a framework of love upon which mutual trust and a sense of belonging resulted. It was the principle upon which we defined ourselves as a community.

Education, when at its best as a system, is a co-laborer with parents and guardians, all parties invested in the shaping and well-being of our nation's children. There are several proverbs relative to various African cultures that reinforce the popularized phrase, *It takes a village to raise a child.*[2] Although authenticating the African origins of that phrase is complex, in northern Tanzania there is a proverb that suggests "a child's upbringing belongs to the community", irrespective of parentage; also from Tanzania is the proverb, "One knee doesn't bring up a child"; finally, from East and Central Africa comes the proverb, "One hand does not nurse a child."[3] These proverbs compliment a curriculum of agape since love, like learning, is a socially motivated construct that is fruitless outside of a community.[4] Love and learning require subject and object, therefore, community becomes a necessity for both. Further, I have taught classes of four students and classes of over 40; it is not the quantity of community membership that I found most relevant but the quality of the relationships—those multidimensional interactions among diverse members that inspired a sense of connectedness and mutual self-actualization. Quality is where agape intersects with community and determines its substance and value system.

One aspect of "quality" that remains a tripwire to establishing a sound learning community is the monocular lens through which curriculum and pedagogical "best practices" are established.[5] "Something is fundamentally amiss in the dominant education systems of the United States."[6] Students whose cultural identities are minimized or erased from the learning space and place in favor of a socioeconomically and politically powerful Eurocentric worldview, find little sense of trust, safety, belonging or love, which we will later discuss as deleterious to self-actualization and positive learning outcomes.[7] Love, as defined in Part II, that regards a "neighbor" as highly as "self", is immediately extinguished by the expectation that students remain "self-reliant and in direct competition with one another"—behaving as if they are "alone in a crowd."[8] It is further stifled by our current monolithic curricular and pedagogical worldview that does not reflect the cultural diversity of our nation's students or their estimable connection to the history and development of the United States and the world.[9]

According to the National Center for Education Statistics (2021), of the 50.7 million students enrolled in K-12 public schools during 2017, 13.6 million identified as Latino(a)/Hispanic, 7.7 million identified as Black, 2.8 million identified as Asian/Pacific Islander, and half a million identified as Native American/Alaska Native.[10] Two million students identified themselves as belonging to more than one racial or ethnic demographic. These numbers do not reflect the ethnic or racial demographics at the post-secondary, adult, level, but what they do tell us is that over 50% of our elementary and secondary students alone are of color and culturally diverse. A research study that I conducted in 2020 found that across ages, genders, and ethnicities, African American/Black, Latino(a) and White students highly preferred a non-Western learning environment in which the curriculum and pedagogical practice was horizontally relational, community oriented, collaborative instead of competitive, and culturally holistic—inclusive of more positive historical and current contributions from underrepresented racial, ethnic and cultural groups within the United States and abroad.[11]

Related to the injustice of a Euro-Colonial, Western-only approach to teaching and learning is the totalitarianism that educators tend to believe is necessary for learning, whether it results from a deficit mentality around underserved and marginalized groups of students—regarding them as needing "fixing" or "saving"—or an assumption of best practice based on observation.[12] It was a genuine epiphany that helped me realize the beauty of moving away from the "top-down" approach to pedagogy that is painfully adhered to our practice. By mid-career, I had learned that the tight grip I held on my curricular and pedagogical expertise was selfish and in opposition to a curriculum of agape. I began to release my dictatorship in exchange for a horizontal, shared communal labor that allows knowledge, belonging, and trust to shape collaboratively.[13] My revelation was that my students were in my classroom to teach as much as I was—they were often more astute and successful at explaining concepts to one another. I can honestly say that I have learned more about life and about my profession from my children and my students. The quality of the village we call our classrooms is better suited for student motivation and engagement when all have "skin in the game" and work collaboratively towards the common purpose of learning and growing.[14]

My one and only experience teaching at a charter school occurred during the same year I retired to pursue my Ph.D. and a career in teacher education. I was hired to "fix a mess" in the high school Spanish department. The students were not learning. They had become accustomed to a chaotic and undisciplined class culture plagued by disrespect. The result was three levels of Spanish students who had zero to limited proficiency in the language and no understanding of the cultural implications of Spanish. One of these classes of students was to begin their AP level course without hope of successfully preparing for the exam, much less taking it. Harkening back to Lisa Delpit's suggestion in *"Multiplication Is for White People": Raising Expectations for Other People's Children*, knowing our students requires developing relationships with them that understand their political, cultural and intellectual legacy.[15] I began to build my curriculum of agape with a textbook adoption that would better suit the inclusion of cultural and experiential diversity, and open the possibility of dialogue around global social issues.[16] A more engaging and relevant set of materials then reflected the list of rules and the resultant preference for agape over other notions of love.

The ninth grade class was the most culturally diverse class I ever had the pleasure of teaching and one of the most spirited. Whether they were learning, socializing or disrupting, theirs was a high octane enthusiasm that needed harnessing. This bunch internalized and embraced our agape culture with such fervor that when the workload became difficult or some playful verbal sparring erupted, someone would invariably yell out, "Aw c'mon, where's the agape?" That would surely send everyone, including me, into a roar of laughter that lightened the corporate burden or let us all participate in the sparring fun.

I definitely worked them hard; it's my nature to expect much from my students.[17] I would remind my students regularly that my job was to identify greatness in them and yank it out. By the end of the year, all three Spanish classes were on level. The AP class was still unprepared to take an AP exam, except for the students who were already native speakers, but they had pulled their language skills up by two and a half levels to meet the proficiency standards of a level three Spanish student. They also had mastered a comparative awareness of culture and the global issues that concerned Spanish speaking communities. Their character grew exponentially alongside their academic accomplishments.

As a member of that learning community, I had promised my students that I would not ask them to work any harder for me than I was willing to work for them—we would traverse the sometimes scary road of Foreign Language acquisition, often distancing ourselves away from our comfort zones, together. One question loomed large on my mind and involved the inequitable power dynamic that exists between a teacher and a student, even within the best relationships—was I truly meeting the burden of my promise to them?[18] Could they trust my word? Was I properly invested in the interconnectedness that defines unconditional love according to Buddhist, Hindu, and Ubuntu philosophies—one in which suffering and joy are co-experienced?[19]

The same year that I taught at my final school, I was taking voice lessons. I love to sing, mostly in the car, in my house when I think no one can hear me, and in the quiet and secluded presence of my friend and voice instructor. The idea of performing in front of a group invited an immediate nausea and muscle failure in my legs. My voice instructor would present me with regular opportunities to show off my new skills, always with the same response—no. Eventually, she suggested that I sing my newest accomplishment, a Mexican Folk piece, to my students. I admit I did decline at first but, after thinking about my promise and all the times I asked my students to embrace the public vulnerability of speaking an uncertain language in front of their peers, I had to show them that my promise was genuine. It was an agape inspired love song, almost operatic in sections—I was scared.

At the end of the year, I announced that I had a parting gift for them, reminding them of the promise I had made and how proud I was of their bravery all year and their accomplishments. I smiled at each and every one of them, and opened my mouth to the first note of the Mexican folk song, *Pregúntale A Las Estrellas*: *"Pregúntale a las estrellas, si no de noche me ven llorar, Pregúntales si no busco, para adorarte la soledad . . . Ya nunca dudes que yo te quiero, Que por tí muero, loco de amor . ."*[20,21] If you have ever performed, it will probably make sense that I have little memory of my singing debut. The only treasures I manage to retain from that experience are visions of my students, mouths agape, in shock that their teacher could sing to them in that way, and crying, having been profoundly moved by the sentiment. I jumped up and down like an excited child at the completion of the song, admitting to my students that I could not feel my legs, and laughed with them over trampling my fear. Finally, in the most profound way, I was on the path of suffering and joy with my students instead of walking the periphery alongside them.[22]

Although the song was meant to be a gift to them, I believe I am the one who walked away with the bigger prize—an opportunity to work hard and grow WITH my students. When I think about all that occurred during my time with these students, I don't believe that professional bearing, classroom management or my demand for excellence would have been enough to drive a good outcome.[23] I believe it was the relationships we built and the agape community we enforced together that made the greater difference.[24] We were an interdependent agape community when we were overwhelmed and struggling as much as when we were celebrating our breakthroughs.

A just and effective set of mutually negotiated rules and collaborative hard work are salient aspects of a thriving community, be it social or academic.[25] However, for educators, cognition and mastery of the learning objectives as determined by state standards—the primary goal of an academic community—is highly influenced by social factors.[26] Central as hard work and discipline are to the purpose of education, proponents of Social Emotional Learning and Culturally Relevant or Responsive Teaching might agree that cognitive growth is also dependent upon softer skills, socially mediated, non-cognitive communal factors such as: love and belonging, well-being, trust, safety.[27] Maslow's Hierarchy of Needs remains a popular motivation theory within education that enlists a more holistic view of individual accomplishment, specifically as it applies to academic goals.[28] Self-actualization, a student's intrinsic drive to fulfill his or her potential, theoretically, is only possible after basic, communal, social needs have been met.[29] Viewing Maslow's Hierarchy of Needs through the lens of Ubuntu, it is assumed that when students have been prioritized and are physically and emotionally safe and well within a loving learning community, the productivity we expect becomes a natural outflow—people come before profit or product from an Ubuntu perspective.[30]

Noltemeyer et al.[31] conducted an empirical study of 390 students and found there to be a positive relationship between Maslow's descriptions of basic social needs and academic achievement. Fisher and Crawford found similar results when school reforms were situated in a community model based upon Malsow's theory.[32] A student who is hungry, stressed, distrustful, unloved, or estranged in a learning community is more likely to remain in a state of *fight or flight*.[33] Neurologically speaking, *fight or flight* favors hypervigilance and gross motor readiness over cognition since thinking skills are less critical to human survival when a perceived threat is on the horizon.[34] A loveless, insecure environment chronically disrupts learning potential and ultimately academic outcomes.[35]

A learning community can be physically unsafe and stressful, but more subtle and no less harmful is the learning community that lacks emotional, onto-epistemological and axiological safety, belonging, trust and love. Malott's concern regarding the educational experience of Native American students in his book, *A Call to Action: An Introduction to Education, Philosophy, and Native North America*, is that they need to "accommodate" for a Eurocentric learning community in order to excel in public schools, whether on or off reservations. This accomodation encourages a type of persistent cognitive dissonance and is supportive of a systemic oppression that takes the students "out of their natural ways of being and learning."[36] This notion is reflected in the term *entremundos* in which Latino(a) students are trapped between two worlds, necessitating the formation of multiple identities to survive.[37]

The book, *Power and Place: Indian Education in America* describes U.S. education for the Native American student as a "product so refined" that it "has become something different and apart from the lives of the people."[38] Like Carter G. Woodson[39] acknowledges in *The Mis-education of the Negro*, *Power and Place: Indian education in America* recognizes that in a country where over 50% of the students represent non-White acculturations, a culturally incohesive learning community is a loveless, insecure space that plagues all students: "The problem with Indian education in America is really the problem of education in America, regardless of whether recipients of the education are [Native American, Latino(a), Asian, Black or White]."[40]

In *"We Dare Say Love": Supporting Achievement in the Educational Life of Black Boys*, Nasir addresses the fallout for Black young men who are steeped in a lovelessness that is systematic and highly prevalent in U.S. schools. She references Pedro Noguera's standpoint on the necessity for structural and cultural approaches to curricular and pedagogical reforms.[41] According to Nasir, love is a vital aspect of Black student success, but one that is "foreign" to Black males and a source of distrust that is difficult to break through.[42] Stereotype threat, other microaggressions, and lack of curricular and pedagogical cultural inclusions against marginalized groups of students remain at the center of distrust and the *fight or flight* stress response that disenfranchises students from educational spaces and contributes to low academic performance and student dropout rates.[43]

Education, like the medical system, has garnered a historical distrust within specific racial, ethnic and cultural demographics.[44] Incidents of inhumane medical research and treatment over the course of American history has caused many people, including people of color, to become reluctant to receive the COVID-19 vaccine.[45] In a similar way, the U.S. educational system has earned its own reputation for abuses, specifically towards minoritized groups of people, to such an extent that many of our students, as well as their parents, harbor feelings of distrust towards the system and the people who comprise it.[46] It may then stand to reason that with a teaching force over 80% White and female, an extra burden of healing and reconciliation lies on the shoulders of educators—our students and parents need us to re-build their fractured trust.[47] This can feel like a tall order when well-intentioned educators become the targeted objects of student contempt and disrespect.

I recall a situation during parent-teacher conferences when I was to meet with the father of my 9th grade student, Heather. She was not an easy personality to work with and could become disruptive in class with or without provocation. Heather had changed schools enough times that her father had become distrustful of educators and was abusive of the teaching staff. I was unaware of the aggressive altercations during parent-teacher meetings until my principal alerted me and offered to attend my conference with Heather's father. I was concerned that my principal's presence may be misconstrued as an act of aggression on my part and chose to meet with her father alone, promising that I would call the office at the first sign of hostility. There was none. Heather's father was a pleasure to work with, including during the few times when I needed his help to correct a behavior that was interfering with Heather's social or academic well-being. Heather and I had a good relationship. She enjoyed my class, and in relaying her own happiness, she softened her father's distrust, enabling us to work together as an extension of the class community.

Dr. Martin Luther King, Jr. considered that "[w]e are all caught in a network of mutuality, tied in a single garment of destiny." He said, "Whatever affects one directly, affects all indirectly." Consider our current condition from a related perspective that draws from Buddhist, Native American and African worldviews. All things, spiritual and material, are designed to co-exist in a harmonious balance.[48] One thing out of balance affects the individual as well as the whole since the nature of interconnectedness is a ripple effect that none can escape.

Metaphorically speaking, from an ecological point of view, a biome thrives in homeostasis—all life being valuable, mutually beneficial and in balance.[49] When any part of that biome is adulterated, deemed unpleasant, unnecessary, and in need of intervention, the entire system is negatively affected by the imbalance.[50] Life may go on in this biome but the interference that appeals to human ignorance and a self-inflated sense of importance renders it inharmonious and disruptive of the entire ecosystem.[51] If we draw an ecological parallel, allowing us to consider our classrooms as a biome of life and learning, all suffer the self-destructive eventuality that follows a gendered, racialized, socio-politicized imbalance in the educational system. The question may then be, can we succeed in bringing our educational biome, our learning communities, into homeostasis without unconditional love? Theoretically, from Part II, the answer is no.

Practically, the same principal is evident in the comments of a Black tenth grader whom I interviewed as part of a research study. About his non-Black teachers, he said the following, "[W]ith a lot of [White] teachers, there's nothing really there [no relationship or connection to the learning environment] 'cause they don't really know what I deal with. 'Cause, a lot of [White] teachers can't really relate, don't really know ... But then, like, a teacher who is [a different race from me] can try: I know they don't understand, but they'll try to figure it out. And then over time, I feel like they just know exactly what I'm dealing with and it feels like they're just there." There is hope for our students in teachers who love them enough to attempt to know them and build a community of trust.

A more thorough understanding of the impact of *fight or flight* stress responses on cognition can found in my experience teaching Wounded Warriors at Brook Army Medical Center in San Antonio, Texas. My course ran in trimesters and was open to repeat attendance as many times as soldiers needed until their learning outcomes had improved to their satisfaction. Usually, this meant they felt prepared to take an entrance exam to re-classify their job skill in the military or to make use their GI bill for college. The possibility of repeating the course was a necessary allowance in building the program considering the pervasiveness of soldiers with Post Traumatic Stress Disorder (PTSD).

PTSD makes it difficult to concentrate. Similar to a student's elevated anxiety due to culturally incohesive curricula and pedagogical practices or microaggressions like stereotype threat, the trauma of a life-threatening experience often leaves the survivor in a state of regular hypervigilance that disrupts behavior, memory and the ability to focus.[52] Like many of our K-12 students, my Wounded Warrior students were survivors of gun violence, catastrophic accidents, debilitating illness, sexual assaults, and other violent and incomprehensible events to which they were witnesses. When under sustained mental/emotional stress, I would often find my students drifting into their own compensatory mind space or attempting to track every sound and movement in the classroom while simultaneously concentrating on a lecture. To highlight the experience, one might attempt to draw meaning from the following: *a ... only ... hears ... of what the teacher ... saying and loses ... written ... the board.* The students would sometimes suffer skull-splitting headaches trying to patch together what they thought they heard or where they digressed from their work.

A loving, safe community of trust and belonging was essential within these classes. Even my husband and two sons became part of our community, as they were an extension of me in knowing and being. My husband joined our community at least once each trimester to allow the students what was an unusual access to a commissioned officer for the purpose of encouragement and mentorship. The students always approached their initial meeting with restraint but wound up liberated—talking authentically and laughing—overjoyed that someone of my husband's rank genuinely cared about their present as well as their future. My two sons joined the community as tutors, working with whomever wanted extra help and an opportunity to enjoy the fraternity of younger "brothers." We had to use our diverse abilities to instruct one another, reinforce what we learned, encourage each other, and rely on every member to maintain the sanctity and safety of our classroom.

Marty was one of my students in the Wounded Warrior Basic Skills Course who existed in constant motion, tracking every movement in the room and regularly monitoring the door. He was an eager learner who sometimes needed reinforcing in English and in Spanish to assure comprehension and it was distressing me that, as badly as he wanted to learn, his need for safety was robbing him of his opportunities. One class session, I just could not take it anymore;

I had lost count of how many times Marty checked the door behind him. I stopped teaching, leaned over his table, and smiled at him: "Marty, I have your six. I can see that door at all times and trust me, if something bad comes through it, I will be over these tables and at the door before you will. Okay?" Confirmation came from his classmates, "We got you, man," "Hooah." Marty smiled, "Yes, Ma'am," and, with rare exception, that was the end of his focus issues. We knew each other. I knew Marty's background—as did his classmates, many of whom experienced the distractions of PTSD—and he knew I valued him and had his back. He had already seen me risk myself for my students, stomping off in a fury to the battalion command suite when my students' education was being disrupted by unnecessary duties. We also understood our collective being—who we were together: caring, respectful, and responsible for one another.

I was teaching middle school in the Baltimore/Washington area on September 11, 2001, when our nation was attacked by foreign terrorists. Almost one year later, our staff members sat in meetings to decide who would volunteer to lose their lives in case gun fire erupted as we sandwiched our students in between two adults during student arrival and dismissal. Our school was positioned close to Interstate 95 and the D.C. Snipers had taken several lives already and had finally attacked a local school. The sacrificial order of service was: single male teachers, single female teachers, married male teachers, married female teachers, married male teachers with children, and last to serve would be married female teachers with children. I fell in the last category but could not escort my own children out of the elementary building. I had to go through the car line like any other parent to minimize loss in case of violence. I was teaching high school when my school was unprepared for an active shooter event that threatened the entire community, including our school. Students and some unwise staff members ran to the all-glass entryway to watch the drama unfold in the streets as alarmed administrators and well-prepared staff members yelled for everyone to lock the students in their classrooms and turn off the lights.

The threat to our students' lives is now a daily reality in schools as we enter and exit through policed metal detectors and practice for natural disasters, fire, and active shooter events. We understand and respond to the stress and anxiety that impacts our students' sense of physical safety within the learning community. What we seldom consider are those smaller onto-epistemological and axiological events that equally effect our students' stress levels, making it difficult for them to thrive academically. The lesson here in discussing PTSD and the fight or flight response that is more widely understood as associated with actual or perceived physical harm, is to understand their relevance to the physiology of learning when our students and/or the learning environment lack the love, trust, belonging, well-being, and safety of community. Loveless assaults, such as cultural incongruence and other microaggressions, that attack their identity are ruinous to learning.

Two incidences occurred at the high school level that created an onto-epistemological or axiological stress among my students that hindered their engagement in my class. In the first case, my class directly followed a Sexual Education class in which the sophomore class was enrolled. It was misaligned with the knowledge and cultural experience of the students. The instructor failed to engage the students in a way that sought to know and understand them. Additionally, the instructor neglected to establish a safe learning community in which the students' needs, values, and experiences could contribute to the curriculum.

Every day, the sophomores entered my class agitated and unable to concentrate until I realized that their learning would remain obstructed as long as they were unable to debrief their experience. My academic content was inaccessible to my students whose anxiety compelled them to distraction. As I would do again in the second example, I stopped teaching and asked my students to form a Talking Circle.

Talking, or Peacemaking, Circles find their roots and contemporary credit among Native American onto-epistemologies, although similar practices can be found in African cultures. They are a regular part of my pedagogy with my current college students. Talking Circles are useful in helping students to psychologically debrief their feelings, create mutual understanding and forgiveness, and restore the community to harmony.[53]

In that safe space, my students voiced their frustrations over the culturally incohesive content and felt affirmed in their understandings and co-constructed knowledge, resolving their stress as a community. Only then, after their anxieties were relieved, were we able to return to the content of my course successfully and effectively.

Similarly, the same high school secured a motivational speaker who would regularly speak before the entire assembly of middle and high school students, all of whom I taught. The speaker regularly and almost exclusively used football analogies and metaphors to connect the students' prior knowledge to his content. The student body became progressively anxious and disconnected from the speaker and his message since his relationship with the students existed only within the football community and erased any student who did not have a working knowledge of football or was not interested in the game.

Finally, this motivational speaker constructed an analogy that was blatantly racist. He demeaned a Black athlete with whom he had an encounter, describing this athlete within a stereotypical, dehumanizing paradigm. I always sat in the back of the audience and the students knew this. Every student in the audience turned around to find me and looked directly at me with pure heartbreak on their faces. We were, by then, a strong community in my classroom, anchored in a curriculum of agape. My students received the speaker's analogy as a direct attack on one of their community members and they were sickened by it. Worse, was the lack of intervention from the administration.

Once again, my high school class that followed the assembly was unable to settle into learning. They had lost their sense of safety in knowing, being, and valuing and could not concentrate. Many of their peers flooded my room instead of going directly to their classes because they, too, suffered an anxiety that made learning or fear of reprimand for tardiness inconsequential. A Talking Circle once again became necessary to lower the *fight or flight* response they had to a microaggression against me and against their learning community. When the non-cognitive need was met—the stress was relieved, and harmony was restored—my students were able to learn.

Learning how important those soft skills are to proper cognition, I have tried over the years to find creative ways to engage my students in non-cognitive areas that might encourage a sense of community safety, trust, well-being, belonging, and engagement. It has been my habit to attend every sporting or special event at least once, especially when my students ask me to come. During those years prior to entering pre-service teacher education, my subject area specialties and my administrators, with whom I had a trusting and close relationship, afforded me some latitude to build an agape community without departing from the academic curriculum. We connected our state-imposed curriculum to diverse, current experiences and understandings; made cakes to help us understand geometric measurements; and watched culturally cohesive movies together to engage more deeply with our literary works and linguistic skills in English and Spanish. We took field trips to order traditional foods in Spanish within authentic experiential contexts. I cooked for my students, ate with them, danced with them, and traveled with them. It's remarkable the way a community bonds over dancing and food.

As part of our cultural inclusion in Spanish classes, we learned the basics of Flamenco, Salsa and Merengue and experienced some choreographies, which have mathematical application as much as music, dance, or culture. We attended shows to see the masters perform to augment the curriculum. One year, we became the show when I decided to choreograph a fusion piece combining Flamenco with Mexican Folklorico for my eighth grade Spanish I classes, and I danced with them. It was a labor of love for all of us, but come showtime, in full costume, those young people were so excited and cohesive. My young male students, who made classroom disruption their daily occupation, discovered their inner *caballero*[54] and embodied this role with surprising zeal.[55] It was an explosion of movement and color, and was the performance of a lifetime to *Mañana Yo Me Voy Con Cristo*[56] by Rigoberto Amaya.[57] They did such a remarkable job that one of the audience members asked if we would perform it at their church service. We were on stage the following Sunday before a packed audience.

After learning that laughter and digestion mitigate stress, to offset the stress response to test anxiety and the hindrance it causes to knowledge production, I let the students eat chips or fruit during exams and gave them stress balls to calm their nerves; I made sure to include a joke or two in the middle of an assessment.[58] The change of mood in the room was glorious as a domino effect of quiet laughter overtook the room for a few moments. The students looked at each other and at me with joy instead of fear. Pen and pencil drumming was permitted. Kinesthesis is widely accepted as a learning style that informs cognition for some students.[59] Instead of the disruption that occurs when students drum their writing implement on a desk or table, I allowed my students to use their laps as a drum pad. Often, we sat at desks or tables, but sometimes we sat on the floor, and sometimes we chose where we wanted to sit during a lesson. I was surprised by the response of an eighth grade ELRA class who beamed at me with a mix of delight and disbelief when I assigned fifteen minutes of quiet reading wherever they would like to sit. The enthusiasm with which they scrambled to find their places taught me that the *where* of learning might be as important as the *what*.

In almost every middle and high school throughout my career, my students wound up creating what I called *lunch bunch*, as, little by little, more students would pour into my room at lunchtime asking for passes to eat in my room. I had young people as my lunch guests who were not my students but who simply liked being with our agape community. Eventually, we brought board games in and played and talked about whatever was on their minds. If it hadn't been for the lunch bunch and one of our frequent guests who had lived in Germany, I might still be lost in the country to this day. She decided to reciprocate the foreign language instruction and teach me German over lunch when it was clear I was about to move there and was linguistically challenged by Deutsch. It was in this same lunch bunch environment that they began to divulge more vulnerable, many times traumatic, aspects of their lives, solidifying a profound level of safety, trust, belonging, and well-being between my students and me.

Reciprocity seemed to be a natural outgrowth of an agape centered learning community. The students had various tutoring and administrative skills they were happy to share. I came to enjoy the mildly condescending looks of pity when they took over for me, their technologically impaired teacher who could not work the A/V equipment or a computer program. Other than teaching me to speak German, my high school students taught me to play cards. One student took it upon herself to be my daily chef—she took great pleasure in being the one to prepare my lunch salads and would become incensed if I attempted to make my own.

My Wounded Warrior student, Marty, offered to refresh my conversational Spanish when my move to Texas resulted in a lapse of my teaching certification and required me to take certain sections of the Texas state teachers certification exam in order to transfer my credentials to the Texas Education Agency (TEA). Marty had lived most of his life in Argentina and was deeply proficient in Spanish. We would meet for an hour after class until I had successfully completed my exams. When we lost our contract for the Basic Skills Course due to a base realignment effort throughout the Department of Defense, it was my students who surreptitiously went job hunting on my behalf, ultimately presenting me with a yellow sticky note on which a contact at the Veteran's Administration was written. One of my students said, "Call this guy—he wants you to work for the VA." By then, I had acquired several student "tutors" who instructed me in the art of becoming an independent contractor for the government.

One of my adult classes, a math refresher course in Darmstadt, Germany, collectively babysat an infant during class. A soldier assigned to my husband's battalion had to deploy for a short time, leaving her newborn baby without a guardian. I volunteered to care for her child so that she would not face legal action for refusing to deploy, which meant taking the little one to class with me. The weight of an infant can injure your back in remarkable ways after hours of standing. When one of us would tire, someone in the class would say, "I've got her," and we passed her to the next set of loving arms until we completed class. It was truly a "village" moment in my teaching career. Together, we felt responsible for the brand new life that needed our care, and for one another—I needed to be able to teach effectively and my students needed equal opportunities to learn. I am forever in the debt of all these students who made a way out of no way for me at many junctures along my career.

Sacrificial love, without boundaries or limitations of any kind, concerned only with the life and growth of another, calls to us as educators to be responsible to create a safe and trustworthy space and place of community belonging and well-being for our students—one that responds to their expressed or unexpressed needs.[60] It requires that we respect and value each community member, according to his or her uniqueness and without exploitation.[61] Love through community seeks out truth, always protects, always hopes, and always endures.[62] If we are not committed to our students' emancipation as democratic citizens and sacred members of the classroom and global community we call, humanity, it's not love.[63] If our learning communities are not acting bravely on the students' behalf to disrupt social, political, and economic inequities that exploit, manipulate and dehumanize our students, again, we are not engaging in a pedagogy of love.[64] Instead, we are complicit in their failure and cannot feign surprise when our national statistics continue to underperform those of less prosperous countries.[65]

Years ago, I acquired a piece of artwork depicting a fishing village in Senegal. It was as spectacular in its message as it was in its display of color and texture. Central to the composition was an image of a young boy celebrating his introduction to manhood by learning to fish—a life skill that would provide for the future prosperity of the community as much as for the boy. The entire village of men, women, and children of all ages surrounded the youngster to contribute their knowledge, support, and encouragement to the success of his task. The instruction was not merely academic; it was a social event, inclusive of chatter, laughter, food and music. The message to us as educators is this—I am because we are. Learning is situated in safety and belonging and is best shaped by an empowering and loving democratic community, diverse in perspective, experience, skill, and position.[66] The welfare and prosperity of our students and our society rests upon this foundation.

Explore, Think, Act

Further building upon the premise that educators must first know their students if they aim to love them, Chapter 5 explores the intention to love unconditionally through *knowing* by creating a sense of community within our classrooms. Now, explore your own pedagogy through the lens of a curriculum of agape.

(A) Think about the community you have created for your students.

   1. How does the expression, "One knee doesn't bring up a child" correct typical notions of teaching and learning in American schools? How does the Western notion of "teaching" overburden the role of a teacher? How can a non-Western, community-minded model assist you in your practice?

   2. What approach to teaching and learning inspires your class rules? How are your class rules established? Do your students participate in establishing and/or maintaining the rules? In what ways can you alter your pedagogy to allow greater student participation in establishing the rules of your learning community?

   3. What can you do to improve the quality of relationships in your classroom to align with an agape, village model more closely, even if your classrooms are virtual? In other words, how can you increase your students' sense of love, well-being, trust, safety and belonging in their diverse identities?

   4. In what ways can you become more of a co-learner with your students? How might you change the curriculum and your pedagogical practice to ensure that suffering and joy are co-experienced in your classroom?

After you have thought about your responses to the questions in section A, consider sharing your questions with your students to elicit their input; their knowledge will be a more accurate representation of their needs.

(B) Think about how you relate to your students.

   1. Can you identify and list any misplaced assumptions or internal biases regarding who your students are that cause you to want to "fix" them? How might you disrupt these biases in order to value your students more effectively?

Notes

1 Missler, C., & Missler, N. (2014). *The way of agape: King's High Way Ministries.*

2 Cowen-Fletcher, J., & Melia, J. (1994). *It takes a village.* New York, NY: Scholastic.

3 Goldberg, J. (2016, July 30). *It takes a village to determine the origins of an African proverb.* Goats and Soda. Retrieved November 11, 2021, from https://www.npr.org/sections/goats andsoda/2016/07/30/487925796/it-takes-a-village-to-determine-the-origins-of-an-african-proverb.

Healey, J. (1998). *It takes a whole village to raise a child.* African Proverb of the Month. Retrieved 2021, from https://afriprov.org/.

4 Belgrave, F. Z., & Brevard, J. K. (2015). *African American boys: Identity, culture, and development* (2015 ed.). New York, NY: Springer.

Flinders, D., & Thornton, S. (2013). *The curriculum studies reader* (4th ed.). New York: Routledge.

Goldberg, J. (2016, July 30). *It takes a village to determine the origins of an African proverb.* Goats and Soda. Retrieved November 11, 2021, from https://www.npr.org/sections/goats andsoda/2016/07/30/487925796/it-takes-a-village-to-determine-the-origins-of-an-african-proverb.

Guy-Evans, O. (2020). *Bronfenbrenner's ecological systems theory.* Bronfenbrenner's Ecological Systems Theory | Simply Psychology. Retrieved November 10, 2021, from https://www.simplypsychology.org/Bronfenbrenner.html.

Lave, J., & Wenger, E. (1991). *Situated learning: Legitimate peripheral participation.* Cambridge, UK: Cambridge University Press. Reading Chapters 1 and 2.

Mcleod, S. (2016). *Albert Bandura's social learning theory.* Albert Bandura's Social Learning Theory | Simply Psychology. Retrieved November 10, 2021, from https://www.simpl ypsychology.org/bandura.html.

Public Broadcasting Service. (n.d.). *PBS online: Only a teacher: Schoolhouse pioneers.* PBS. Retrieved November 10, 2021, from https://www.pbs.org/onlyateacher/john.html.

Vygotsky, L. (1997). Interaction between learning and development. In N. Gauvain & M. Cole (Eds.), *Readings on the development of children* (pp. 29–36). New York, NY: W.H. Freeman and Company.

Vygotsky, L. S., & Cole, M. (1978). *Mind in society: The development of higher psychological processes.* Cambridge: Harvard University Press.

5 Bergstrom, A., Cleary, L. M., & Peacock, T. D. (2003). *The seventh generation: Native students speak about finding the good path.* ERIC.

Cajete, G. (1994). *Look to the mountain: An ecology of indigenous education.* ERIC.

Cleary, L. M., & Peacock, T. D. (1998). *Collected wisdom: American Indian education.* ERIC.

Darder, A. (2015). *Culture and power in the classroom: Educational foundations for the schooling of bicultural students.* Routledge.

Helfenbein, R. J. (2021). *Critical geographies of education: Space, place, and curriculum inquiry.* Routledge.

Johnson, S. (2020). *Afrocentricity: Student voices on African American identity in multicultural education reform.* The University of Texas at San Antonio.

Malott, C. (2007). *A call to action: An introduction to education, philosophy, and Native North America* (Vol. 324). Peter Lang.

6 Deloria, V., Deloria Jr., V., & Wildcat, D. (2001). *Power and place: Indian education in America* (p. 7). Fulcrum Publishing.

7 Op. Cit., Bergstrom et al. (2003).

   Op. Cit., Cajete (1994).

   Op. Cit., Cleary & Peacock (1998).

   Op. Cit., Deloria et al. (2001).

Op. Cit., Helfenbein (2021).

Op. Cit., Johnson (2020).

Op. Cit., Malott (2007).

Montero-Sieburth, M., & Villaruel, F. (2003). *Making invisible Latino adolescents visible: A critical approach to Latino diversity.* Routledge.

8 Op. Cit., Darder (2015), p. 35.

Johnson, S. C. (2019). U.S. education and the persistence of slavery. *Journal of Curriculum and Pedagogy*, 1–20, p. 6. https://doi.org/10.1080/15505170.2019.1618757.

9 Apple, M. W., & Beane, J. A. (2007). *Democratic schools: Lessons in powerful education*: Heinemann.

Arredondo, P., Gallardo-Cooper, M., Delgado-Romero, E. A., & Zapata, A. L. (2015). Latino worldviews and cultural values. *Culturally Responsive Counseling with Latinas/os*, 15–30.

Beane, J. A. (2005). *A reason to teach: Creating classrooms of dignity and hope: The power of the democratic way.* Heinemann Educational Books.

Beyer, L. E. (1996). *Creating democratic classrooms: The struggle to integrate theory and practice* (The practitioner inquiry series). ERIC.

Joselowsky, F. (2007). Youth engagement, high school reform, and improved learning outcomes: Building systemic approaches for youth engagement. *NASSP Bulletin*, 91(3), 257–276. https://doi.org/10.1177/0192636507306133.

King, J. E., & Swartz, E. E. (2015). *The Afrocentric praxis of teaching for freedom: Connecting culture to learning.* Routledge.

Ladson-Billings, G. (2009). *The dreamkeepers: Successful teachers of African American children.* Somerset, USA: Wiley.

Op. Cit., Montero-Sieburth & Villaruel (2003).

Murrell Jr., P. C. (2002). *African-centered pedagogy: Developing schools of achievement for African American children*: SUNY Press.

10 NCES-National Center for Education Statistics (2021). *Analyzing teacher mobility and retention: Guidance and considerations report 1–2.* Retrieved May 28, 2021, from https://nces.ed.gov/pubsearch/index.asp?HasSearched=1&searchcat2=subjectindex&L1=49&L2=19.

11 Op. Cit., Johnson (2020).

12 Op. Cit., Apple & Beane (2007).

Au, W., Brown, A. L., & Calderón, D. (2016). *Reclaiming the multicultural roots of US curriculum: Communities of color and official knowledge in education.* Teachers College Press.

Op. Cit., Beane (2005).

Op. Cit., Beyer (1996).

Op. Cit., Joselowsky (2007).

Op. Cit., King, J. E., & Swartz (2015).

Op. Cit., Ladson-Billings (2009).

Op. Cit., Murrell Jr (2002).

13 Op. Cit., Ladson-Billings (2009).

Op. Cit., Montero-Sieburth & Villaruel (2003).

Op. Cit., Murrell Jr (2002).

14 Gill, J. H. (2002). *Native American worldviews an introduction.*

Op. Cit., Joselowsky (2007).

Op. Cit., King, J. E., & Swartz (2015).

Op. Cit., Ladson-Billings (2009).

Op. Cit., Montero-Sieburth & Villaruel (2003).

Price, M., Kallam, M., & Love, J. (2009). The learning styles of Native American students and implications for classroom practice. In *Eighth Native American Symposium and Film Festival: Images, Imaginations, and Beyond.*

15 Delpit, L. (2013). *"Multiplication Is for White people": Raising expectations for other people's children.* New York, USA: The New Press.

16 Taylor, K. B., & Reynolds, D. J. (2019). Dissonance. In rethinking college student development theory using critical frameworks. *Journal of College and Character, 21*(3), 234–236.

17 Rojas, L., & Liou, D. D. (2017). Social justice teaching through the sympathetic touch of caring and high expectations for students of color. *Journal of Teacher Education, 68*(1), 28–40.

18 Donnelly, D. F., McGarr, O., & O'Reilly, J. (2014). 'Just Be Quiet and Listen to Exactly What He's Saying': Conceptualising power relations in inquiry-oriented classrooms. *International Journal of Science Education, 36*(12), 2029–2054.

Manke, M. (1997). *Classroom power relations: Understanding student-teacher interaction.* Routledge.

19 Lipner, J. (1998). Capturing gods: The god of love and the love of god in Christian and Hindu tradition. *Boardman Lectureship in Christian Ethics. 3.* Retrieved May 26, 2021, from http://repository.upenn.edu/boardman/3.

Nhat Hanh, T., & DeAntonis, J. (2014). *How to love.* USA: Parallax Press.

20 Translation: O Ask of the Stars, Beloved: "Ask of the stars, beloved, who see me weeping the long night through; they know that I'm ever seeking but to adore thee in solitude . . . O doubt it never that I adore thee. My life for thee love, I'd gladly give."

21 Kilenyi, E. (2001). *Pregúntale A Las Estrellas.* Hal Leonard Corporation (Original work published 1917).

22 Tshivhase, M. (2018). Love as the foundation of Ubuntu. *Synthesis Philosophica, 65*(1/2018), 197–208. https://doi.org/10.21464/sp33112.

23 Cheng, Y. C. (1996). Relation between teachers' professionalism and job attitudes, educational outcomes, and organizational factors. *The Journal of Educational Research, 89*(3), 163–171. https://doi.org/10.1080/00220671.1996.9941322.

Robinson-Morris, D. W. (2018). *Ubuntu and Buddhism in higher education: An ontological (re) thinking.* Routledge.

24 Op. Cit., Rojas & Liou (2017).

25 Op. Cit., Delpit (2013).

Dustova, G., & Cotton, S. (2015). Classroom management strategies. *The CTE Journal, 3*(2), 32.

26 Op. Cit., Belgrave & Brevard (2015).

Flinders, D., & Thornton, S. (2013). *The curriculum studies reader* (4th ed.). New York: Routledge.

Op. Cit., Guy-Evans (2020).

Op. Cit., Lave & Wenger (1991).

Op. Cit., Mcleod (2016).

Op. Cit., Vygotsky (1997).

Op. Cit., Vygotsky & Cole (1978).

27 Au, W. (2017). When multicultural education is not enough. *Multicultural Perspectives, 19*(3), 147–150. https://doi.org/10.1080/15210960.2017.1331741.

Gay, G. (2018). *Culturally responsive teaching: Theory, research, and practice.* Teachers College Press.

Ladson-Billings, G. (2014). Culturally relevant pedagogy 2.0: aka the remix. *Harvard Educational Review, 84*(1), 74–84.

Op. Cit., Montero-Sieburth & Villaruel (2003).

Weissberg, R. P., Durlak, J. A., Domitrovich, C. E., & Gullotta, T. P. (2015). Social and emotional learning: Past, present, and future. In J. A. Durlak, C. E. Domitrovich, R. P. Weissberg, & T. P. Gullotta (Eds.), *Handbook of social and emotional learning: Research and practice* (pp. 3–19). The Guilford Press.

Yeager, D. S., & Dweck, C. S. (2020). What can be learned from growth mindset controversies?. *American Psychologist, 75*(9), 1269.

28 Kline, T. (n.d.). *Applying Maslow's hierarchy of needs in our classrooms.* ChangeKidsLives. Retrieved November 11, 2021, from http://www.changekidslives.org/actions-4.

29 Ibid.

30 *Chapter four: The African Ubuntu philosophy.* (n.d.). Retrieved January 4, 2022, from https://repository.up.ac.za/bitstream/handle/2263/28706/04chapter4.pdf?sequence=5.

31 Noltemeyer, A., Bush, K., Patton, J., & Bergen, D. (2012). The relationship among deficiency needs and growth needs: An empirical investigation of Maslow's theory. *Children and Youth Services Review, 34*(9), 1862–1867. https://doi.org/10.1016/j.childyouth.2012.05.021

32 Fisher, M. H., & Crawford, B. (2020). "From School of Crisis to Distinguished": Using Maslow's hierarchy in a rural underperforming school. *The Rural Educator (Fort Collins, Colo.), 41*(1), 8–19.

33 Bluestein, J. (2008). *The win-win classroom: A fresh and positive look at classroom management.* Corwin Press.

Hammond, Z. (2014). *Culturally responsive teaching and the brain: Promoting authentic engagement and rigor among culturally and linguistically diverse students.* Corwin Press.

Willis, J. (2010). The current impact of neuroscience on teaching and learning. In *Mind, brain and education: Neuroscience implications for the classroom* (pp. 45–68).

34 Op. Cit., Bluestein (2008).
Op. Cit., Willis (2010).

35 Op. Cit., Bluestein (2008).
Op. Cit., Hammond (2014).
Op. Cit., Johnson (2019).
Op. Cit., Willis (2010).

36 Op. Cit., Malott (2007), p. 128.
Op. Cit., Taylor & Reynolds (2019).

37 Op. Cit., Montero-Sieburth & Villaruel (2003).

38 Op. Cit., Deloria et al. (2001), p. 42.

39 Woodson, C. G. (1933). *The mis-education of the Negro.* Washington, D.C.: Associated Publishers.

40 Op. Cit., Deloria et al. (2001), p. 9.

41 Nasir, N. S. (2019). *"We dare say love": Supporting achievement in the educational life of Black boys*. New York, NY: Teachers College Press.

42 Ibid., p. 2.

43 Aronson, J. (2002). Stereotype threat: Contending and coping with unnerving expectations. In *Improving academic achievement* (pp. 279–301). Academic Press.

Aronson, J., Quinn, D. M., & Spencer, S. J. (1998). Stereotype threat and the academic underperformance of minorities and women. In *Prejudice* (pp. 83–103). Academic Press.

Op. Cit., Cajete (1994).

Op. Cit., Deloria et al. (2001).

Op. Cit., Delpit (2013).

Huynh, V. W. (2012). Ethnic microaggressions and the depressive and somatic symptoms of Latino and Asian American adolescents. *Journal of youth and adolescence, 41*(7), 831–846.

Op. Cit., Johnson (2019, 2020).

Op. Cit., Malott (2007).

44 Armstrong, K., Rose, A., Peters, N., Long, J. A., McMurphy, S., & Shea, J. A. (2006). Distrust of the health care system and self-reported health in the United States. *Journal of General Internal Medicine, 21*(4), 292–297.

Armstrong, K., Ravenell, K. L., McMurphy, S., & Putt, M. (2007). Racial/ethnic differences in physician distrust in the United States. *American Journal of Public Health, 97*(7), 1283–1289.

Op. Cit., Nasir (2019).

45 Op. Cit., Armstrong (2006, 2007).

Op. Cit., Nasir (2019).

Willis, D. E., Andersen, J. A., Bryant-Moore, K., Selig, J. P., Long, C. R., Felix, H. C., ... & McElfish, P. A. (2021). COVID-19 vaccine hesitancy: Race/ethnicity, trust, and fear. *Clinical and Translational Science, 14*(6), 2200–2207.

46 Larson, C. L., & Ovando, C. J. (2001). *The color of bureaucracy: The politics of equity in multicultural school communities*. Taylor and Francis Group.

Op. Cit., Nasir (2019).

Walton, G. M., & Cohen, G. L. (2007). A question of belonging: race, social fit, and achievement. *Journal of Personality and Social Psychology, 92*(1), 82.

47 García, E., & Weiss, E. (2019). *U.S. schools struggle to hire and retain teachers: The second report in 'The perfect storm in the teacher labor market' series*. Economic Policy Institute. Retrieved November 10, 2021, from https://www.epi.org/publication/u-s-schools-struggle-to-hire-and-retain-teachers-the-second-report-in-the-perfect-storm-in-the-teacher-labor-market-series/.

Op. Cit., NCES (2021).

48 Op. Cit., Cajete (1994).

Op. Cit., Cleary & Peacock (1998).

Mayaka, B., & Truell, R. (2021). Ubuntu and its potential impact on the international social work profession. *International Social Work, 64*(5), 649–662.

Ramose, M. B. (2014). Ubuntu. In *Degrowth* (pp. 240–242). Routledge.

Robinson-Morris, D. W. (2018). *Ubuntu and Buddhism in higher education: An ontological (re) thinking*. Routledge.

49 Trojan, P., & Przemysław, T. (1984). *Ecosystem homeostasis*. Springer Science & Business Media.

50 Ibid.

51 Di Marco, M., Venter, O., Possingham, H. P., & Watson, J. E. (2018). Changes in human footprint drive changes in species extinction risk. *Nature Communications, 9*(1), 1–9.

    McGowan, P. J. (2016). Mapping the terrestrial human footprint. *Nature, 537*(7619), 172–173.

    Ibid.

52 Op. Cit., Huynh (2012).

    Jelinek, L., Jacobsen, D., Kellner, M., Larbig, F., Biesold, K. H., Barre, K., & Moritz, S. (2006). Verbal and nonverbal memory functioning in posttraumatic stress disorder (PTSD). *Journal of Clinical and Experimental Neuropsychology, 28*(6), 940–948.

    Moradi, A. R., Doost, H. T. N., Taghavi, M. R., Yule, W., & Dalgleish, T. (1999). Everyday memory deficits in children and adolescents with PTSD: Performance on the rivermead behavioural memory test. *The Journal of Child Psychology and Psychiatry and Allied Disciplines, 40*(3), 357–361.

53 Op. Cit., Mayaka & Truell (2021).

    Op. Cit., Robinson-Morris (2018).

    Talking Circles Overview. First Nations Pedagogy Online Project. (n.d.). Retrieved January 13, 2022, from https://firstnationspedagogy.ca/circletalks.html.

54 Translation: chivalrous gentleman.

55 Op. Cit., Arredondo (2015).

56 Translation: Tomorrow, I Am Going With Christ.

57 Amaya, R. (2004). Mañana Yo me voy con Cristo. *Para ti lo mejor*. Berea Music.

58 Berk, R. A. (2000). Does humor in course tests reduce anxiety and improve performance? *College Teaching, 48*(4), 151–158. https://doi.org/10.1080/87567550009595834.

    Pines, A. & Gal, R. (2006). The effect of food on test anxiety. *Journal of Applied Social Psychology, 7*, 348–358. https://doi.org/10.1111/j.1559-1816.1977.tb00759.x.

    Strategies to reduce test anxiety. LSU Health New Orleans. (2021). Retrieved November 11, 2021, from https://nursing.lsuhsc.edu/AcademicSuccessProgram/StrategiesTestAnxiety.aspx#:~:text=Integrating%20relaxation%20techniques%20into%20your,Maintain%20a%20realistic%20viewpoint..

59 Lengel, T., & Kuczala, M. (2010). *The kinesthetic classroom: Teaching and learning through movement*. Corwin Press.

60 Freire, P. (1993). *Pedagogy of the oppressed* (New Rev 20th-Anniversary ed.). New York: Continuum.

    Fromm, E. (2000). *The art of loving: The centennial edition*. A&C Black.

61 Op. Cit., Fromm (2000).

62 Op. Cit., Missler & Missler (2014).

63 Darder, A. (2011). Chapter 9: Teaching as an act of love: Reflections on Paulo Freire and his contributions to our lives and our work. *Counterpoints, 418*, 179–194.

Forbes, J. D. (2001). Indigenous Americans: Spirituality and ecos. *Daedalus: Journal of the American Academy of Arts & Sciences*. Retrieved May 26, 2021, from www.amacad.org/publication/indigenous-americans-spirituality-and-ecos.

Op. Cit., Freire (1993).

Op. Cit., Fromm (2000).

Op. Cit., Tshivhase (2018).

64 Op. Cit., Darder (2011).

Darder, A. (2017). *Reinventing Paulo Freire: A pedagogy of love*: Taylor & Francis.

Op. Cit., Freire (1993).

Freire, P. (2005). *Teachers as cultural workers: Letters to those who dare teach with new commentary by Peter McLaren, Joe L. Kincheloe*: Westview Press.

65 Balingit, M., & Dam, A. V. (2019). *U.S. students continue to lag behind peers in East Asia and Europe in reading, math and science, exams show*. The Washington Post. Retrieved November 11, 2021, from https://www.washingtonpost.com/local/education/us-students-continue-to-lag-behind-peers-in-east-asia-and-europe-in-reading-math-and-science-exams-show/2019/12/02/e9e3b37c-153d-11ea-9110-3b34ce1d92b1_story.html.

Ladson-Billings, G. (2006). From the achievement gap to the education debt: Understanding achievement in U.S. schools. *Educational Researcher, 35*(7), 3–12.

66 Op. Cit., Taylor & Reynolds (2019).

Op. Cit., Tshivhase (2018).

Vygotsky (1997).

Vygotsky & Cole (1978).

Part III

MEET THEM WHERE THEY ARE

"For all students to excel, teachers must learn about them and connect with each child. This is not just about finding out how they learn, but it is finding out who they are." (George Curos)[1]

· 6 ·

UNDERSTANDING EQUITY

From the perspective of many African and Native American societies, education should support the quest to determine *who* the child is not *what* the child is assumed to be—a journey along a unique path where the student learns to be fully human in harmony with spirit, community and the creation.[1] Scholars of Democratic Schooling and Emancipatory Pedagogy insist that any transformative education should be rooted in a curriculum of liberty, treating students as individual human beings rather than commodified widgets along a curricular and pedagogical assembly line.[2] The average American classroom today is more diverse than ever.[3] Our students are not the products of a single cultural, cognitive, or ideological cookie cutter. Social, economic, and political disparities are, in part, the visible results of an educational system that expects the students to fit the prescribed curricular and pedagogical standards instead of flexing those standards to fit the students.[4] This idea of a "one size fits all" education is a null-curriculum of anti-love that teaches us to disregard the uniqueness of each student and his or her sense of promise, agency, and self-determination and is central to many scholars' critiques of our current, and historical, system of education.[5]

Educators cannot expect all the children to be well when we approach their education from an equality standpoint without balancing it with one of equity. Theoretically, an equality only education that imposes onto-epistemological and axiological limitations of sameness upon all students is centered in a curricular lovelessness since love can never be self-gratifying.[6] For example, I love my two sons unconditionally, with a desperation that only a parent can know, but they are such different personalities that it's impossible to love them in the exact same way. I remember my mother telling me that I would know my children even from within the womb—who they were as I carried them in pregnancy would be the same people that I would know in their adulthood. Nothing could have turned out to be truer.

My eldest is still the unhurried, laid-back adult that he was when I carried him. I poked at my belly and pushed him around periodically just to make sure he was still responsive in there. My stomach moved like a gentle wave as he would stretch and turn over or withdraw his body away from my prodding. He had no interest in upsetting his sleepy, tranquil space that was my womb so, as his due date approached and he was clearly unmotivated to meet the world, my doctor and I chose to evict him with and intravenous push of Pitocin. Not much has changed—he still loves a good sleepy, tranquil space and I still have to verbally poke and push, to his annoyance.

My youngest was so active—he beat my bones up like a martial artist, and he was in such a hurry. I had to be medicated and put on bedrest to keep him in place until his lungs were developed enough to survive. When it was finally safe to enter the world, he wasted no time—my doctor was still putting on his gloves as my son shot out of my body. The doctor threw himself around and caught my son in the air like a football. To this day, my husband and I fuss at our grown young man, "Slow down, son!" He talks fast, walks fast and has 25 tabs open on his laptop at any one time. He is who he always has been, and like his brother, is the delight of my life.

If someone were to ask me if I love my sons equally, I would not hesitate to respond with a "Yes, absolutely." The implication would not be that I love them exactly alike. Instead, my response would reflect my equal responsibility for them and investment in them.[7] They have an equal hold on my heart and are equally known, valued, accepted and cared for, except the manifestation of that equal love is an expression of equity not equality.[8] My sons are brothers, children shaped by the same home and parentage, with the same impartation of cultural ideology and expectation, but they are very different people with differing needs and aspirations. Were I to manifest my love equally, someone would remain stunted in his development for never having received in love what he uniquely needed. Perhaps my oldest son, who thrives on quality time and words of affirmation, may have found himself stifled if limited to those kisses and hugs that are vital only to my youngest. The opposite might also be true for my youngest son.

Although the expressions of love may not be limited to five as suggested in the bestselling books by Gary Chapman, theoretically, they speak to the unique individuality that not only expresses love but interprets it as well.[9] Like our children, students need an equality of love that is equal in responsibility, investment, knowledge, respect, and care.[10] They need to have hold of our hearts equally, but the manifestation of that same love ought to be grounded in equity.[11]

A curriculum of unconditional love evokes a concern for the needs of the other person, respecting his or her values as a person according to his or her uniqueness, without exploitation. Its framework is freedom not domination; it's an act of bravery on the part of educators to disrupt social, political, and economic inequities that exploit, manipulate, and dehumanize students, with the expectation that suffering and joy are co-experienced.[12] We need to meet students where they are and love them in their individuality. We must know them, respect them, care for and educate them, understanding that their academic, social, and behavioral needs are complicated by the uniquely diverse conditions affecting their lives, yet taking care not to conflate the impulse to "fix" our students with empowering them.[13]

Jesus was quoted to have said, "Greater love has no one than this: to lay down one's life for one's friends."[14] The Buddhist and Ubuntu imperative to alleviate another's suffering shares a similar implication. Chögyam Trungpa Rinpoche, a Buddhist teacher, said, "The bodhisattva vow is the commitment to put others before oneself. It is a statement of willingness to give up one's own well-being, even one's own enlightenment, for the sake of others." It is not an easy undertaking to love equitably. Central to the selflessness of unconditional love is the willingness to step out of our comfort zones, forsaking our own needs for that of another, whether we "get it" or not. I would be a rich woman were I to have collected a dime for every time I reminded myself that my providential placement in my classroom was not about me. In some ways it was an adventure and a pleasure to step outside of myself to enjoy my students within their individual frames of reference. However, their various needs did not always make sense and sometimes incited an ideological self-conflict. Since my actions had the potential to reflect either a curriculum of selfishness or selflessness, in every case, I felt it necessary to overcome myself for their sakes.

Essential to increasing student motivation and engagement is a protective and supportive environment of love and belonging that is situated in an ethos of equity.[15] A curriculum of agape provides this via a profound respect for our students and a knowledge of who they are in their multiple, intersectional identities, what they value, and what they uniquely need to ignite a holistic sense of confidence, agency, self-determination and academic self-efficacy. Connecting this idea to my own practice, this meant magnifying their strengths and providing learning opportunities in their weaknesses by equitably supporting their academic, social and cultural identities, and understanding their behavior.

Explore, Think, Act

Part III suggests that we fail to love unconditionally through knowing if we neglect to meet our students where they are. Chapter 6 of Part III explores the limitations of knowing and loving our students solely based upon a curriculum of equality and, instead, examines a curriculum of agape as it brings equality into balance with equity. Consider the ways in which equality may overshadow equity in your own classroom.

(A) Think about the words *equal* and *equitable*.
   1. Find the definition of *equal* and *equitable* in the dictionary. How do the dictionary definitions alter your understanding of the relationship between these two words as they relate to your students?
   2. In what ways can a curriculum be self-gratifying to teachers, administrators and policy makers when it is exclusively based on *equality*? How are these detrimental to the student?
   3. In what ways are curricular and pedagogical practices of *equality* more easily self-gratifying for you in your classroom?
   4. In what ways do you maintain an environment of equality in the face-to-face or virtual classroom?
   5. In what ways do you maintain an environment of equity in the face-to-face or virtual classroom?
(B) Consider those areas where you believe you may strive for equality in your classroom without considering the need for equity. Make a list of those areas and then talk to your students. Share the definitions of *equal* and *equitable* with them.
   1. In what ways do your students say they need a better sense of equality in your learning community?

2. In what ways do your students say they need a better sense of equity in your learning community?

Compare your students' answers to your list. How might you improve upon your curricular and pedagogical practices in light of the responses to sections A and B?

Notes

Part III

1 Curos, G. (n.d.). *What makes a master teacher.* George Couros. https://georgecouros.ca/blog/archives/9978

Chapter 6

1 Cajete, G. (1994). *Look to the mountain: An ecology of indigenous education.* ERIC.

Delpit, L. (2013). *"Multiplication Is for White people": Raising expectations for other people's children.* New York, USA: The New Press.

2 Apple, M. W., & Beane, J. A. (2007). *Democratic schools: Lessons in powerful education.* Heinemann.

Beane, J. A. (2005). *A reason to teach: Creating classrooms of dignity and hope: The power of the democratic way.* Heinemann Educational Books.

Beyer, L. E. (1996). *Creating democratic classrooms: The struggle to integrate theory and practice* (The practitioner inquiry series). ERIC.

Freire, P. (1993). *Pedagogy of the oppressed* (New Rev 20th-Anniversary ed.). New York: Continuum.

Giroux, H. A. (2004). Critical pedagogy and the postmodern/modern divide: Towards a pedagogy of democratization. *Teacher Education Quarterly, 31*(1), 31–47.

Neill, A. S. (1960). *Summerhill; a radical approach to child rearing.* New York: Hart.

Pinar, W. (2004). *What is curriculum theory?*. Routledge.

3 Nasir, N. S. (2019). *"We dare say love": Supporting achievement in the educational life of Black boys.* New York, NY: Teachers College Press.

4 Op. Cit., Neill (1960).

5 Brown, K. D., Brown, A. L., & Grant, C. A. (2015). *Black intellectual thought in education.* Routledge.

Cleary, L. M., & Peacock, T. D. (1998). *Collected wisdom: American Indian education.* ERIC.

Gill, J. H. (2002). *Native American worldviews an introduction.*

Johnson, S.C. (2019). U.S. education and the persistence of slavery. *Journal of Curriculum and Pedagogy,* 1–20. https://doi.org/10.1080/15505170.2019.1618757.

Malott, C. (2007). *A call to action: An introduction to education, philosophy, and Native North America* (Vol. 324). Peter Lang.

Merry, M., & New, W. (2008). Constructing an authentic self: The challenges and promise of African centered pedagogy. *American Journal of Education, 115*(1), 35–64. https://doi.org/10.1086/590675.

Murrell Jr, P. C. (2002). *African-centered pedagogy: Developing schools of achievement for African American children.* SUNY Press.

6 Missler, C., & Missler, N. (2014). *The way of agape.* King's High Way Ministries.

7 Fromm, E. (2000). *The art of loving: The centennial edition.* A&C Black.

8 Ibid.

9 Chapman, G. (2009). *The five love languages: How to express heartfelt commitment to your mate.* Moody Publishers.

Chapman, G. D. (2010). *The five love languages of teenagers: The secret to loving teens effectively.* Moody Publishers.

Chapman, G., & Campbell, R. (2008). *The five love languages of children.* Moody Publishers.

10 Darder, A. (2011). Chapter 9: Teaching as an act of love: Reflections on Paulo Freire and his contributions to our lives and our work. *Counterpoints, 418,* 179–194.

Darder, A. (2017). *Reinventing Paulo Freire: A pedagogy of love.* Taylor & Francis.

Op. Cit., Freire (1993).

Freire, P. (2005). *Teachers as cultural workers: Letters to those who dare teach with new commentary by Peter McLaren, Joe L. Kincheloe.* Westview Press.

Op. Cit., Fromm (2000).

11 Johnson, K., & Williams, L. (2015). *When treating all the kids the same is the real problem.* SAGE Publications, Ltd. https://doi.org/10.4135/9781452286914.

12 Op. Cit., Darder (2011, 2017).

Op. Cit., Freire (1993, 2005).

Lipner, J. (1998). Capturing gods: The god of love and the love of god in Christian and Hindu tradition. *Boardman Lectureship in Christian Ethics, 3.* Retrieved May 26, 2021, from http://repository.upenn.edu/boardman/3.

Nhat Hanh, T., & DeAntonis, J. (2014). *How to love.* USA: Parallax Press.

13 Op. Cit., Apple & Beane (2007).

Arredondo, P., Gallardo-Cooper, M., Delgado-Romero, E. A., & Zapata, A. L. (2015). Latino worldviews and cultural values. *Culturally Responsive Counseling with Latinas/os,* 15–30.

Au, W., Brown, A. L., & Calderón, D. (2016). *Reclaiming the multicultural roots of US curriculum: Communities of color and official knowledge in education.* Teachers College Press.

Op. Cit., Beane (2005).

Op. Cit., Beyer (1996).

Copple, C., & Bredekamp, S. (2009). *Developmentally appropriate practice in early childhood programs serving children from birth through age 8.* National Association for the Education of Young Children. 1313 L Street NW Suite 500, Washington, DC 22205-4101.

Op. Cit., Fromm (2000).

Op. Cit., Johnson & Williams (2015).

Joselowsky, F. (2007). Youth engagement, high school reform, and improved learning outcomes: Building systemic approaches for youth engagement. *NASSP Bulletin, 91*(3), 257–276. https://doi.org/10.1177/0192636507306133.

King, J. E., & Swartz, E. E. (2015). *The Afrocentric praxis of teaching for freedom: Connecting culture to learning.* Routledge.

Ladson-Billings, G. (2006). From the achievement gap to the education debt: Understanding achievement in U.S. schools. *Educational Researcher, 35*(7), 3–12.

Ladson-Billings, G. (2009). *The dreamkeepers: Successful teachers of African American children.* Somerset, USA: Wiley.

Montero-Sieburth, M., & Villaruel, F. (2003). *Making invisible Latino adolescents visible: A critical approach to Latino diversity.* Routledge.

Murrell Jr, P. C. (2002). *African-centered pedagogy: Developing schools of achievement for African American children.* SUNY Press.

14 New International Version. (2021). John 15:13.

15 Op. Cit., Nasir (2019).

Op. Cit., Delpit (2013).

Degruy-Leary, J. (2017). *Post-traumatic Slave Syndrome: America's legacy of enduring injury.* Portland, OR: Joy DeGruy Publications Inc.

Op. Cit., Montero-Sieburth & Villaruel (2003).

· 7 ·

SOCIAL AND ACADEMIC BELONGING

Increasing a student's sense of belonging also increases the likelihood that the student will feel resilient and academically motivated towards stronger GPAs, and graduation.[1] Students need to see themselves as socially and academically connected to the content of their coursework as well as the overall learning environment.[2] The concern is that in academic settings, students who are more uncertain of the quality of their social bonds become more sensitive to issues of social belonging and risk factors for lower performance increase.[3] Those risk factors further increase when students are unsure of their academic self-efficacy, their belief that they are inherently capable of achieving academic success.[4] A strong sense of academic self-efficacy is the highest predictor for positive learning outcomes.[5] Considering that our students do not come to us equally, having benefitted from equal exposures, opportunities or academic experiences, educators must maintain social and academic equity to provide their students with appropriate access to belonging and learning, according to their needs.

My sons were also my students. One of my teaching assignments was in a moderately sized private school in San Antonio, Texas. I was eventually the only Spanish teacher from kindergarten to twelfth grade and, at the time, one of my sons was in upper elementary, and the other was in eighth grade taking high school Spanish. Social equity being vital to me, I maintained a learning environment in which my sons were indistinguishable in preference from the rest of the student body. One visiting student who was unaware of our relationship had partnered for the day with my eldest son to preview the school. The young man hustled into Spanish class with the rest of my students, all making their normal lively entrance. My attention was, of course, on welcoming him as he took his seat next to my son. At the end of class, my son was clearly infuriated, so as with any student, I held him after class to see if I could help. At some point during class, our visitor whispered that the Spanish teacher was "hot," sending my son into an offended furry. I smiled and chuckled a bit, reassuring my son that the comment was innocent. The young man did enroll and became my permanent student. It was inevitable that one day he would be confused by an exchange he did not yet understand, when the whole class would blurt out in chorus, "She's his MOM!"

Equity meant that my new student became the object of my greater attention, as his sense of belonging was at stake, having embarrassed himself with his comment to my son. Establishing a safe place for him became reminiscent of the Christian biblical story when Jesus leaves the 99 people who are well to tend to the one who needs a rescue. It wasn't long before our new class member was a valued member of our classroom community. This situation occurred because an equitable learning environment in my classroom relied upon the relationship of *mom* never being leveraged as social or academic privilege. Although, that special relationship remained accessible when necessary to satisfy a real need, like when my son's behavior was in need of correction and, with the coveted teacher face that we all are advised to establish our first year as teachers, I would jokingly say, "You do know you have to go home with me, right?" Many of my colleagues have admitted to the impossibility of teaching their own children for risking the relationship, but my sons and I worked well together in the classroom and those moments when I was clearly identified as *mom* were lighthearted and a source of collective joy within the learning space—everyone got a sweet laugh out of our banter.

To further highlight the importance of disrupting social and academic privilege for equitable belonging, my son had as much access to me as his teacher as any of my other students. He did not enjoy a privilege that could not be shared with his classmates, including tutoring. I suppose he was demonstrating a lack of motivation at some point because my husband suddenly began to query me about the current assignments, not understanding why I was unwilling to oversee my son's home study. I assured him that I provided tutoring after school for any student who felt the need or was summoned due to declining grades. No one would have known if I had managed my son's homework production or prepared him for upcoming assessments, but the temptation to favor my son instead of laying my life down to serve the interests of academic equity would have been a hypocritical injustice on my part, and my son's, against our class community. We still laugh today as I relive the memory of my husband fussing at my son in his room, "Don't you realize that your mother is going to fail you!" My husband had to assume the parental role of monitoring our son's progress because, for equity's sake, even at home, I needed to remain his Spanish teacher.

Unfortunately, this was not the point of view of two of my colleagues who were both longstanding and favored teachers of my younger son and whose sons I also taught. In both cases, and on separate occasions, a repetitive disruptive behavior needed correction and resulted in their sons attending a detention with me after school. The first colleague verbally attacked me in the hallway, and also in profoundly, inflammatory, and defaming letters to the principal. She inappropriately assumed that her son was due a privilege, exceptional treatment, according to his elevated status as the child of a staff member. In the second case, my student's athletic coach was his father in whose care he would normally be after school—his father did not object to the detention when I alerted him to the situation. It wasn't too long before I received a mysterious knock at the classroom door. There was his mother, my colleague, in the hallway, publicly yelling at me in the most dismissive and unprofessional way because she also assumed her son to be an exception to our class culture.

In my experience, it is not unusual for parents to demand inequitable privileges for their children. Their misplaced expectations always seemed to emanate from a place of protection, particularly as our educational system has been consumed by biases and misplaced meritocracy and competitiveness. The irony is that I never, in my entire career, experienced an irate, non-staff parent whose anger I was unable to diffuse through a loving and supportive discussion regarding our mutual investment in his or her child.

Socially or academically privileging certain students, even when welcomed on the part of the student, in truth, is an act of selfishness that avoids the work of meeting students where they are and is counterintuitive to cognitive growth and self-empowerment as much as unconditional love.[6] Inequitably privileging our students disrupts the individual integrity and communal nature of Native American worldview as well as the Umbutu notion of "I am because we are."[7] Instead, it teaches an ideology of self-gratification, "I am because I am." Every part of the creation, according to Native American worldview, has a sacred path that is especially designed for its divine purpose, and through which a providential, harmonious balance is intended.[8] To inequitably privilege a student or leave a real need unmet is to alter that student's good path, possibly to catastrophe.[9] One disturbing example of the casualty of inequitable privilege regards a discussion which occurred after several weeks of teaching a cohort of Wounded Warriors in my Basic Skills Course.

Two of my students moaned and groaned about the hard work that was required and often defaulted to clever schmoozing tactics to avoid pulling their academic weight. This is an unfortunate survival tactic to mask a lack of interest and confidence; one that I have seen too many times in those students whose academic self-efficacy has been neglected.[10] After a few weeks of realizing their own growth, one of the students initiated a dialogue that captured the whole class:

> You know, I wasn't good at academics; I never did my homework, and my teachers would just let me get away with that because I was a star athlete and they liked me. Now I see they didn't care about me at all.

Several classmates concurred with this student's experience, realizing at this late hour in their lives that they had been shortchanged by a curriculum of lovelessness and were now trying to make up for it when their livelihoods were suddenly threatened. The main contributors to the discussion, including one student whose public education occurred on a Navajo reservation, were all from underserved, underfunded communities whose education did not provide them with equitable access to sociocultural or academic empowerment. The "privilege" these athletes experienced only exacerbated the systemic inequities that disregard and under educate minoritized communities.

A second example of the harm done to the individual and the community when we inequitably privilege our students by refusing to meet them where they are occurred in a high school Spanish class, populated by high-achieving, upper middle class students. The students entered Spanish II ill-prepared for the content of the course and worked hard with me to pull themselves up to level during the first nine weeks. Since their grades were a few points lower than was traditional for this group of students, the principal decided to privilege only their class with a grade inflation. My other Spanish classes did not get a similar benefit and had to be satisfied with the grades they earned. We enjoyed a bond of love and respect in my Spanish II class, as in my other Spanish classes, and upon realizing that the principal had given them an inequitable dispensation, every student's countenance had fallen to shock and sickness. They had to carry the burden of this guilt for nine more weeks until they had accomplished what would have been an eventual lifting of their grades, had they just been left alone to work for it.

The curricular message in both of these examples is that when students are perceived to be incapable, building a dishonest sense of self-gratification—anti-love—is of greater salience than investing in self-efficacy. The critical question we should return to is this: what knowledge is valued in inequitably privileging the students in these examples, and who does it benefit in the short run and in the long run?[11] Academic equity assumes that not all students come to us with the same experiences, understandings, and opportunities. We have to make those opportunities and root them in who our students are according to their onto-epistemes, interests, and values. Since it is a sacrificial act on the part of the teacher, a curriculum of agape, as it relies on academic and social equity, is an enterprise that requires commitment. The following stories highlight a few examples at the adult education level.

I teach at a Hispanic Serving Institution. It is not unusual to encounter students who struggle to successfully code-switch, moving between two or more languages, when engaged in academic writing, although it is rare to find their writing unintelligible. Recently, I taught a graduate class in which one of my students, Rose, struggled to produce acceptable written work. Attempting to code-switch from Black vernacular to academic vernacular was a profound battle for her. She was brilliant! Her insight into the social, political, and economic nature of education in America was awe inspiring. Rose's trouble was in articulating her knowledge on paper. She was defensive. She felt undervalued and threatened in her identity when required to write in colonial language, but knowing her and the importance of her voice, I choose to do something unusual.

Office hours were insufficient to help Rose, so we made an appointment on a Saturday during which I asked Rose to look at her writing and speak it to me aloud. "What did you intend to tell me here?" I asked this question in every section of her paper until she was able to edit the whole thing with a few hurried grammar lessons. Two hours later, Rose had a solid paper and a plan for future papers. She lamented her primary and secondary schooling for not taking the time to develop her understanding of language and composition to ensure her survival in academic spaces, as well as her undergraduate program which continued that trend and left her unknowingly deficient in her writing skills. Professors do not invest this kind of time in correcting graduate students' writing. As a rule, students are referred to the Writing Center—but Rose needed something more than a grammar tutor. She needed someone to believe in her, to love her unconditionally, and take the time to mentor her.

The Wounded Warrior Basic Skills Course lasted from 8:00 a.m. to 12:00 p.m. each day of the work week. Math skills began at addition and ended with basic geometry and Algebra I. Nathan, a highly capable student with a natural affinity for math, had designs on becoming a nurse and wanted to apply to the Army Nursing program. This was a notoriously rigorous program with high expectations for incoming candidates. Nathan was motivated, but the Basic Skills Course curriculum was not designed to cover Algebra II or pre-calculus. Once again, Nathan was a product of an uninspiring public education that did not love him and, therefore, left him to squander his intelligence. The act of loving Nathan unconditionally resulted in our agreement to continue to augment his math skills after class until 4:00 p.m. Nathan and I worked through lunch for four hours every day until he had completed the course and had also mastered the necessary Algebra II and pre-calculus skills to sit for his nursing school exam. He disappeared out of my life when the trimester ended until I received a phone call from him months later telling me that he had passed his exam and was on his way to Bethesda, Maryland, to begin the Army Nursing program. Nathan is now a pediatric nurse and, without a doubt, a blessing to his young patients.

A former Basic Skills Course classmate of Nathan's, whose name was Anthony, was similarly loved unconditionally right through to the completion of his bachelor's degree in Criminal Justice. Like Nathan, Anthony needed someone to know him and see him for all of his potential, but equitably educating him required much more than a single trimester of extra tutoring. Anthony had an amazing mind that became disrupted between his PTSD and his prior education. He needed someone to walk with him through his personal life and the entirety of his education. Anthony needed tutoring and additional familiar relationships to expand his sense of possibilities. It has been a rocky road loving Anthony unconditionally, requiring long hours and years of tutoring, counseling and patience for the impulsive and unwise decisions he would sometimes make. Most of my students never needed this depth of involvement, but Nathan and Anthony did. Nathan surprises me with a phone call now and again to check in, and Anthony has become a "bonus son" to my husband and to me; he is now the first in his family to complete a college degree and to buy a home.

At the secondary level, I taught an Algebra I class which the school assumed to be developmentally appropriate for all eighth grade students—the fallacy of the cookie cutter model of educating. It did not take long before a chasm was evident between those students who were ready for the level of abstraction involved in algebra and those who were not. I was caught between meeting the needs of both groups. I could not hold one part of the class back or leave the other behind so, we sought the help of two parents who were available during our class time and were excellent tutors in general mathematics and algebra. I introduced each new concept as a group and during the independent practice phase of the lesson plan, the two parents took the students who needed extra time and attention to the room across the hall from me where they could concentrate, and I was still able to see and hear them. I worked with the accelerated group and traveled between the two classrooms to answer questions and maintain our community cohesion—I needed to make certain that equitably meeting all of my students' needs would not be confused with erasing some of them.

In another instance, I had a Spanish II student, Sue, who had been adopted from a Chinese orphanage. She was touched as an infant only to be fed and changed, which disrupted some of the areas of her brain that governed cognition. I did not know at the time that the loving touch of a parent or guardian was necessary for healthy cognitive development. Sue struggled to learn in her first language, English. Learning a foreign language with the endless lists of vocabulary and grammatical rules was a mountain climb at best. I met regularly with the Special Education team and with her tutor who had been with her since infancy. Sue was a real Titan, often refusing her accommodations, but she needed an abundance of patience when responding to oral drills, group work, and independent written classwork. We upheld our class culture of interconnectedness and unconditional love, equitably supporting and empowering her to reach her full potential. Sue held at minimum a B average all year and her achievements in Spanish II were nothing short of inspirational.

Steven and Zafar were Spanish I students whose personalities preceded them into the classroom. They attended separate schools and were tremendous joys, full of life and energy—way too much energy. When I think of what it was like to teach them, I imagine chasing a runaway ping-pong ball that suddenly and unsuspectingly changes height and direction on you. Educating overly energetic students is an exhausting task that ends in disciplinary action for so many young male students, especially if they are students of color.[12]

Misunderstood and mishandled, these young men are more susceptible to dis-engagement, truancy, and prison.

Instead of sending Steven and Zafar to the office on a regular basis, I decided to try physical nearness to help keep them on task and lessen the compulsion to violate one of their classmate's personal space. All of my students had my attention via proximity, but Steven and Zafar needed a bit more. In those moments of nearness, we got to know and appreciate one another tremendously, which seemed to aid in their academic progress. In Steven's case, giving him opportunities to get out of his seat to pass out papers, or other tasks, helped him manage his excessive energy. He took great pride in his job as "assistant." Still, he was unable to hold his attention long enough to succeed in the class without extra help.

Much like my Wounded Warrior students with PTSD, Steven needed extra, individual attention and repetition. We agreed that we would eat lunch together a few times per week in my classroom to review his content and assure his success in the course. Zafar, on the other hand, simply needed a loving, attentive relationship to spark engagement and motivation. Steven's and Zafar's classmates had every right to feel annoyed by their overwhelming presence, but the agape culture provided just enough patience, forgiveness and valoriza-tion, creating a sense of equitable belonging as members of our class commu-nity, that the students learned to enjoy them more often than tire of them.

Often, when talking about academic equity, terms like cognition and schema—cultural capital—are at the forefront of the conversation. Experience has shown me that students are not only unique in cognitive growth and cul-tural capital; they are equally diverse in emotionality, which demands as much in the way of equity as any other aspect that affects learning.

Becca was one of my eighth grade English students who required emotional equity as it related to her public speaking requirement. Western culture has generally privileged written knowledge over oral tradition except in the area of oral demonstrations of knowledge that are assertive, typically in the form of public presentations.[13] The assumption is that a public display of knowledge is coherent with all students' cultural worldviews and emotional constitutions. Consider Native American worldview in which cultural norms may instill a profound sense of humility.[14] For some Native American students, to stand up before a group of peers and a teacher to pontificate upon ideas would be insult-ing.[15] Further, for some Native American communities, speaking is a function of readiness and is predicated upon having something meaningful and contrib-utory to say.[16] Becca was not emotionally ready to speak.

Becca was to present her findings on an essay topic, as many of her class-mates had done successfully despite experiencing various degrees of nervous-ness and anxiety. When it was her turn to present, she was nowhere to be found. She had signed out to use the bathroom and disappeared. After alerting the office, Becca was found and arrived at my classroom door on the phone with her mother shrieking hysterically. It was a shocking display. She had expe-rienced a panic attack over the thought of having to speak before her peers. Still, she had to satisfy the assignment. Unfortunately, it was a course require-ment that she would face again in high school. Becca needed to succeed for her own growth and continued progress in her academic future.

Had I felt a greater sense of teacher autonomy, I might have approached this assignment from the perspective of Native American culture and allowed those students to speak who were ready; for those who were not, an option to have a classmate present on their behalf would have satisfied the assignment and the opportunity for corporate learning that is embedded in a public share of knowledge. To address the need for emotional equity, we agreed that Becca would bring one guest of her choosing to my room during an off period to pres-ent her work. As was the case with Rose, Nathan, Anthony, Sue, Steven and Zafar, a curriculum of unconditional love obligated me as her teacher to know her, be responsible to meet her needs, respect her for who she was, and care for her so her learning experience would encourage and empower her. Becca successfully presented her work in a less threatening environment.

Meeting the needs of language-diverse students can feel insurmountable, a topic which I will further explore in the next chapter. I am a linguist by pro-fession and nature, so accessing languages outside of English is typically fun for me, even if I do horrible justice to them in my poor execution. Just as I am unique to my knowledge, way of being, and value system, every teacher is as well, and, therefore, not necessarily prepared to access secondary and tertiary languages. Despite my comfort with many languages, my students' language needs have not always aligned with my abilities.

In the case of Marty, a student in the Wounded Warrior Basic course, I was able to meet his linguistic needs with relative ease. Marty was a pleasure. He was one of my most engaged students who took his educational opportunity seriously. He was humble, respectful, outgoing and the life of the classroom. He also had a terrible time concentrating and experienced the short term memory loss that is typical of students with PTSD. Equally disruptive to his learning was Marty's difficulty with English comprehension. He was born and raised in Argentina until he came to the United States as an adult to serve in the military. I remember looking at Marty on many occasions and seeing the blank gaze that I have displayed myself when confronting a lack of understanding due to language barriers. The obstacle was overcome since I spoke Spanish and could quickly re-teach the content in Marty's native language. Our class was founded upon the principals of an agape curriculum and was patient and supportive, understanding the importance of equitably educating all students, including Marty.

I was not as confident when my eighth grade English student, on exchange from China, introduced himself. Heng had very little mastery of the English language. Upon his introduction, I realized my own curricular and pedagogical insufficiency and was fearful that I would not be able to equitably meet his social or academic needs. I spoke a little Japanese but not a word of Mandarin and contemplated my failure even before I began to teach Heng. How would I facilitate access to a curriculum of agape or the state curriculum for eight grade English Language Arts and Reading when I could not communicate with him?

Students are amazingly resilient and the culture of agape that my English speaking students embraced and welcomed Heng, making him a celebrated and integral part of our classroom culture without my intervention. Language is not an obstacle to love, and Heng's classmates were not afraid to love him unconditionally. I taught in English while he took notes in Mandarin, so I was never able to know whether he correctly annotated moments of direct instruction. To ensure equity and comprehension, I used my cell phone to translate content or playful communications, sometimes eliciting the help of a neighbor whose children attended a local bilingual Chinese school. I was shameless in asking for help wherever resources were available; equally shameless was the way I butchered Mandarin. Heng found my linguistic abuses to be a source of entertainment and a bond of fun between the two of us. With the help of a tutor, we managed to keep his grades up and Heng returned to China having conquered eighth grade English in an American school.

According to Maslow's Hierarchy of Needs, students must perceive themselves to be loved and physically and emotionally safe before they can consider meeting their academic potential.[17] While our students are uncertain of their academic and social belonging, their positive learning outcomes remain at risk.[18] Thus, student motivation and engagement are directly influenced by curricular and pedagogical practices that are rooted in providing an individualized, protective, and supportive environment of love and belonging.[19] A curriculum of agape opposes the self-gratifying, historical, and contemporary approach to education that inequitably privileges certain students or forces them all, despite their unique and complex onto-epistemological and axiological needs, into a curricular and pedagogical box of sameness.[20] Love in education must produce equality for students in responsibility, investment, knowledge, respect, and care while equitably catalyzing a holistic sense of social belonging and academic self-efficacy.[21] To accomplish this and realize every student's potential, educators must do the hard work of knowing each student, finding out who each student is, and esteeming him or her above normalized curricular and pedagogical biases.

Explore, Think, Act

Chapter 7 of Part III explores equity through *belonging* as it is a conduit for student engagement and motivation. Knowing our students and equitably meeting them where they are helps us to foster social and academic belonging more effectively and is a direct reflection of a curriculum of agape and our unconditional love for our students. Consider your own pedagogy and the degree to which you cultivate student belonging in the learning space.

(A) Think about your own experiences as a student.
  1. Have you ever experienced an inequitable privileging as a student? If so, how did you feel about it? Why do you think the inequitable privileging occurred?
(B) Think about your students who are socially or academically struggling.
  2. Are there areas of social or academic inequity that may contribute to their lower performance?
  3. How might you verify if your students are suffering from social or academic inequities?
  4. Are you inequitably privileging certain students? If so, think, and try to get to the root of why you choose to privilege those students. In what ways can you change your behavior? Brainstorm the conversation you will have with your students in which you will explain your change of behavior for the sake of their growth.
(C) Create an action plan to equitably address your students need to *belong.*

Notes

1 Bluestein, J. (2008). *The win-win classroom: A fresh and positive look at classroom management.* Corwin Press.

    Walton, G. M., & Cohen, G. L. (2007). A question of belonging: Race, social fit, and achievement. *Journal of personality and social psychology, 92*(1), 82.

2 Ibid.

3 Op. Cit., Walton & Cohen (2007).

4 Johnson, S. (2020). *Afrocentricity: Student voices on African American identity in multicultural education reform.* The University of Texas at San Antonio.

5 Ibid.

6 Yeager, D. S., & Dweck, C. S. (2020). What can be learned from growth mindset controversies?. *American Psychologist, 75*(9), 1269.

7 Cleary, L. M., & Peacock, T. D. (1998). *Collected wisdom: American Indian education.* ERIC.

    Gill, J. H. (2002). *Native American worldviews an introduction.*

    Tshivhase, M. (2018). Love as the foundation of Ubuntu. *Synthesis Philosophica, 65*(1/2018), 197–208. https://doi.org/10.21464/sp33112.

8 Op. Cit., Cleary & Peacock (1998).

9 Ibid.

10 Platt, T., Wagner, L., & Ruch, W. (2016). The association between class clown dimensions, school experiences and accomplishment. *Learning and Individual Differences, 51*, 327–332.

11 Kridel, C. (2010). Currere. In *Encyclopedia of curriculum studies* (Vol. 1, pp. 178–178). SAGE Publications, Inc. https://doi.org/10.4135/9781412958806.n102.

    Pinar, W. (2004). *What is curriculum theory?.* Routledge.

12 Gregory, A., Skiba, R. J., & Mediratta, K. (2017). Eliminating disparities in school discipline: A framework for intervention. *Review of Research in Education, 41*(1), 253–278.

    Losen, D. J., Hodson, C. L., Keith II, M. A., Morrison, K., & Belway, S. (2015). *Are we closing the school discipline gap?.*

13 Op. Cit., Cleary & Peacock (1998).

    Op. Cit., Gill (2002).

    Johnson, S. C. (2019). U.S. education and the persistence of slavery. *Journal of Curriculum and Pedagogy*, 1–20. https://doi.org/10.1080/15505170.2019.1618757.

    Op. Cit., Johnson (2020).

    Malott, C. (2007). *A call to action: An introduction to education, philosophy, and Native North America* (Vol. 324). Peter Lang.

14 Op. Cit., Cleary & Peacock (1998).

15 Ibid.

16 Ibid.

17 Kline, T. (n.d.). *Applying Maslow's hierarchy of needs in our classrooms.* ChangeKidsLives. Retrieved November 11, 2021, from http://www.changekidslives.org/actions-4.

18 Op. Cit., Johnson (2020).

    Montero-Sieburth, M., & Villaruel, F. (2003). *Making invisible Latino adolescents visible: A critical approach to Latino diversity.* Routledge.

    Op. Cit., Walton & Cohen (2007).

19 Op. Cit., Cleary & Peacock (1998).

Delpit, L. (2013). *"Multiplication Is for White people": Raising expectations for other people's children*. New York, USA: The New Press.

Degruy-Leary, J. (2017). *Post-traumatic slave syndrome: America's legacy of enduring injury*. Portland, OR: Joy DeGruy Publications Inc.

Op. Cit., Montero-Sieburth & Villaruel (2003).

Nasir, N. S. (2019). *"We dare say love": Supporting achievement in the educational life of Black boys*. New York, NY: Teachers College Press.

20 Brown, K. D., Brown, A. L., & Grant, C. A. (2015). *Black intellectual thought in education*. Routledge.

Op. Cit., Cleary & Peacock (1998).

Fromm, E. (2000). *The art of loving: The centennial edition*. A&C Black.

Op. Cit., Gill (2002).

Op. Cit., Johnson (2019).

Op. Cit., Malott (2007).

Merry, M., & New, W. (2008). Constructing an authentic self: The challenges and promise of African centered pedagogy. *American Journal of Education, 115*(1), 35–64. https://doi.org/10.1086/590675.

Missler, C., & Missler, N. (2014). *The way of agape*. King's High Way Ministries.

Murrell Jr, P. C. (2002). *African-centered pedagogy: Developing schools of achievement for African American children*. SUNY Press.

Neill, A. S. (1960). *Summerhill; a radical approach to child rearing*. New York: Hart.

21 Darder, A. (2011). Chapter 9: Teaching as an act of love: Reflections on Paulo Freire and his contributions to our lives and our work. *Counterpoints, 418*, 179–194.

Darder, A. (2017). *Reinventing Paulo Freire: A pedagogy of love*. Taylor & Francis.

Freire, P. (1993). *Pedagogy of the oppressed* (New Rev 20th-Anniversary ed.). New York: Continuum.

Freire, P. (2005). *Teachers as cultural workers: Letters to those who dare teach with new commentary by Peter McLaren, Joe L. Kincheloe*. Westview Press.

Op. Cit., Fromm (2000).

Op. Cit., Johnson (2020).

Johnson, K., & Williams, L. (2015). *When treating all the kids the same is the real problem*. SAGE Publications, Ltd. https://doi.org/10.4135/9781452286914.

Walton, G. M., & Cohen, G. L. (2007). A question of belonging: Race, social fit, and achievement. *Journal of Personality and Social Psychology, 92*(1), 82.

· 8 ·

CULTURAL BELONGING—"SAWUBONA: I SEE YOU"

My cousin had occasion to live in Zimbabwe and South Africa with her family. One of the stories her husband shared with me regarded the unique and beautiful way the African people in these regions greeted one another. In English, "I see you," was the customary greeting, and it spoke to a sense of belonging. The Zulu greeting, "*Sawubona* [I see you]," is an ideological embracing of each person as uniquely valuable and acceptable as they are. The response in English was, "I see you, too" or "I'm here," as if to call the person into the fullness of existence now that he or she was *seen* authentically by another. Although Americans do not address one another in such affirming terms, *seeing* each other for who we are does amplify our existence, and we are diminished by those who erase our identity. We do not escape the damage done to our students by not *seeing* them simply because our traditional greetings, "Hi" or "Hello," allow us to evade our responsibility when generalizing who they are and/or relegating them to the curricular and pedagogical periphery.

From a Buddhist perspective, a person cannot love if that person doesn't understand.[1] Understanding encapsulates Fromm's four basic elements of love—care, responsibility, respect, and knowledge—and is a natural outgrowth of deeply and intentionally *seeing* a person and listening to discover who he or she is.[2] Love through cultural equity demands that a teacher first *see* students in order to liberate their distinctive, existential purpose and global value.

I learned to dislike history in middle school. It was a distaste that would not resolve itself until Dr. Caminera's vibrant and identity-affirming Latin American History courses in college. Mr. Mac was my history teacher who presented one Eurocentric battle after another in the quest to conquer the land and peoples of what we now call America, which included the quest to conquer my people. Consistent with the student interview comments from chapter 3, middle school history was date heavy, boring, and terribly oppressive from my vantage point. We arrived at the moment in history in Mr. Mac's class where one of America's favorite rivalries emerged—the West Virginia clash between the Hatfields and McCoys.[3] Finally, a positive connection between who I was and my middle school history curriculum. I raised my hand to announce that I was Hatfield on my mother's side of the family. Storytelling was a vital aspect of my family culture and our understanding of our lineage—I knew who I was, the descendant of a Blackfoot and Hatfield union. Mr. Mac quickly corrected me and told me before my classmates, with emphasis, that I was mistaken.

Mr. Mac did not *see* me. He saw only what fit his own personal schema. In his mind, my brown skin could not possibly find belonging in these Appalachian American darlings. Three errors of anti-love occurred here that disenfranchised me from my learning environment: a biased assumption was made regarding my Black identity based upon an essentialized notion of Blackness, a devaluation of my identity occurred as a result of my teacher's disrupted, racist paradigm, and I was publicly humiliated to ensure no harm was done to my classmates' White supremacist mis-education. Stolen was my classmates' opportunity to engage in an authentic dialogue around the realities of our pluralistic interconnectedness as human beings and citizens within the United States, and stolen was my opportunity to belong—to connect—with my middle school curriculum.

According to William Pinar, if what American students know about themselves is "deformed by absences, denials, and incompleteness, then [their identity] as individuals and Americans [in their lack of curricular and pedagogical representation] is fragmented."[4] A "fragmented self" is a "repressed" self in which a void is created, disallowing full access to "self" and the world.[5] This repression disrupts the capacity for intelligence, informed action, and simple functional competence.[6] As stated earlier, minimizing or erasing student identity from the learning space and place in favor of a monolithic worldview destabilizes the trust, safety, belonging and love, necessary for self-actualization and positive learning outcomes.[7] It goes without saying that my middle school history grades reflected my disconnection.

A curriculum of agape is supportive of cultural equity in that it defies our biases by valuing and upholding the expressed individual and collective identities of our students. It is a correction upon the areas of disconnection experienced by students, such as the interview participants from Chapter 3. A curriculum of agape favors equitable curricular and pedagogical integrations of student cultural identity that foster human connection.

Color blind, spiritually separated, canceled culture, that relegates non-Eurocentric funds of knowledge to an isolated and discretionary, superficial celebration of foods, heroes, and "traditional" clothing is neither loving nor restorative.[8] Instead, this delivers the very stereotypical message of "other" that is incongruent with unconditional love, engagement, and motivation, and that we, as educators, ought to dismantle. To uphold a curriculum of agape, love that connects us all to one another in society and in the classroom, it is necessary to be embracive of all that makes our students culturally unique and autonomous, even against our own self-interest, points of view, and understandings. A curriculum of agape cannot exist in cultural fear or inequity.[9] It exists in bravery and freedom—providing honesty and restoration regarding race and ethnicity in society, spiritual accessibility and integration, and cultural consciousness and inclusivity.[10]

Seeing Our Students' Racial-Ethnic Identities

Contrary to our professional programming, and to the most recent political efforts to remove discussions of race and racism in school curriculum, evading race or ethnicity in the learning environment is shown to be harmful to academic progress, particularly for students of color.[11] Three aspects of racial-ethnic-cultural identity are most pertinent to student engagement and motivation: social belonging, academic belonging or self-efficacy, and an honest reflection regarding the realities of systemic racism.[12] Students need to be *seen*, able to exist, in the realities that are their life experiences. Race, ethnicity and culture are inherent and many times influential aspects of who our students are and how they experience and interpret social, economic and political phenomena.[13] When students ask the question, "Do I belong?" they are also asking, "Does my group belong?"[14] Academic engagement and motivation are enhanced when our students perceive their racial, ethnic and cultural selves as positively valued and occupying a place of curricular and pedagogical belonging.[15] The converse is true when that curricular and pedagogical place of racial, ethnic and cultural belonging is withheld. The strongest predictor of success in education is a student's perception of academic belonging [self-efficacy].[16] When a student views high academic achievement as being inherent to his or her race, ethnicity or culture, the direct result is an increase in engagement and motivation.[17]

Part of establishing a learning community that is supportive of a curriculum of agape is to facilitate honest dialogue that supports and restores racial and ethnic identity as it is situated in curricular and pedagogical connections. An example of this is the use of Talking, or Peacemaking, Circles to help students process their experiences and feelings relative to social topics and texts within the curriculum in a way that builds knowledge, humility, understanding and unity.[18] If we are to properly address curricular and pedagogical equity at the K-12 levels, we must engage in transformative dialogues as pre-service and in-service teachers. Dialogue around social inequities that includes White privilege, gender, language and ability inequities, to name a few, can be tricky and highly emotional since feelings of guilt and anger can accidentally divide instead of unify. For this reason, within a clear and established ethos of agape, I use Talking Circles in clusters of 4–5 to build small group trust and openness that eventually lead to medium and large group talks. Students are often guarded at the onset of the semester but quickly bond with one another as they listen to diverse perspectives and, ultimately, realize the depth of commonality in their joys and hurts across life's experiences. Tissue boxes become centerpieces within our Talking Circles as comments such as, "I never knew they felt this way, too" and "I just didn't realize" emerge in response to finally seeing their classmates across races, ethnicities, genders, abilities, and the like. Color blindness and the fear that births it is replaced with *seeing* and the ability to safely acknowledge and accept the life experiences of people in this country who are weighed down by systemic social inequities, particularly through our educational system. Further, Talking Circles provide a basis for action as these dialogical spaces become fodder for transforming current practices within their own classrooms.

An example of a similar restorative activity at the middle school level arose out of an obligation to include *The Pearl* by John Steinbeck as a literary source for a discussion about the ills of greed. The department head, a Ph.D. who retired from college level instruction to enjoy retirement from a high school classroom, expected me to approach the conversation of greed through the story of an indigenous population that had become ruined by their own sense of greed. In truth, it was colonial greed that incited a desperate attempt to save the life of an indigenous baby to the ultimate ruination of the family. Many of my students shared Latino(a) heritage and a few were of African American descent. I could not in good conscience approach the curriculum from a colonial male perspective without neglecting to *see* my female students or students of color and the many perspectives that any of my students might bring to the text. I refused to participate in fragmenting my students' identities. We read, we contemplated many vantage points through which to view the literature, and we connected our themes to our contemporary concerns in society.

It was during this study that riots erupted in response to the shooting death of Michael Brown. A colleague who shared the same group of students in his bible class blurted out to the class, "I don't know why these people keep tearing up their neighborhoods." THESE PEOPLE was the only part of that sentence I truly heard when my students reported what had transpired in their class. It angered me to think of my Black and brown students who were reduced to THESE PEOPLE, and my White students for whom THESE PEOPLE would become yet another normalized statement of othering and individualized erasure that would foment their dysconcious, racist notions, whether they wanted the bias or not.

Out of love for my students, we created Talking Circles where we connected our literature study to the results of colonialism in America across multiple racial-ethnic demographics. The purpose of the activity was to answer the question: Why do "these people" riot? After investigating and discussing with their group the historical and current conditions of their demographic at the hands of American colonialism, they presented the findings of their research to the class and shared what they learned. We satisfied the prescribed curriculum. We read the required text and discussed the topic of greed, but we did so in a manner that *saw* all students as individuals and allowed each to be present with the curriculum and with each other so that their content was honest, relevant, and restorative, unblinded to the neutralization of the realities of women and people of color in this nation and beyond.

Seeing Our Students' Religious Identities

Seeing our students in their religious identities through our curriculum and our pedagogical approach to education supports cultural equity and, thus, agape.

When our educational spaces are inclusive of diverse, spiritual perspectives, we restore divested areas of cognition and a sense of onto-epistemological belonging that has been lost in the separation of church and state. The Constitution of the United States is inarguably a foundational sociopolitical document, aligning American culture with the ideals and preservation of a democracy. Yet, there exists in education, a type of psychic dissonance as students are, in many cases, forced to navigate the confusing space between our democratic ideology and practice.

Perhaps the chasm between profession and practice lies in a lack of certainty over the definition of a *democracy*.[19] Our founding documents demand the establishment of "justice", "insure domestic tranquility", "promote the general welfare", and assume that "all men are created equal" with rights to life, liberty and the pursuit of happiness. U.S. public education, being an extension of the nation's socioeconomic and political systems, becomes problematic when curriculum is said to be reflective of democratic ideals while it is at the same time upholding colonial and/or imperialistic ideals.[20] Particularly concerning is the way in which the application of the First Amendment of the United States Constitution creates this very conflict and is prone to leave Black, Latino(a), and Indigenous students uniquely open to fragmented identities in the learning space, and the disenfranchisement and underperformance that follow.[21]

The First Amendment states that the government, including state boards of education, shall make no law respecting an establishment of religion. Imagining that the silencing of religion is a type of "establishment" unto itself, in order to defeat religious hegemony and Judeo-Christian favoritism, it appears that schools have also taken Thomas Jefferson's intentions out of context and disrupted two vital components of student identity: students' freedoms of religion and speech.[22] As a woman of color, I do not approve of Thomas Jefferson's hypocrisy and inhumanity, but since our First Amendment law is founded upon his words, it is essential to know that his intention, albeit limited, was not to disallow a full dialogue that would otherwise participate in the democratic process by celebrating the diversity of a civic community. His objective was only to moderate opinion when necessary to protect people from mean-spiritedness: ". . . overt acts against peace and good order . . ."[23] In its current practice, "freedom of religion" in education has rendered itself undemocratic, possibly unconstitutional, and serves as a source of curricular psychic dissonance that is disruptive of non-western worldviews and the learning outcomes of predominantly Black and brown students.[24]

Intersecting Pinar's theory of identity repression with the misapplication of Thomas Jefferson's "separation of church and state" and its repression of religious identity in the learning environment, the imposition of the First Amendment upon education cast out the curricular and pedagogical imperialism of Christian thought but also, metaphorically, "threw the baby out with the bathwater." The application of the law repressed all students.[25] This misapplication then contributes to false narratives around student disengagement and poor academic outcomes that especially place blame upon students of color instead of the meaningless, repressive, curriculum that racially, ethnically, and culturally disconnects students from their realities.[26]

The fact is, religious identity may be as important an intersectionality to student engagement and motivation as other identity markers such as race, ethnicity, gender, nationality, etc. The Black church is often central to the African American community, creating strong extended family bonds referred to as one's "church family."[27] For those African American students whose spiritual orientation is an integral part of knowing and being, the cognitive and intellectual divestiture of spiritual and ethnic identities precipitates a struggle for self-empowerment.[28] Racial-ethnic identities and intellectual identities "forever pitted against each other" cognitively disenfranchises these students from the learning space since "both these two conceptual orientations have contributed profoundly to the formation of Black identity in America."[29]

A similar curricular psychic dissonance occurs for Native American students whose onto-epistemological norms are predicated upon an understanding of material and spiritual interconnectedness within all phenomena.[30] Latino(a) spiritual worldviews are closely related to those of Native Americans in many respects and for many Middle Eastern students, spiritual orientation highly moderates onto-epistemological and axiological understandings.[31] One study found that, among African American, Latino(a) and White students, curricular and pedagogical inclusiveness of diverse spiritual understandings is preferred and is supportive of student engagement, motivation and resilience.[32]

In addressing student perspectives on the importance of spiritual identity and its relevance to proper connection to the learning environment, student interviews conclude that spiritual identity is integral to the schema of learners.[33] These perspectives are consistent with the theoretical position that when "pitted against" intellectual notions in the classroom, the resulting curricular psychic dissonance interrupts proper engagement and motivation.[34] Interestingly, the notion of a curricular psychic dissonance is most evident when participants attempt to cherry pick aspects of their identities that might pacify ideological conflicts or federal law within the public classroom.[35] Despite admissions of connection in learning spaces that invite open discourse and integration of diverse spiritual understandings—acknowledging the benefits of integrating spiritual identity into the curriculum—students may reject its applicability in fear of retribution or discord.[36]

Examples of student connections between the learning space and religious identities are as follows:

> "I've been a part of church ever since I came out the womb . . . Me, being a part of that community, learning how to take on those leadership roles, has better prepared me to be outside of the church walls within the community and my school."[37]
>
> "I identify as Black or African American and it's important to me because that's who I am; it makes me part of who I am. And, my religious and spiritual self is important to me also. I'm a Christian and that's also part of who I am at home and in school."[38]
>
> "I wouldn't say I'm very religious or spiritual . . . but I would like to hear your ideas or your spirituality or your religion and I'll compare the two and I'll say, '[O]kay, well I see both of your guys' points and I see what you sayin'.'"[39]
>
> "[L]ike, I know there's not just one religion. So, I understand that, but I feel like it shouldn't have been [completely outlawed] . . . I feel like in those types of ways, I'm no longer represented."[40]
>
> "[R]eligion is a key source in my life . . . [Y]ou can't live without it . . . It's an important part of my cultural identity because my family and the people around me do religion . . . So, yeah, I guess it goes hand in hand [with the curriculum]."[41]

Additionally, when surveyed, African American students demonstrate a moderately high to high preference for a curriculum that is inclusive of diverse spiritual identities "where spiritual understanding is not subjugated to or separated from the understanding of the material world."[42] White and Latino(a) students also demonstrate a moderate to high preference for the same.[43]

A curriculum of agape as it supports cultural equity through the curricular and/or pedagogical inclusion of individual spirituality does not demand or specify any particular spiritual practice, or lack thereof, but allows for dialogue, recognizing the importance of this aspect of student identity. I have to be honest in saying that my intentions to uphold this aspect of agape through cultural equity have not always come easily. I had to grow in this area as I struggled with my own fears and reservations amidst the myriad of student spiritual practices that have not always aligned with my own.

I was challenged to love my students unconditionally, *seeing* them selflessly, and allowing them to be present and valuable to me while meeting them where they were. In one such case, a high school Spanish student, Rashid, trembled furiously as he handed me an invitation to a Hindu celebration of the guru. I had heard the term *guru* and even had used it loosely now and again to describe specific relationships, but I did not truly understand the construct of a guru from a Hindu standpoint. The chasm between Hinduism and my spiritual practice had me confused and conflicted while I debated attending a spiritual ceremony that was so diametrically opposed to my own sense of truth. I decided to try to understand the guru from Rashid's perspective and was stunned by the beauty and the importance of a teacher in the spiritual life of my student. With my husband's encouragement, I decided to attend the celebration. I remained cognizant of how nervous Rashid was in extending the invitation, a clear importance which I could not ignore. I went for Rashid's sake.

I learned that, within Hinduism, the term teacher and guru are synonymous. Guru is a Sanskrit word that refers to someone who dispels darkness. Different from a Western standpoint regarding the profession of teaching, Hinduism views the role of a teacher, or guru, as divine since a teacher not only imparts academic wisdom and knowledge to their students, but also guides them along a right path of life.[44]

The ceremony to express gratitude for the teacher who invests his or her life in the student was inspiring, profoundly informing my agape centered approach to education. Rashid's invitation was not simply to observe; he regarded me as his guru and had chosen me to participate as an honoree. I was called to the stage where I was given a handful of rice and instructed to throw the rice upon my student while speaking a prayer over his life. I was never asked if my spiritual practice aligned with his, if my prayers would appropriately fit their beliefs to be heard and answered beyond the material veil. It was assumed that I was sufficiently spiritually interconnected with my student. Rashid walked up to me and prostrated himself at my feet to honor my place in his life and receive his blessing from me. I have never been so humbled and honored. This moment became the rudder by which my practice of unconditional love in my classroom steered my research interest towards understanding the profound place that spiritual beliefs occupy within the cultural identity of my students.

When Emad, a ninth grade Spanish student, approached me with an offer to cantor his Islamic prayers, which he was learning as a rite of passage, he had little doubt in his mind that I would be honored to receive his gift. I had at that point learned from my experience with Rashid, and my students were accustomed to freely sharing their spiritual perspectives as it related to their subject matter or their personal lives, which often resulted in a fascinating, multidimensional dialogue. Since this opportunity was not linked to our content in any way, I agreed upon a day when we would finish our lesson with time to spare so that Emad's prayer would not disrupt his classmates' learning or their right to not partake. Those who were curious joined us in the back of the classroom to listen to Emad proudly showcase his cantoring skills. It was rich and not without criticism from some of his Muslim classmates who felt it was their duty to correct him. Part of maintaining an agape community is to mediate those disagreements into support and valorization of diverse experiences and bodies of knowledge—this was not their moment; it was Emad's. We clapped and cheered as Emad stood confidently, swollen with pride and a smile along the whole of his face. The more inclusive I became, the freer my students became in sharing those risky parts of themselves that mattered but were acculturated to be taboo in school.

According to Thomas Jefferson, the mind was created to be free—no one should tell another what to think or believe, but ". . . all men shall be free to profess, and by argument to maintain, their opinions in matters of Religion . . ."[45] Jefferson was not afraid of diverse spiritual ideologies or their impact on civil harmony. It was professionally enriching for me one day to hear another teacher, whose classroom I happened to visit during a school tour, ask her students during a discussion, "What spiritual notions do you think might have influenced this [phenomenon]?" I pulled her aside after class and shared a high five with her for freeing her students' spiritual intellect in her classroom. As a democracy, by definition, requires the unhindered participation of "difference," from a curricular standpoint and definitely one that is situated in unconditional love, so should the public educational system that feeds and perpetuates it. If Jefferson's intention had been to liberate religious or spiritual dialogue, an intention that the high school students highlighted in this chapter and those in my own personal classrooms seemed to embrace, Separation of Church and State, in its current obstructive application, must, therefore, be fueled by some other ethos—one that separates and subdues religious or spiritual identity as something "other" than intellectual goods.

Although the inequity of evangelistic privilege that was Christianity in public schools needed to be corrected, Separation of Church and State has erased equity, disrupting democratic values and fracturing student identity, making it impossible for religious freedom to co-exist with freedom of speech. Students remain invisible, *unseen*, in a crucial area of their identity. The curricular psychic dissonance that may follow this lovelessness begs the question: who benefits from such a contemporary misrepresentation of Thomas Jefferson's speech and a constitutional law that makes a hypocrisy of them both? Judeo-Christian thought, still the dominant influencer within western society, is threatened by curricular repression, especially for students of color whose worldviews are intricately tied to their spiritual understandings, but its social position of privilege supports its normative voice and reaches across American culture. More profound is the harm to those non-Western onto-epistemes that rely on a unification of the material and spiritual and to the people whose intellectual growth and self-empowerment depend on them.

Seeing the Intricacies of Students Identity

Our classrooms should make sense to the learners who inhabit them. A student whose inherent cultural curriculum—the inner ecosystem in which he or she has been raised—has fostered cognition through storytelling and other aspects of oral tradition, or collaborative efforts centered in collective harmony, familial relationships and mentoring, might find it hard to impossible to learn in a highly individualistic, meritorious environment that is exclusively reliant on written forms of knowledge.[46] This student may come to learn and understand the world through direct intervention or, indirectly, via strict adherence to non-interference.[47] Similarly, for students who understand phenomena as a symbiotic dynamic between the spiritual and material realms, the dissonance that results from a forced separation has already been established to be disruptive to proper cognition.[48] Our pedagogical goal, stemming from a curriculum of agape, is to know our students' cultural worldviews, and the ways in which they impact knowledge construction, and equitably give place to those cognitive processes as part of a diversified program of cultural inclusiveness. Yet, in doing so, care has to be taken to avoid assumptions based on stereotyping or overgeneralizations.

When onto-epistemological and axiological aspects of identity become essentialized due to prior experiences, media propaganda or other innate social, political or economic biases, student engagement, motivation and positive academic outcomes are at risk.[49] Mistaken assumptions as to who our students are, even when well intentioned, reduce the students, rendering them invisible—the students cease to be in the learning space while their individualities remain *unseen*. Although there is immense pride in the expressed commonalities that cement ones' membership to a cultural group and distinguishes them as "a people"—social norms, dialect, music, foods, history, heroes, etc.—love, through cultural equity, must maintain an awareness of shared cultural community norms while seeking to know the individualized and intersectional ways of knowing and being of each student.[50]

There is something terribly askew in our current American culture that requires us to categorize and label everything: Black, White, liberal, conservative, woke, ally. It is necessary to find ways to articulate our experiences and understandings, and a common lexicon helps us accomplish this. The trouble arises from stratification, the lines in the sand that force the human experience into boxes with binary labels—if we're not all the way in, we're out. If we don't live on the res, we're not Indian. If we "talk White" or "look White" we're not Black. If we are Christian, we are also republicans—conservative across the board. If we say we're Latino(a), we automatically speak Spanish and relate to *machismo*[51] or *marianismo*.[52,53] Notions such as these are borne out of selfish, loveless pursuits that refuse to *see* people through the lens of human complexity and are detrimental to the personal and academic development of our students. An example of this occurred when my brother was minimized by his elementary teacher who publicly insisted that he confused his breakfast meal with his dinner.

The students were asked to share what they had for breakfast that morning and my brother volunteered, "chicken and green beans." The assumption that our family meals were consistent with American eating patterns caused Steve's teacher not to *see* him, and under protest, in that moment, he became culturally invisible. The reality was that we ate the heavier dinner fare in the morning and a lighter breakfast-like meal in the evening. An understanding of metabolism, being at its peak earlier in the day and trailing off towards the average dinner hour, inspired my mother to schedule our meals in a way that cooperated with the human design. We also enjoyed an international exposure to food choices, unlike many of our peers. To further this point, I recently purchased a delightfully provocative sketch in which multiple figures with super-sized pencils, imperiously box themselves off from one another. A Jesus-type figure is at the same time erasing those lines. A curriculum of agape should do the same. It should erase those hard lines that compartmentalize and leave students on the margins of their existence with limited belonging.

Language is often one of those significant and celebrated aspect of students' cultural identity and community belonging.[54] One of the ways I attempt to meet my students where they are is through diversifying the languages with which I engaged them during class. I speak to my students in as many languages to which I have had exposure. Sometimes I speak in sentences, other times I can only produce a loving word or two. Regardless, my goal is to *see* my students, to engage in a curriculum of agape through valorizing their language capital. I never assume my students speak their heritage languages. I simply toss a diverse cross section of languages out into the learning environment and when a student responds in kind, I know they feel safe and that I am supporting them. As they become more comfortable in their agape learning community, my students often volunteer their home languages.

As mentioned earlier, accommodating language diversity is sometimes scary to do and I fall flat on occasion. I never did get the hang of the one Romanian greeting I worked on for an entire high school year, but my student smiled brilliantly each time I tried and failed—he knew, underneath it all, that what I was actually trying to say was that I *saw* him and loved him, unconditionally. I don't think I understood the full relevance of my efforts until I received the following email from one of my pre-service, undergraduate students who commented upon the meaningfulness of experiencing cultural equity in this way: "You made my life and my presence feel like it mattered. With cultural inclusion being shown in your classroom daily, whether it be through PowerPoint slides or your occasional salutations and farewells in different languages, you embraced the beauty of diversity."

A favorite memory of mine occurred in a ninth grade Spanish class— another class of spirited students whose energy fluctuated primarily at the whim of a few fidgety young men. Early in the year, when I was still shaping our agape culture, I had enough of the play. I decided to try something different. I knew enough Arabic to correct my students in their own language. I was not sure how many of my young men spoke Arabic at home, but I knew I would certainly capture their attention and might contribute something positive to our relationship in valuing their language. "Habibi, khalas,"[55] I said gently. The room erupted in shock and cheering. One of the young men rose up from his seat out of sheer emotion at hearing his home language. The phrase was translated for the rest of the class, expanding everyone's cultural knowledge and then the whole room got back to work.

There are no words to express what this moment did to solidify a year-long mutual respect, admiration and engagement. In contrast, I knew I was hearing one of my tenth graders speaking in a language that reminded me of Arabic, but it was different somehow. My student told me I was hearing Farsi and when I agreed that I needed to learn, he said with a melted countenance, "Oh no, ma'am, you don't want to learn my language." I questioned him as to why and, reflective of a post-911 world, he told the class about the airline staff in one of our major U.S. international airports who asked his family to move their seats because their conversation in Farsi was upsetting the other passengers. The outrage we felt as a class community was palpable. A corporate embrace of his cultural identity as a result of this oppressive experience forged our relationships and created an openness, transparency and cohesiveness that I'm not certain would have existed otherwise.

Through the whole of my career, learning to *see* each other in an agape learning community introduced a richness of intersectionalities that defied so many normative ideas about what it meant to belong to a particular culture, within cultures and across cultures. We learned that ethnic ties to India did not necessarily predispose a person to Hinduism or that a person can be Jewish and still find their favorite holiday to be Christmas with their extended family. Our Asian classmates sometimes get Cs by the skin of their teeth, too. Our Latino(a) classmates may need help with their Spanish homework like anyone else. Our non-African American classmates are also tormented by colorism within their ethnic groups, and our Black classmates may not know how to rap or ball but might instead skateboard and scream every line of *Assistant To The Regional Manager* by The Devil Wears Prada. We learned that *seeing* requires us to develop a cultural consciousness and inclusivity that sheds our preconceived ideas about who we are and how we interact within distinct cultures. Never was this more impactful than when I took my students to Puerto Rico as a capstone to two or three years of in-class Spanish.

It would have been more familiar and generally easier to have taken my students to Mexico. The area of Texas where I lived and taught at the time was heavily influenced by Mexican culture, with many of my students coming from Mexican backgrounds. I decided that Puerto Rico provided a more complete learning opportunity because the culture was less known to this group of students. The dialect, the foods, the topography and the racial blend was more distal to my students' local experiences and provided an equitable learning opportunity for everyone. Puerto Rico's colonial history and its current socio-political and economic relationship with the United States as a territory also provided an opportunity for students to critique and challenge their understandings of their own country's activity as a world power. The objective was to recontextualize our curriculum of agape and apply who we were as a class community to the greater global community through a living classroom experience—I wanted my students to *see* the Puerto Rican people.

By this point, my students recognized that *seeing* others required dialogue. They had to know the Puerto Rican people to understand and value them for who they are. They also had to approach this in a way that was sacrificial and selfless, esteeming the lives of the people they encountered as intrinsically connected to their own. Dialogue, asking open ended questions, and listening to the stories of the people as we did in Talking Circles allowed my students to accomplish a cultural consciousness through relationship with their Puerto Rican hosts. My students conversed with as many guides and restaurant staff as they could, observing and listening to their language patterns, social interactions, histories, and their current political, economic, and ecological concerns. They volunteered at a local orphanage where they worked, played, and talked with young children and their caretakers, trying to understand how social conditions left the children abandoned. The primary rule of the orphanage was that volunteers refrain from touching the children. My students' attempts to know and understand the children and the circumstances around their placement in the orphanage provoked little hugs everywhere that my students could not help but return. They developed a new perspective regarding the conflict between love and a world power that exploits a people and leaves them in a socio-political and economic grey area. They felt their human connection and obligation to nature as they explored rainforests, barrier reefs and marine life causing them to reconsider the human footprint that is rooted in the loveless ideology of manifest destiny.

Our curriculum of agape, as it intersected with the land and people of Puerto Rico, changed my students' paradigm so significantly that our last meeting before returning to the United States was overrun by sobs. They had experienced an ideological shift that created a moral and ethical dilemma in the face of their return home. "We'll never be the same," one of my students summarized on behalf of her classmates. Little did they know that the whole point of a curriculum of agape was to make sure they would "never be the same." These students were supposed to demonstrate proficiency in the grammatical and cultural content of their course while also demonstrating an other's centered concern for "the life and growth" of another.

Connected to the state standards in my classroom is a curriculum of agape: the expectation that students will measurably seek out truth, exhibiting care, respect, and knowledge of others as evidenced through an ethos of persistent humility, trust, patience, kindness, hopefulness and forgiveness. The goal is to deconstruct the lovelessness that currently shapes the knowing and being of our students in educational spaces and rebuild the learning environment with a curriculum that taps into it and builds their humanity—a curriculum that is shaped by a mutually empowering and loving, democratic community, diverse in perspective, experience, skill and position that engages them and motivates them in safety and belonging to be the diamonds they are created to be.

Explore, Think, Act

Chapter 8 of Part III continues to explore equity through *belonging* by establishing the connection between crucial aspects of our students' identities, and academic engagement, and motivation. Biased assumptions and erasures fail to meet students where they are. They disrupt our students' sense of belonging and are a result of a curriculum of anti-love that devalues their specific funds of knowledge and ultimately dehumanizes them, particularly if they are underserved and/or marginalized. Examine your practice as an educator and consider the ways in which a curriculum of agape restores dignity and humanity to your students and to their learning environment through racial-ethnic-cultural belonging.

(A) Select and think about one unit of study within your curricular cannon for a face-to-face or virtual course of your choosing. Now, think about your students who are enrolled in this course.
  1. Are your students' intersectional identities positively valued and represented in this unit of study?
  2. Are your students fully able to connect who they are with the content or are they erased in some way? Does the content of this unit *see* each of your students?
  3. What about your pedagogy? Are your students fully able to connect who they are with the manner in which you instruct them on this unit? Is there something about your way of being as an instructor that erases your students?
(B) Make a list of your students' names in this course. Next to each name identify the ways in which the content of this unit and your pedagogy *see* the student. Identify the ways they might erase or makes assumptions about the student.
(C) Create a mailbox for your class that you can set out before you begin to teach this unit of study (shoeboxes work well when teaching in person and there are several online tools to achieve the same).
  1. Ask your students if they feel erased in any way regarding the topic of the unit and to write those erasures on a piece of paper,

anonymously, and deposit them in the mailbox. They can submit them virtually as well.

2. Ask your students what they would like to know regarding this unit. Have them write their responses on a piece of paper, anonymously, to be deposited in the mailbox. They can also submit their ideas virtually.

Compare your responses from parts A and B to your students' responses. Use this information to reshape *what* and *how* you will teach this unit to your students.

Notes

1 Robinson-Morris, D. W. (2018). *Ubuntu and Buddhism in higher education: An ontological (re) thinking*. Routledge.

2 Ibid.

3 A&E Television Networks. (n.d.). *The Hatfield & McCoy feud*. History.com. Retrieved February 7, 2022, from https://www.history.com/shows/hatfields-and-mccoys/articles/the-hatfield-mccoy-feud.

4 Pinar, W., Reynolds, W., Slattery, P., & Taubman, P. (2008). *Understanding curriculum: An introduction to the study of historical and contemporary curriculum discourses* (Vol. 17, p. 328). Peter Lang.

5 Ibid. p. 328.

6 Ibid.

7 Bergstrom, A., Cleary, L. M., & Peacock, T. D. (2003). *The seventh generation: Native students speak about finding the good path*. ERIC.

   Cajete, G. (1994). *Look to the mountain: An ecology of indigenous education*. ERIC.

   Cleary, L. M., & Peacock, T. D. (1998). *Collected wisdom: American Indian education*. ERIC.

   Deloria, V., Deloria Jr, V., & Wildcat, D. (2001). *Power and place: Indian education in America*. Fulcrum Publishing.

   Helfenbein, R. J. (2021). *Critical geographies of education: Space, place, and curriculum inquiry*. Routledge.

   Johnson, S. C. (2019). U.S. education and the persistence of slavery. *Journal of Curriculum and Pedagogy*, 1–20. https://doi.org/10.1080/15505170.2019.1618757.

   Johnson, S. (2020). *Afrocentricity: Student voices on African American identity in multicultural education reform*. The University of Texas at San Antonio.

   Malott, C. (2007). *A call to action: An introduction to education, philosophy, and Native North America* (Vol. 324). Peter Lang.

   Montero-Sieburth, M., & Villaruel, F. (2003). *Making invisible Latino adolescents visible: A critical approach to Latino diversity*. Routledge.

8 Op. Cit., Johnson (2020).

9   Freire, P. (1993). *Pedagogy of the oppressed* (New Rev 20th-Anniversary ed.). New York: Continuum.

Fromm, E. (2000). *The art of loving: The centennial edition.* A&C Black.

Missler, C., & Missler, N. (2014). *The way of agape.* King's High Way Ministries.

Tshivhase, M. (2018). Love as the foundation of Ubuntu. *Synthesis Philosophica,* 65(1/2018), 197–208. https://doi.org/10.21464/sp33112.

10 Op. Cit., Freire (1993).

Op. Cit., Fromm (2000).

11 Op. Cit., Johnson (2000).

Op. Cit., Montero-Sieburth & Villaruel (2003).

Zou, I. (2021). *Texas Senate bill seeks to strip required lessons on people of color and women from "Critical race theory" law.* The Texas Tribune. Retrieved November 11, 2021, from https://www.texastribune.org/2021/07/09/texas-critical-race-theory-schools-legislation/.

12 Op. Cit., Johnson (2020).

13 Ibid.

14 Walton, G. M., & Cohen, G. L. (2007). A question of belonging: Race, social fit, and achievement. *Journal of personality and social psychology,* 92(1), 82.

15 Op. Cit., Johnson (2020).

16 Ibid.

17 Ibid.

18 *Talking circles overview.* First Nations Pedagogy Online Project. (n.d.). Retrieved January 13, 2022, from https://firstnationspedagogy.ca/circletalks.html.

19 Price, J. M. (2007). Democracy: A critical red ideal. *Journal of Thought,* 42(1/2), 9–25.

20 Op. Cit., Johnson (2019).

Darder, A. (2019). *Decolonizing interpretive research: A subaltern methodology for social change* (1st ed.). Routledge.

21 Arredondo, P., Gallardo-Cooper, M., Delgado-Romero, E. A., & Zapata, A. L. (2015). Latino worldviews and cultural values. *Culturally Responsive Counseling with Latinas/os,* 15–30.

Op. Cit., Darder (2019).

Op. Cit., Deloria et al. (2001).

Op. Cit., Johnson (2020).

Op. Cit., Malott (2007).

Nelson, B. (2013). *Elevating student voice: How to enhance student participation, citizenship and leadership.* Taylor and Francis.

Op. Cit., Pinar et al. (2008).

Ragosta, J. (2014). *Virginia statute for establishing religious freedom (1786).* Retrieved from http://www.EncyclopediaVirginia.org/Virginia_Statute_for_Establishing_Religious_Freedom_1786.

22 Op. Cit., Nelson (2013).

Op. Cit., Ragosta (2014).

23 Op. Cit., Ragosta (2014).

24 Op. Cit., Johnson (2020).

25 Op. Cit., Johnson (2020).

Op. Cit., Pinar et al. (2008).

26 Op. Cit., Darder (2019).
        Op. Cit., Deloria et al. (2001).
        Op. Cit., Johnson (2019).
        Op. Cit., Malott (2007).
        Op. Cit., Montero-Sieburth & Villaruel (2003).
        Op. Cit., Nelson, B. (2013).
        Op. Cit., Pinar et al. (2008).
27 Op. Cit., Johnson (2020).
28 Op. Cit., Darder (2019).
29 Ibid. p. 105.
30 Op. Cit., Deloria et al. (2001).
        Op. Cit., Malott (2007).
31 Op. Cit., Arredondo et al. (2015).
        Awad, G. H. (2010). The impact of acculturation and religious identification on per-
        ceived discrimination for Arab/Middle Eastern Americans. *Cultural Diversity and Ethnic
        Minority Psychology, 16*(1), 59.
32 Op. Cit., Johnson (2020), unpublished data.
33 Ibid.
34 Ibid.
35 Ibid.
36 Ibid.
37 Ibid. p. 102.
38 Ibid. p. 106.
39 Ibid. p. 113.
40 Ibid. pp. 123–124.
41 Ibid. p. 126.
42 Ibid. p. 150.
43 Ibid. unpublished data.
44 *Guru purnima 2021: Date, history, importance and significance.* The Indian Express. (2021,
        July 23). Retrieved January 4, 2022, from https://indianexpress.com/article/lifestyle/
        life-style/guru-purnima-2021-date-history-importance-and-significance-7393152/.
45 Op. Cit., Ragosta (2014).
46 Op. Cit., Arredondo et al. (2015).
        Degruy-Leary, J. (2017). *Post-traumatic slave syndrome: America's legacy of enduring injury.*
        Portland, OR: Joy DeGruy Publications Inc.
        Op. Cit., Cajete (1994).
        Chapter four: The African Ubuntu philosophy. (n.d.). Retrieved January 4, 2022, from
        https://repository.up.ac.za/bitstream/handle/2263/28706/04chapter4.pdf?sequence=5.
        Op. Cit., Cleary & Peacock (1998).
        Gill, J. H. (2002). *Native American worldviews an introduction.*
        Op. Cit., Johnson (2019, 2020).
        Op. Cit., Malott (2007).
        Op. Cit., Robinson-Morris (2018).
47 Op. Cit., Cleary & Peacock (1998).

48 Op. Cit., Arredondo et al. (2015).
    Op. Cit., Cajete (1994).
    Op. Cit., Chapter 4
    Op. Cit., Cleary & Peacock (1998).
    Op. Cit., Degruy-Leary (2017).
    Op. Cit., Gill (2002).
    Op. Cit., Johnson (2019, 2020).
    Op. Cit., Malott (2007).
    Op. Cit., Robinson-Morris (2018).

49 Aronson, J. (2002). Stereotype threat: Contending and coping with unnerving expecta-tions. In *Improving academic achievement* (pp. 279–301). Academic Press.
    Aronson, J., Quinn, D. M., & Spencer, S. J. (1998). Stereotype threat and the academic underperformance of minorities and women. In *Prejudice* (pp. 83–103). Academic Press.
    Op. Cit., Bergstrom et al. (2003).
    Op. Cit., Cajete (1994).
    Delpit, L. (2013). *"Multiplication Is for White people": Raising expectations for other people's children*. New York, USA: The New Press.
    Op. Cit., Deloria et al. (2001).
    Huynh, V. W. (2012). Ethnic microaggressions and the depressive and somatic symp-toms of Latino and Asian American adolescents. *Journal of Youth and Adolescence*, *41*(7), 831–846.
    Op. Cit., Johnson (2019, 2020).
    Op. Cit., Malott (2007).
    Op. Cit., Walton & Cohen (2007).

50 Op. Cit., Arredondo et al. (2015).
    Op. Cit., Johnson (2020).
    Op. Cit., Montero-Sieburth & Villaruel (2003).

51 Translation: Male chivalry, social preeminence and expectation of strength as protector and provider.

52 Translation: Female submissiveness, purity and sacrificial maternal expectation.

53 Op. Cit., Arredondo et al. (2015).
    Op. Cit., Montero-Sieburth & Villaruel (2003).

54 Op. Cit., Cleary & Peacock (1998).
    Op. Cit., Montero-Sieburth & Villaruel (2003).

55 Translation: stop it, enough, my love.

· 9 ·

INTERPRETING THEIR BEHAVIOR

While we often think in terms of race, ethnicity, religion, language or gender when discussing diversity, the term also captures differences in wealth, health, geography and life experiences. Some students live happily with one or two cisgender parents, some with two same-sex parents. Some come from enormous families with strong communal ties and others have no extended family. Some students endure abuse or neglect by at least one entrusted adult. Some students are homeless, live in rural communities, or in ghettoized circumstances that limit access to food and other basic resources. Some students are survivors of acts of violence where others have every advantage that a prosperous life affords yet still struggle from disfunction. The complexities with which students live, especially in the midst of a global pandemic, not only produce diverse academic, social, and cultural needs but diverse behavioral needs as well.[1]

Agape rests in an interconnectedness that co-experiences suffering and joy and centers itself in the life and growth of another human being.[2] For many students, particularly those who have been historically disempowered and marginalized, the relationship with their teachers is directly related to successful learning outcomes.[3] Often these positive relationships include aspects of advocacy and mentorship and rely on positive teacher attitudes towards their students.[4]

Teachers often feel undervalued, underpaid, and under-supported, which can cause a strain on student-teacher relationships.[5] The juxtaposition between the high sacrifice of the profession and feelings of irrelevance may explain the high attrition rate—most teachers who leave the field do so within three to five years of service.[6] I have always understood the stress of the job, but what I could not understand was the lovelessness with which my colleagues, year after year, irrespective of the level or location of the school, discussed the students. I found that I was uncomfortable among my professional peers who spent their planning and lunch periods disparaging our students, and fearing any transference of attitude towards the students we had in common, I began to spend my breaks in my classroom. Behavioral equity as an outgrowth of an agape curriculum views poor teacher-perceptions of students as disruptive to effective teaching.[7] Educators who embrace behavioral equity share an equal love for all students while concurrently seeking to know, understand, and meet the individualized behavioral needs of their students, for the sake of their respective lives and growth, but also for the interconnected potential for joy between the student and teacher.

The earlier statistics regarding our national K-12 population of students do not speak to demographics such as wealth, health condition, or life experience. They do not help us to understand how many of these students suffer from emotional and physical stress resulting from "structural phemonena."[8] We do know, however, what our response is to the resultant behaviors.

Currently, African American, Latino, and Native American students are disproportionately overdisciplined, suspended or expelled; these same groups are far more likely to be placed in special education or to drop out of school altogether.[9] Exclusively addressing student behavior that precipitates a suspension, the California Department of Education concluded that compared to 3% of White students, African American students received 9.4% of state suspensions, Native American/Alaskan Native students received 7.2%, Pacific Islander students received 4.7%, and Latino(a)/Hispanic students received 3.6%.[10] In the California study, it was determined that Native American/Alaskan Native males were 4.2 times more likely than females to receive a suspension.[11] On a national level, 15% of Black male students suffered a suspension as compared to 7% of Latino students and 5% of White male students.[12]

A similar asymmetrical pattern of school disenfranchisement is evident in national dropout rates for these same groups of students with Native American/Alaskan Native students being two times more likely to drop out of school, surpassing all other demographics.[13] Dominant colonial norms that have historically informed the egregiously inequitable power and social dynamics within U.S. school culture have cultivated a learning environment of curricular and pedagogical anti-love, especially as it affects Black and brown students, and more closely mirrors prison culture than an educational one.[14]

I agree with Gloria Ladson-Billings' assertion that educators cannot allow students to "get away with murder" in our classrooms.[15] Allowing students to misbehave in the classroom because the teacher feels sorry for the students is not loving them—pity is not equity; it's anti-love because love is corrective. To not correct our students signals a lack of concern that students interpret as such.[16] At the same time, our use of punishment cannot continue to be rooted in our stereotypical notions, the consequence of misunderstanding behaviors, that assume certain groups of children to be a model of innate genius and respectability while other groups are immoral, illiterate, jihadist, lazy, "savages", troublemakers, slow, or academically inferior.[17] Behavioral equity calls a teacher again to question what knowledge is valued and is of most worth, and for whom it is most beneficial as it directly connects to a curriculum of agape.[18] It identifies and acknowledges our own dysconcious biases while we come to know our students and their unique needs, and it responds to behavior in a way that does not default to punitive convenience—busy work, loss of privileges or trips to the principal's office—but seeks to correct in a way that understands and mutually empowers the student as a member of the greater learning community and the world.[19]

My first teaching assignment, outside of my graduate internship, was a middle school Spanish position in Upper Marlboro, Maryland. My own education from kindergarten through college took place in majority White, upper middle class environments where the administration consisted of only White men. This was my first experience entering a school in which the White student population was in the minority and the principal was a female and Black. I could not have had a better introduction to my career, as I shaped my curricular and pedagogical practice around equity and inclusion in support of student identity.

It took a long time for me to realize how much my time working under this principal had influenced my understanding of agape and its curricular implications. She only wore heels to administrative meetings. Otherwise, we would find her in her suit and sneakers moving through the hallways, speaking to the students during bell changes and encouraging them to be their best selves. She was our village leader and knew everyone by name. Staff meetings were conducted as a multidisciplinary learning community during which students and their progress were discussed as a team. We had a working culture in which no one person's knee was relied upon to meet the needs of the students. We leaned on each other's strengths and interpersonal relationships with the students to impart knowledge and shape the being of every young learner.

My initiation to understanding the importance of equity when it comes to student behavior began on my first day of teaching in Upper Marlboro. Into my eighth grade class walked students whose behavior closely modeled the familiarity of my majority White school culture that I had become dysconciously accustomed to, despite the devastation to my own self-identity it produced.[20] Interspersed with the socially normalized behaviors attributed to middle class whiteness in an academic setting was, for me, a more awkward display of gum popping and eye rolling from my students of color.[21] They sauntered into the class dismissing my happy greetings as irritatingly odd and inconsequential. It was later in the year, after the closeness of our agape class community was solidified, that I attributed the initial behavior of my non-White students to simple distrust.[22] One of my seventh grade classes smelled the blood in the water—my own—of my novice classroom experience and decided to exploit it with a daily hijacking of my class. My principal would have come to my aid in this second circumstance but, in both cases, the students' sense of respect for me and confidence in me as their teacher would only improve as I strengthened my relationship with them on my own.[23] Thus began my intentional focus on equitably understanding student behavior—behavior that is often misunderstood through the lens of cultural dominance and the stereotypical false narratives it weaves and sustains.[24] A curriculum of agape required me to know my students, inclusive of their behaviors that I did not understand because their academic outcomes depended upon it.[25]

Having lived and worked in many places and spaces within the United States and abroad, I was exposed to enough cultural difference that I became less reliant on my Apprenticeship of Observation and my colonial American understandings and more flexible—welcoming of behavioral "oddities". I was most interested in understanding these nuances and making them a part of my pedagogical practice. The more I collected in my pedagogical trick bag, the more effective I might be at meeting the diverse needs of my students.

Where the dominant American acculturation taught me it was rude and dismissive not to look an adult in the eye, Native American and Middle Eastern culture reframed my ontological understandings. Now I consider the possibility that my students choose not to look me in the eye because to do so might be to look into my soul, or imply rudeness and, in both cases, would be an abominable disrespect.[26] As incomprehensible as this might be to some of our competing worldviews, selflessness acknowledges, accepts, and values other ways of knowing and being. To this point, a middle school student of mine was not permitted to participate in our class video because her family's Hindu practice considered a camera to be soul snatching. Loving her unconditionally, she was honored with the job of video director and producer.

Furthermore, pointing at my students can be misconstrued as an insult, as can asking personal questions of students whose culture values privacy.[27] From a Native American point of view, to firmly shake hands might signal aggression, or to speak before having something important to say could relay a lack of humility on the part of the student.[28] Silence, a lack of eye contact, or unwillingness to interrupt during lectures or class discussions is not necessarily an indication of disengagement from the learning environment; it could very easily be the result of an offense or a function of humility and observation before action. Unfortunately, I learned this lesson the hard way.[29]

My youngest son attended my elementary Spanish classes over a three year period. As was typical of my colonial pedagogical framework that measured student engagement by the eyes of the room on the teacher and hands eagerly raised to contribute to the lesson, I observed my son to be withdrawn—to my frustration, his eyes were rarely on me, nor was his hand raised in anticipation of sharing his insight. Eventually, after many prompts to "pay attention", I finally stopped my direct instruction to reprimand him for his poor behavior. "Kyle, you have not paid attention to one thing I've said up here." First, I admit that calling him out in front of the class was an opportunity for humiliation that I never repeated. I regret my actions to this day. Second, my son, in response, repeated back to me everything that had thus far been presented to the class, making me the one to finally end up embarrassed. My son's behavior was actually conducive to his learning, unknowingly, a behavior I was pressed to disrupt. In correcting my son's behavior, I also risked a sense of shame brought upon him had he not been prepared to respond to my accusation. Like some Native American communities that insist upon competence before any action, or risk *shunning* or *shaming*, had my son displayed a lack of competence in the presented material, he would likely have felt ashamed before me and his classmates.[30]

Unlike Growth Mindset which teaches students to embrace failure, some Native American students seek to avoid failure.[31] Other students are acculturated not to acknowledge failures because, as is the case with Native American worldview, failure brings shame upon them and possibly their families.[32]

Sometimes the shame or embarrassment that a student feels is hard to detect and may present itself as a smile instead of the aggression that Western educators are trained to recognize.[33] Putting students "on the spot," as I had done with my son, Kyle, including openly rewarding them for individual accomplishments, may result in a misunderstood behavior of withdrawal or resistance.[34]

Additionally, capitalistic, meritocratic systems of education, as we experience in the U.S., that count on staunch individualism, selfish pursuits and student competition are often disruptive to Native American onto-epistemologies, as they are to Latino(a) and many other students of color, where a sense of individualism is traditionally situated in collective collaboration for the common good and is central to their worldview.[35] "[A]ssessing students through competitive test taking and grading may not contribute to student motivation" and may, therefore, undergird misunderstood behaviors.[36] Becca's earlier story highlights the need for behavioral equity in a way that helps students save face.[37] When I surveyed African American, Latino(a) and White students across two Title 1 high schools within different areas of the United States, student responses to a preference for the current individualistic and highly competitive pedagogy were overwhelmingly low.[38] Inclusive of all demographics, students highly preferred a collaborative, familial learning environment where the interconnectedness that is common to many Native American, Latino(a) and African communities was evident and supportive of a curriculum of agape.[39]

One departure from what may appear to be an act of cooperation involves "helping."[40] Native American worldview is often known for its ideological leanings towards noninterference when it comes to correcting learning or behavior, unless the behavior is perilous.[41] The idea is to make mistakes without intervention or scorn so individuals can forge their own path as they learn from their choices.[42] Along our diverse spectrum of students, from a Native American perspective, teachers or classmates who attempt to "help" leave themselves open to possible disagreement or hidden disgust because their help may be received as an intrusion or a criticism of incompetence.[43] In this case, the help becomes an issue of disrupting a student's providential purpose and invalidating his or her dignity and worth as a person, a student, and a unique personality.

To highlight this idea, it was determined that my niece was in need of Special Education benefits throughout most of her elementary and secondary schooling. By mid-high school, I had become her math tutor and our sessions were taken up by rants of complaining that her Special Education teachers interfered with her learning. If she wanted their help, it was only to answer a question. Instead, they were giving her too much help and derailed her efforts to navigate her math problems on her own until she understood the concepts. Her Special Education teachers were unwilling, even under fierce and, at times, disrespectful protest, to let my niece make mistakes and learn from them. Whether through a deliberate or mistaken selfishness, it was more convenient to show or tell her what to do than to let my niece figure it out and only interfere as much as she would allow.

Thankfully, instead of disengaging from her learning space, my niece became brutally determined to pull herself up academically so she could liberate herself from Special Education. Different from the overwhelming statistic of students who do disengage, some to the point of dropping out of school, because they have become weary of the "meddling" or lack of challenge that often accompanies low teacher expectations, my niece had an unusual experience; her anger compelled her to persist all the way to an ivy league college.[44] My student, Sue, had a similar disposition yet, in contrast to my niece's experience, I gave Sue permission to dictate when and how much she wanted my help or help from her classmates. Sue thrived in Spanish class when she was allowed to make mistakes and learn from them, and when she was not required to speak until she felt competent to do so.

When considering anti-colonial ways of being, there are generalized areas of intersection between non-Western worldviews that help us as educators to consider other ways of approaching unfamiliar student behavior. It is important, however, to remember that although the overlap is helpful, any overgeneralizations tend to erase those valuable nuances that distinguish cultural ways of being. Cautiously, it can be said that African, Middle Eastern and Native American ontologies share a unique perspective on time, and Africans and Native Americans similarly value intrinsic reward, humor, and the long tradition of oral storytelling, a practice that challenges our western insistence on endorsing only what is written.[45]

African and Native American concepts of time are best explained from a circular point of view—past, present and future are omnipresent so that time is relational.[46] Western thought maintains a linear, chronological framework of time based on logic and rationality, whereas non-western frameworks consider time to be more negotiable.[47] Unhurried contemplation must precipitate action in some Native American points of view and relationships outweigh the hands on a clock in many African and Middle Eastern societies—"late" is almost meaningless.[48] Points of time are relative to events and the interpersonal experiences that surround those events.[49] People, particularly families, are the central priority for many non-western cultures, making relationships the gateway to enterprise and not the reverse.[50]

I had occasion to invite a dear South African friend to dinner. He let me know that he was running late and, after he arrived 30 minutes late, proceeded to apologize throughout the evening. I finally smiled and asked him, "If you were in South Africa, invited to a party as the guest of honor, would you apologize for being late?" He laughed and explained that it is frowned upon to arrive on time in South Africa because the implication is one of desperation, which is rude. His introduction to American culture occurred in an all-White place and space where he learned that lateness was unacceptable. I reassured my friend that our home was one of color and an "emancipated space" where we shared cultural traditions around time. I relayed a term, specific to the Black community, that is an intracultural joke and speaks to the relaxed notions of time that may have roots in our African ancestry. My friend unapologetically enjoyed the rest of the evening with my family.

It may be worth mentioning that not only is it unlikely that a meeting in many African countries will take place "on time," in a similar vein, some Middle Eastern cultures prefer interpersonal relationship over punctuality as well.[51] My husband has lived in several North African and Middle Eastern countries. Stories abound regarding the frustrations of American business people who remained vexed by the tardiness of their hosts who insisted upon several servings of tea and informal chatter before tending to a business agenda. Most important is the understanding that for our students whose ontological orientations include a less linear view of time, showing deference for a schedule over proper rumination or a human exchange in any one moment is disruptive to the harmonious interconnection between our humanity and other forms of existence—it risks the whole order of things.[52]

To understand the ways in which these behavioral differences affect some African American students in the classroom, it is first essential to make the ontological connection between African cultures and African American or Black culture. Remnant threads of African culture are said to have persisted in African American culture.[53] "The aspects of African culture that survived may have been so subtle and so ingrained in Black behavior patterns that they are not thought of as Africanisms. They may simply be thought of as 'the way' that Black people cook, walk, dance, dress, and talk."[54] This is not to confuse being African with being African American, broad brushing Black culture or dismissing the infinite variations of Black expression in America.[55] The intention is simply to acknowledge a historical connection that may explain certain commonalities in cultural behaviors.[56] For example, oral communication within the Black community is traditionally very direct.[57] Strong relational bonds that extend well beyond the nuclear family, the spontaneity and participatory nature of speech within the Black community, including storytelling and call and response, are age old traditions handed down from one generation to another.[58] High volume cross-talking with interruptions and animated body language are often intrinsic to some aspects of the community dynamic and, in some cases, can be socially expected even among formal interactions, such as a church service.[59]

Loquacity is also not unusual among Middle Eastern and Latino(a) communities. *Respeto*, a deep honor and respect for elders as well as family and friends, is common to Latino(a) families and is akin to Middle Eastern and Asian cultures.[60] Personal interaction flows out of *respeto* and the resultant socializing is meant to honor a person's good nature and caring; it is not intended to be disruptive.[61] Middle Eastern culture often values spoken language and so encourages oral expression, including an outspokenness that can, at times, dominate a conversation.[62] Traditionally, proverbs or stories that are at the core of teaching and learning for Black and Native American culture also operate as curricula for right living within Latino(a) communities in the form of *dichos*.[63,64] These behaviors among African American, Latino(a) and Middle Eastern students, that often facilitate cognition, are typically foreign to White middle-class standards and, at times, are a source of immediate devaluation, labeled behavioral problems that hasten disciplinary action.[65]

One of my favorite comparisons to share with my pre-service teachers to help them connect lived experiences with these ideas is a description of family gatherings with my Black and Latino(a) family, or with my Middle Eastern and Spanish friends. The environment is loud and energetic. Everyone is talking at once and overtop of one another. It is not unusual for multiple conversations to co-exist around one large table. Not all my family members enjoy the fervency—we are many individuals within one people group—but those quiet spirits who would rather "contemplate" than act quickly to talk simply endure the overwhelmingness of it all. A person who expects to wait his or her turn to speak will struggle to find a quiet entry point into a conversation. Any of my college students who come from these backgrounds eventuate into laughter, shaking their heads in agreement since they experience something similar in their own relational circles. This frenzied oral exchange between extended family and friends is not exclusively reserved for certain racial-ethnic groups.

It can be a familiar way of being for any of our students, leading teachers to misinterpret behavioral norms as signs of insolence.

I also reinforce with my pre-service teachers the need to be direct when presenting expectations. Depending on students' cultural orientations, presenting an expectation or a directive as a choice is a pedagogical bear trap that can lead to unfair disciplinary action.[66] Suppose I need my students to indicate that they are finished working their sample problems during a check for understanding and I say to them, "Would you like to give me a thumbs up when you're finished?" Certain students may properly infer that hidden in the question is a directive because this operation is culturally familiar, but, again, the classroom has a power dynamic to it that is mostly contextualized by a White-centric frame of reference.[67]

The ambiguity in a directive that appears to provide a choice is foreign to much of African American culture.[68] Black children who respond, "no," are likely to face disciplinary consequences because they fail to adapt to an unfamiliar frame of reference.[69] Related to this, western worldview's direct usage of "no" can be interpreted as rude and shameful for students whose cultural orientation requires a softer, more indirect manner of negation.[70] These students will circumvent a "no" response when answering a prompt that correctly requires a negative utterance; similarly, a teacher who responds to a student with a "no" might accidentally offend and be perceived to be rude and inharmonious.[71] In any case, there is no behavioral equity, therefore no love, in prematurely assuming a student to be disrespectful before first understanding whether the error is situated in a cultural misunderstanding.

Second to conversational survival skills, gatherings such as I described above also require everyone to have thick skin—the kidding knows no mercy. Humor plays a strong role in the Black community, and is often expressed as *playing the dozens* or *signifying*.[72] Mutually negotiated and reciprocated humor in the form of teasing is not unusual, as is the case among many of the Native American nations as well.[73] Friendly humor strengthens the interpersonal bond between community members and is not typically mean-spirited.[74] Humor is a cultural tool that warms the learning environment and facilitates learning.[75] Aside from needing to address profanity and inappropriate crudeness, it is important for teachers to know and understand the difference between destructive and malicious targeting between students and a familiar cultural practice that increases engagement and motivation.

Once more, behavior equity is a function of unconditional love, the sacrifice being putting our own selves—our own biased worldviews—aside to know and understand our students and the origin of their behavior. I have found that this takes an intentional, focused effort because it is not always easy to do. During my years in the K-12 classroom, I had students and full classrooms of students whom I routinely prayed over simply to learn to like. I too know what it means to be grateful to the heavens when certain "pot stirrers" are absent. My need to get outside of myself did not come from logic or reason. It came from my sense of regard for every student as a gift. I approached my student roster not as the result of an existential accident but a deliberate assignment for which I was responsible. My prayers never went unanswered, perhaps because my students changed or, more likely, because I did.

What we need to consider is that our system of education expects Euro normative motivators—extrinsic reward such as grades, test scores and awards—to be sufficient and appropriate for all learners when, in fact, considering that some cultures do not highly esteem material possessions, it is possible that our methods of rewarding behavior or academic progress do more to offend students.[76] Instead, many students are culturally inclined towards love and are intrinsically motivated by relationships.[77] Engagement in learning and the motivation to perform academically may situate itself more effectively in mutual belongingness and self-determination.[78]

Two memories stand out in my mind in this regard. The first relates to a high school Spanish student, Jennifer, who was unmanageable for any of the teaching staff. Jennifer was precocious, hostile and overly assertive, often disrespecting her classmates and elders. I had to write discipline reports for inappropriate language, "making out" in the hallways and stairwells, disrespect, and disobedience. I prayed about Jennifer every day, probably more for my own well-being than hers. I always seemed to be the one to catch her in the wrong act, and I began to think I was missing the point of my relationship with her— perhaps I was the only teacher who had the patience to love this young lady. Eventually, I turned my prayers around, asking for a glimmer of anything in her I could love. I was asking for change within myself instead of a change in her. Jennifer had an amazingly mature, administrative gift, so I started giving her clerical responsibilities that allowed her strengths to shine.

Our relationship improved to the degree that other staff members sent her to me when they could no longer tolerate her antics. We would talk, and her better self would materialize, often to the point of an apology to the referring teacher. I learned to love Jennifer unconditionally, and she was a constant joyful presence in my classroom. What behavioral equity taught me about Jennifer was that she was the youngest of several grown brothers, with a mother who loved her, but who left her unparented. Her mother allowed her every latitude, and it angered Jennifer to be left to the wind to grow and mature. Jennifer was responsible for every aspect of her own upbringing, making decisions that no young person ought to make alone. She would never have worn down from punishments—nothing would have improved for Jennifer as long as discipline referrals to the principal remained our primary response to her behavior. She needed love, first, and out of that love, the safety of mentorship and structure. When I last heard from Jennifer, she had become an airline attendant with one of the leading U.S. airline companies.

Second is the story of my previously mentioned 7th grade Spanish class in Upper Marlboro, Maryland. There were enough students in this class who had no interest in allowing me to teach. Not only were they robbing themselves of their education, they were also taking the rest of the class down with them. There was an interesting power struggle going on in my class, one that I knew I had to get under control, so I could motivate my students to learn.[79] Every day, I became deflated at the end of the preceding class because I knew my 7th graders were coming and that their disruptive behavior was going to ruin the rest of my day. This class exhausted me. The students were loud, talking across me, and their classmates to get a laugh instead of progressing with the lesson. Finally, I chose to make use of two relational, cultural practices that are common to some Native American, Latino(a) and African communities: *shunning* and *restorative justice*.[80]

I could not remove students completely from the class—that would have solved nothing and would not have been in their best interest—but I had to make it clear that my hijackers would no longer be welcome as part of the learning community. At the beginning of class, I asked, "Who wants to learn?" I identified those students who indicated a want to learn Spanish and the rest I escorted to the back wall of the room where I had arranged desks for them. I told my students they would all remain in the class but would not be permitted to participate until they could observe the agreed upon learning culture which we had worked so hard to establish. Only those students in the front of the room who had indicated a want to learn would be called on to participate in class. When students attempt to hijack a class, it is, in my experience, usually socially driven—it's relational. Students who no longer have the support of their comrades lose interest in disruptions as they are a lost source of entertainment; the hijackers lose their motivation.

Spanish class began to move smoothly and the students who wanted to learn were unwilling to address any attempts to disrupt the learning space.

It took less than a week for students in the back to request restoration to the front of the room. They were always welcomed back with the caveat that they must demonstrate good classroom citizenship or face a return to the back of the room. Central to this non-western experiment was restorative justice, a practice that is fundamental to Ubuntu and to many Native American cultures.[81]

Because every member of a community is considered to be sacred, a vital contributor to the overall well-being and vitality of a society, reconciliation in many African and Native American cultures is a priority when an offense has been committed.[82] Where Western ideology is predominantly punitive, all of the worldviews that assist in theorizing a curriculum of agape are reconciliatory in their being.[83] Unconditional love requires forgiveness, which is complete and fully restorative as if nothing ill has occurred.[84] My students needed to be utterly forgiven by me and by their classmates so that their hearts remained intact and, therefore, they would not suffer in a state of stress that might compete with their cognitive process. By the second week, all of my students were in the front, learning and enjoying Spanish class, and in return, I got to enjoy my 7th graders.

Relationship, knowing your students and allowing them to know you, directly parallels any successes in managing behavior.[85] Trust, respect, safety, and interconnectedness are necessary ingredients to motivation in the classroom even when extrinsic rewards are appropriate.[86] One of my tenth grade Spanish students in a school that required a dress uniform was causing me great pains in the amount of paperwork I had to file to document his refusal to wear the proper uniform. Despite numerous trips to the office, as was required by the school for a uniform violation, this young man, Brian, continued to come to class without a tie and/or a belt. It became apparent to me that the abrupt loss of his father created a level of grief that left the household emotionally crippled and unable to value the importance of something so mundane as a tie. It was a miracle that Brian made it to school each day.

On a daily basis, Brian forgot the particulars of his uniform, forgot his books, forgot to brush his hair, forgot everything in the abyss that was his sorrow. He was also struggling privately with his sexuality, which only added insult to injury. We already had a bond of unconditional love between us, although it was not enough to overcome his propensity to forget his tie or to hold the tie down with a paperclip. I found a very inexpensive stainless steel tie bar through Amazon.com that would come with engraving if I chose. I purchased it, had his initials engraved, and took it to school. I took him aside on morning before classes began and presented him with his tie bar. He was elated almost to tears. The tie bar was to stay on my desk where he could retrieve it and wear it whenever he was properly in uniform. At the end of the year, the tie bar was his to keep. It wasn't a perfect execution, but I wrote far fewer discipline referrals, and Brian's textbooks were suddenly in his hand each day to aid his learning.

Even college students push the boundaries now and again. In my experience, the most frequent infringements tend to defy attendance policies either coming late to class or missing class altogether. Being the stickler for professionalism and responsibility that I am, my patience has been tried. As an instructor at a Hispanic Serving Institution, what I came to understand about the Latino(a) community from a generalized perspective is that, related to Ubuntu and many Native American communities, family comes before all else. *Familismo*, the strong commitment and loyalty to family, varies widely among younger generations of Latino(a) students in America but is still an impactful cultural norm for many.[87] This profound devotion that subordinates individuality to the needs of the familial group, particularly to parental and grandparental authority, is also pertinent to Middle Eastern and Asian worldviews.[88]

My Latino(a) students were not necessarily indicating their lack of concern for their course or for me by their absences; when the family needed help, they were obligated to answer that call. As in many Middle Eastern families, parental authority is absolute, particularly if the student is the eldest sibling or female.[89] In light of a curriculum of agape at the college level, outside of an abuse of my desire to accommodate unfamiliar acculturations, I learned to dialogue with my college students as I did with my elementary and secondary students to understand the behavior and equitably respond to it. Now I give my students two free absences per semester, no questions asked, to allow for those emergencies and preserve the culture and dignity of my students.

As I come to the end of this chapter, I find myself thinking about my experiences as an instructional coach, a high school student mentor, or a researcher in predominantly Title 1 schools. I have heard stories and have witnessed the most outrageous displays of student behavior, from language that would have flushed the faces of my Wounded Warrior students to dancing on the desks and threatening to violate teachers' and classmates' mothers. One such case was so egregious that I recommended administrative help to remove the student from the class until she could bring herself to make better choices. The novice teacher under my mentorship was in her first year of teaching and was told that the disruptive student had been a truancy case who, for the first time, was coming to school. The administrator did not want to encourage a resurgence of absences by coming to the aid of his teacher. The student remained in the class to torture everyone while the teacher repeatedly told her students who were struggling to concentrate above the outbursts of expletives, "Just focus on me." I was at a loss as to how to help this young teacher without taking control of her class myself.

A similar story was relayed to me in a district that demanded a statistical improvement on disciplinary action. The remedy was to outlaw suspensions across the board, correcting the numbers but not the students. Teachers were left to the same mantra in an attempt to rescue their learning environment, "Don't pay any attention to him; focus on me." There are extreme cases when disciplinary measures must be available to teachers. I share exasperation with those who are trapped in seemingly impossible behavioral situations without the proper support of their leadership. The only reasonable advice I could offer would be to seek local counsel and support from those highly effective teachers and coaches on campus who have established a good rapport with your students and do not view them as lost causes but rather diamonds in the rough. Positive collaboration is not a sign of weakness. It is part of the maturity process for every educator and fills in those pedagogical gaps that we all experience as we grow in our craft.

An occasion where an intervention of this nature was called for involved a substitute teacher who shared a dividing wall with me in one of my middle schools. Beyond relationship with my own students, I had somehow captured the respect of the larger student body in the school. Students whom I did not teach or know were regularly in my room, but they were as welcomed as my Spanish students. My colleague on the other side of the wall was out of school for several days, leaving her students with a male substitute who was intimidating in size and bearing on a good day. During one of my 8th grade classes, we could hardly concentrate or hear each other for the shouting and chaos next door. The substitute was struggling to manage his class. His aggression and intimidation were ineffective, which is not unusual. Students do not typically respond well to mean-spirited or aggressive threats. I would never suggest that a contemporary teacher do what I did. In fact, I advise my education students against ever leaving a class unattended, but I told my own students that they were to maintain our good class culture and continue working while I went next door to rescue the substitute. My students knew me well, as I knew them, and they knew I meant business.

I admit that I lost my temper with the students next door, indicating that their behavior was appalling and unacceptable for the village culture that was our middle school. The demand for appropriateness in the learning environment was answered with a "yes, ma'am," I believe, because I had a relationship with those students, which the substitute did not, and I represented a standard they knew to be true about our way of being as a school. The substitute teacher only needed a momentary helping hand from a colleague with relational and positional leverage. After that one intervention, he was in good shape and there was peace on the other side of the wall.

Similarly, a high school in Charlotte, North Carolina utilizes a novel approach to discipline within the Science Department. The science teaching staff is led by a seasoned teacher who is agape oriented in her approach to teaching and learning. Strong relationship with her students is evident by the number of students who open her door to say hello or to visit. Her science colleagues maintain similar relational ties as part of their communal instructional culture.

The Science Department functions as a village where behavioral equity is an integral part of knowing, understanding and correcting students. They do not typically refer disciplinary offenses to the office for counseling or suspension—the department has an almost zero suspension rate. Instead, when an offense occurs that is best treated by *shunning*, removing the student from the environment, they call on one another to see who has a vacant seat during that period. The student is removed to attend another science class, whether it is for a moment or for several days. Since the students have existing relationships with staff members who are within the same subject area and can monitor their work, the students respond with compliance and do not lose their place within the village or their learning opportunities. Restoration quickly follows when the student is ready to participate more appropriately. It's a similar mode of operation as when my husband comes to me regarding one of our sons and says, "You need to go talk to him because I just can't get through anymore." My husband and I are a unified front. We do not compete with each other. We collaboratively and strategically use each other's skills and strengths to meet the behavioral needs of our sons when one of us is at a loss. The science staff is baffled by their colleagues in other subject matter areas who complain about classroom management and the number of discipline referrals among the same group of students while refusing to implement a non-western pedagogy that has demonstrated effectiveness for the Science Department.

Engaging in behavioral equity requires work and out-of-the-box thinking—the type of contemplation that is inspired by Native American worldview and prevents hasty, precipitous, and punitive action that catalyzes

the type of disharmony that is evident within U.S. education.[90] As an outgrowth of a curriculum of unconditional love, it takes courage.[91] Behavioral
equity is not limited by the monocular lens of equality. It examines behavior through cultural and individual uniqueness and demands sacrificial acts of
patience and kindness that do not seek self-gratification or result in quick anger.
It forgives all, seeks out truth, always protects, trusts, hopes and endures.[92] It
sees the student as sacred, a valuable and necessary addition to the learning
community, and seeks to correct behavior in a way that is mutually instructive,
empowering and restorative of the values and harmony that precipitate effective learning and good citizenship.

Explore, Think, Act

Chapter 9 of Part III explores the idea of behavioral equity, addressing questionable student behavior from the standpoint of diverse cultural norms and
situational needs of our students. None of us wants to teach in a chaotic environment, but before we look to punitive measures that possibly exert unnecessary and unloving, dogmatic control, educators should consider meeting their
students where they are to *see* them and understand the behavior. The experiences I have shared were unique to the students, the time, the spaces and
places—they provide a prospective not a prescription. Explore your own experiences with questionable student behavior as they are specific to your students,
your spaces, places and moments in time.

(A) Think about the diverse cultures and life experiences of your students.
   1. Is it possible that their behaviors are the result of cultural norms
      with which you are unfamiliar? How can you respectfully deter-
      mine if this is the case?
   2. Are your students struggling with life experiences that overshadow
      the value of your class content, or education in general? How can
      you respectfully determine if this is the case?
   3. Is it possible that your students' behaviors are a result of your rela-
      tionship with them? What specific aspects of relationship might
      you improve to uphold a curriculum of agape to foster better
      engagement and motivation?
(B) Try a new pedagogical approach that may more effectively meet the
   needs of your students.

1. Keeping in mind the theoretical aspects of unconditional love, begin a journal in which you reflect upon each of your students in a positive way. Identify their strengths and areas where you appreciate them that go beyond cursory or superficial thought. Consider sharing your journal entries with your students.
2. Adjust the learning environment using some of non-western approaches from this chapter to stimulate engagement and motivation. This will be most effective if you elicit student participation and feedback.

(C) Every educator finds himself or herself outmatched by a student or students at some point along a career path. If you need help:

1. Make a list of your coworkers who know the student(s) and can help you with creative solutions to improve your relationship(s).
2. Arrange to meet with those coworkers who have relational or positional leverage with the student(s) and be sure to keep your conversations positive. Your students are diamonds; they may just still be in the rough.

Notes

1 Cleary, L. M., & Peacock, T. D. (1998). *Collected wisdom: American Indian education*. ERIC.

Delpit, L. (1995). *Other people's children: Cultural conflict in the classroom*. New York: New Press.

Delpit, L. (2013). *"Multiplication Is for White people": Raising expectations for other people's children*. New York, USA: The New Press.

Gill, J. H. (2002). *Native American worldviews an introduction*.

Johnson, K., & Williams, L. (2015). *When treating all the kids the same is the real problem*. SAGE Publications, Ltd., https://dx.doi.org/10.4135/9781452286914.

2 Amidon, J. (2013). Teaching mathematics as agape: Responding to oppression with unconditional love. *Journal of urban mathematics education*, 6(1), 19–27.

Freire, P. (1993). *Pedagogy of the oppressed* (New Rev 20th-Anniversary ed.). New York: Continuum.

Fromm, E. (2000). *The art of loving: The centennial edition*. A&C Black.

Lipner, J. (1998). Capturing gods: The god of love and the love of god in Christian and Hindu tradition. *Boardman Lectureship in Christian Ethics*, 3. Retrieved May 26, 2021, from http://repository.upenn.edu/boardman/3.

Missler, C., & Missler, N. (2014). *The way of agape*. King's High Way Ministries.

Nhat Hanh, T., & DeAntonis, J. (2014). *How to love*. USA: Parallax Press.

Wivestad, S. M. (2008). The educational challenges of agape and phronesis. *Journal of Philosophy of Education*, 42(2), 307–324. https://doi.org/10.1111/j.1467-9752.2008.00626.x.

3 Bluestein, J. (2008). *The win-win classroom: A fresh and positive look at classroom management*. Corwin Press.

Op. Cit., Cleary & Peacock (1998).

Degruy-Leary, J. (2017). *Post-traumatic slave syndrome: America's legacy of enduring injury*. Portland, OR: Joy DeGruy Publications Inc.

Malott, C. (2007). *A call to action: An introduction to education, philosophy, and Native North America* (Vol. 324). Peter Lang.

Montero-Sieburth, M., & Villaruel, F. (2003). *Making invisible Latino adolescents visible: A critical approach to Latino diversity*. Routledge.

Nasir, N. S. (2019). *"We dare say love": Supporting achievement in the educational life of Black boys*. New York, NY: Teachers College Press.

4 Op. Cit., Montero-Sieburth & Villaruel (2003).

Op. Cit., Nasir (2019).

5 Ingersoll, R. M., & Smith, T. M. (2003). The wrong solution to the teacher shortage. *Educational Leadership, 60*(8), 30.

Marvel, J., Lyter, D. M., Peltola, P., Strizek, G. A., Morton, B. A., & Rowland, R. (2007). *Teacher attrition and mobility: Results from the 2004–05 teacher follow-up survey. NCES 2007–307*. National Center for Education Statistics.

6 García, E., & Weiss, E. (2019). *U.S. schools struggle to hire and retain teachers: The second report in 'The perfect storm in the teacher labor market' series*. Economic Policy Institute. Retrieved November 10, 2021, from https://www.epi.org/publication/u-s-schools-struggle-to-hire-and-retain-teachers-the-second-report-in-the-perfect-storm-in-the-teacher-labor-market-series/.

Neason, A. (2020). *Where have all the black and brown teachers gone?* The Hechinger Report. Retrieved November 23, 2021, from https://hechingerreport.org/black-brown-teachers-gone/.

Williams, C. S. (2011). *Combating teacher burnout*—THE Journal. Retrieved from https://thejournal.com/articles/2011/11/03/teacher-burnout.aspx.

7 Arredondo, P., Gallardo-Cooper, M., Delgado-Romero, E. A., & Zapata, A. L. (2015). Latino worldviews and cultural values. *Culturally Responsive Counseling with Latinas/os, 15–30*.

Op. Cit., Degruy-Leary (2017).

Ladson-Billings, G. (2009). *The dreamkeepers: Successful teachers of African American children*. Somerset, USA: Wiley.

Op. Cit., Montero-Sieburth & Villaruel (2003).

8 Op. Cit., Gill (2002).

Op. Cit., Nasir (2019), p. 5.

9 Faircloth, S. C., & Tippeconnic, J. W. (2009). *The dropout/graduation crisis among American Indian and Alaska native students: Failure to respond places the future of native peoples at risk*. Civil Rights Project/Proyecto Derechos Civiles. Retrieved December 1, 2021, from https://eric.ed.gov/?ff1=eduHigh%2BSchools&q=source%3A%22civil%22%2B-source%3A%22center%22%2B-source%3A%22perspective%22%2B-source%3A%22arts%22&id=ED511323.

Op. Cit., Nasir (2019).

10 *2017–18 suspension rate.* Suspension Rate—State (CA Dept of Education). (n.d.). Retrieved December 1, 2021, from https://data1.cde.ca.gov/dataquest/dqCensus/DisSuspRate.aspx-?year=2017-18&agglevel=State&cds=00.

11 Ibid.

12 Op. Cit., Nasir (2019).

13 Op. Cit., Faircloth & Tippeconnic (2009).

14 Meiners, E. R. (2010). *Right to be hostile: Schools, prisons, and the making of public enemies.* Routledge.

15 Op. Cit., Ladson-Billings (2009).

16 Ibid.

   Dee, T. S. (2004). Teachers, race, and student achievement in a randomized experiment. *The Review of Economics and Statistics, 86*(1), 195–210. https://doi.org/10.1162/003465304323023750.

   Op. Cit., Delpit (2013).

17 Awad, G. H. (2010). The impact of acculturation and religious identification on perceived discrimination for Arab/Middle Eastern Americans. *Cultural Diversity and Ethnic Minority Psychology, 16*(1), 59.

   Brown, K. D. (2013). Trouble on my mind: Toward a framework of humanizing critical sociocultural knowledge for teaching and teacher education. *Race Ethnicity and Education, 16*(3), 316–338.

   Op. Cit., Delpit (2013).

   Op. Cit., Gill (2002), p. 167.

   Li, G. (2005). Other people's success: Impact of the" model minority" myth on under-achieving Asian students in North America. *KEDI Journal of Educational Policy, 2*(1).

   Op. Cit., Malott (2007).

   Op. Cit., Montero-Sieburth & Villaruel (2003).

18 Kridel, C. (2010). Currere. In *Encyclopedia of curriculum studies* (Vol. 1, pp. 178–178). SAGE Publications, Inc., https://www.doi.org/10.4135/9781412958806.n102.

   Pinar, W. (2004). *What is curriculum theory?.* Routledge.

19 Op. Cit., Bluestein (2008).

20 Op. Cit., Brown (2013).

   Op. Cit., Delpit (1995).

21 Op. Cit., Delpit (1995).

22 Op. Cit., Cleary & Peacock (1998).

   Op. Cit., Malott (2007).

   Op. Cit., Montero-Sieburth & Villaruel (2003).

   Op. Cit., Nasir (2019).

23 Op. Cit., Delpit (1995).

   Op. Cit., Nasir (2019).

24 Op. Cit., Cleary & Peacock (1998).

   Op. Cit., Degruy-Leary (2017).

   Op. Cit., Delpit (1995; 2013).

   Op. Cit., Malott (2007).

   Op. Cit., Montero-Sieburth & Villaruel (2003).

    Op. Cit., Nasir (2019).

25 Op. Cit., Degruy-Leary (2017).

    Op. Cit., Nasir (2019).

26 *Arabic customs and traditions.* Arab Academy (2017, May 15). Retrieved February 9, 2022, from https://www.arabacademy.com/arabic-customs-traditions/.

    Op. Cit., Cleary & Peacock (1998).

27 Abi-Raad, M. (2019). Western organizational theories: Middle Eastern style: How much do you know about the culture. *The Journal of Organizational Management Studies, 2019,* 1–16.

    Op. Cit., *Arabic customs* (2017).

    De Mente, B. L. (2016). *Etiquette guide to China: Know the rules that make the difference!.* Tuttle Publishing.

28 Op. Cit., Cleary & Peacock (1998).

29 Cajete, G. (1994). *Look to the mountain: An ecology of indigenous education.* ERIC.

    Op. Cit., Cleary & Peacock (1998).

30 Op. Cit., Cleary & Peacock (1998).

31 Op. Cit., Cleary & Peacock (1998).

    Yeager, D. S., & Dweck, C. S. (2020). What can be learned from growth mindset controversies?. *American Psychologist, 75*(9), 1269.

32 Op. Cit., Abi-Raad (2019).

    Op. Cit., De Mente (2016).

33 Op. Cit., De Mente (2016).

34 Op. Cit., Abi-Raad (2019).

    Op. Cit., Cleary & Peacock (1998), p. 34.

    Op. Cit., De Mente (2016).

35 Op. Cit., Abi-Raad (2019).

    Op. Cit., Arredondo et al. (2015).

    Op. Cit., Cajete (1994).

    Op. Cit., Degruy-Leary (2017).

    Johnson, S. (2020). *Afrocentricity: Student voices on African American identity in multicultural education reform.* The University of Texas at San Antonio.

    Op. Cit., Malott (2007).

    Op. Cit., Montero-Sieburth & Villaruel (2003).

36 Op. Cit., Cleary & Peacock (1998), p. 44.

    Johnson, S. C. (2019). U.S. education and the persistence of slavery. *Journal of Curriculum and Pedagogy,* 1–20. https://doi.org/10.1080/15505170.2019.1618757.

    Op. Cit., Johnson (2020).

    Op. Cit., Montero-Sieburth & Villaruel (2003).

37 Op. Cit., Abi-Raad (2019).

    Op. Cit., Cleary & Peacock (1998).

38 Op. Cit., Johnson (2020).

39 Op. Cit., Cajete (1994).

    Op. Cit., Degruy-Leary (2017).

    Op. Cit., Gill (2002).

    Op. Cit., Johnson (2020), unpublished data.

    Op. Cit., Montero-Sieburth & Villaruel (2003).

40 Op. Cit., Cleary & Peacock (1998), p. 33.

41 Ibid.

42 Ibid.

43 Ibid.

44 Ibid. p. 33.
     Op. Cit., Johnson (2020).
     Op. Cit., Montero-Sieburth & Villaruel (2003).

45 Op. Cit., Abi-Raad (2019).
     Op. Cit., Cleary & Peacock (1998).
     Op. Cit., Degruy-Leary (2017).
     Op. Cit., Gill (2002).
     Op. Cit., Johnson (2019, 2020).
     Op. Cit., Malott (2007).

46 Op. Cit., Cleary & Peacock (1998).
     Op. Cit., Degruy-Leary (2017).
     Op. Cit., Johnson (2019, 2020).

47 Ibid.

48 Op. Cit., Abi-Raad (2019).
     Op. Cit., Cleary & Peacock (1998).
     Op. Cit., Degruy-Leary (2017).
     Op. Cit., Johnson (2019, 2020).

49 Op. Cit., Abi-Raad (2019).
     Chapter four: The African Ubuntu philosophy. (n.d.). Retrieved January 4, 2022, from https://repository.up.ac.za/bitstream/handle/2263/28706/04chapter4.pdf?sequence=5.
     Op. Cit., Cleary & Peacock (1998).
     Op. Cit., Degruy-Leary (2017).
     Op. Cit., Gill (2002).
     Op. Cit., Johnson (2019, 2020).

50 Op. Cit., Abi-Raad (2019).
     Op. Cit., Arredondo et al. (2015).
     Op. Cit., *Chapter four.*
     Op. Cit., Montero-Sieburth & Villaruel (2003).

51 Op. Cit., Degruy-Leary (2017).

52 Op. Cit., Cleary & Peacock (1998).
     Op. Cit., Degruy-Leary (2017).
     Op. Cit., Johnson (2019, 2020).

53 Op. Cit., Degruy-Leary (2017).
     Hale, J. E. (1982). *Black children, their roots, culture, and learning styles.* Provo, Utah: Brigham Young University Press.
     Op. Cit., Johnson (2019, 2020).

54 Op. Cit., Hale (1982), p. 10.

55 Op. Cit., Johnson (2019, 2020).

56 Op. Cit., Johnson (2020).

57 Op. Cit., Delpit (1995).

58 Op. Cit., Johnson (2019).

59 Ibid.

60 Op. Cit., Abi-Raad (2019).
   Arabic customs and traditions. Arab Academy (2017, May 15). Retrieved February 9, 2022, from https://www.arabacademy.com/arabic-customs-traditions/.
       Op. Cit., Arredondo et al. (2015).
       Op. Cit., De Mente (2016).

61 Op. Cit., Arredondo et al. (2015).

62 Kayi-Aydar. (2018). Teaching and learning styles in Middle-Eastern cultures. In *The TESOL encyclopedia of English language teaching* (pp. 1–5). John Wiley & Sons, Inc. https://doi.org/10.1002/9781118784235.eelt0800.

63 Translation: proverbs.

64 Op. Cit., Arredondo et al. (2015).
       Op. Cit., Cleary & Peacock (1998).
       Op. Cit., Gill (2002).
       Op. Cit., Malott (2007).
       Op. Cit., Montero-Sieburth & Villaruel (2003).

65 Op. Cit., Arredondo et al. (2015).
       Op. Cit., Degruy-Leary (2017).
       Op. Cit., Johnson (2019).

66 Op. Cit., Delpit (1995).

67 Ibid.

68 Ibid.

69 Ibid.

70 Op. Cit., Abi-Raad (2019).
       Op. Cit., *Arabic customs* (2017).
       Op. Cit., De Mente (2016).

71 Ibid.

72 Schwegler, A. (2007). Black Ritual Insulting in the Americas: On the Art of "VociferaR" (Colombia), "Vacilar" (Ecuador) and "Snapping", "Sounding" or "Playing the Dozens" (USA). *Indiana*, 24, 107–155.

73 Op. Cit., Cleary & Peacock (1998).

74 Op. Cit., Cleary & Peacock (1998).
       Op. Cit., Schwegler (2007).

75 Op. Cit., Cleary & Peacock (1998).

76 Op. Cit., Cleary & Peacock (1998).
       Op. Cit., Delpit (1995, 2013).
       Op. Cit., Degruy-Leary (2017).

77 Op. Cit., Abi-Raad (2019).
       Op. Cit., *Arabic customs* (2017).
       Op. Cit., Arredondo et al. (2015).
       Op. Cit., Cleary & Peacock (1998).
       Op. Cit., Delpit (1995, 2013).
       Op. Cit., Degruy-Leary (2017).
       Op. Cit., Montero-Sieburth & Villaruel (2003).

78 Op. Cit., Cleary & Peacock (1998).
    Walton, G. M., & Cohen, G. L. (2007). A question of belonging: Race, social fit, and achievement. *Journal of Personality and Social Psychology, 92*(1), 82.
79 Op. Cit., Bluestein (2008).
80 Op. Cit., Cleary & Peacock (1998).
    Zehr, H. (2015). *The little book of restorative justice: Revised and updated.* Simon and Schuster.
81 Graybill, L. S. (2002). *Truth and reconciliation in South Africa: Miracle or model?.* Lynne Rienner Publishers.
    Mayaka, B., & Truell, R. (2021). Ubuntu and its potential impact on the international social work profession. *International Social Work, 64*(5), 649–662.
    Robinson-Morris, D. W. (2018). *Ubuntu and Buddhism in higher education: An ontological (re) thinking.* Routledge.
    Talking circles overview. First Nations Pedagogy Online Project. (n.d.). Retrieved January 13, 2022, from https://firstnationspedagogy.ca/circletalks.html.
82 Ibid.
83 Ibid.
84 Op. Cit., Missler & Missler (2014).
85 Op. Cit., Bluestein (2008).
86 Ibid.
87 Op. Cit., Arredondo et al. (2015).
    Op. Cit., Montero-Sieburth & Villaruel (2003).
88 Op. Cit., Abi-Raad (2019).
    Op. Cit., Arabic customs (2017).
89 Op. Cit., Abi-Raad (2019).
    Op. Cit., *Arabic customs* (2017).
    Op. Cit., Arredondo et al. (2015).
    Op. Cit., Montero-Sieburth & Villaruel (2003).
90 Op. Cit., Cajete (1994).
    Op. Cit., Cleary & Peacock (1998).
91 Op. Cit., Freire (1993).
    Op. Cit., Fromm, E. (2000).
92 Op. Cit., Missler & Missler (2014).

Part IV
FORGIVE AND FORGET

"He who is devoid of the power to forgive is devoid of the power to love." (Dr. Martin Luther King, Jr.)[1]

· 1 0 ·

LOVE FORGIVES ALL

My life as a teacher has been brilliant, deeply rewarding, but also hard and, on occasion, out of balance. One thing about unconditional love is that it exposes the heart, making us vulnerable to hurt. My heart has broken many times. My students have broken my heart over their behavior or poor choices. I have also lost students to untimely deaths by war or disease. Other times my heartbreak has been associated with my own failings as a teacher where exhaustion or the learning curve, that is a teacher's perpetual measure of growth, disrupted my path towards curricular and pedagogical agape. I have not always successfully loved and motivated my students. Forgiveness has been a necessary tool to dig my way out of the dark and despairing places that are sometimes an inescapable part of the teaching experience.

Anger, hurt, disappointments and failures are going to impact the learning environment at some point. What becomes more impactful than the injury itself is that without forgiveness, unconditional love is an impossibility. Unconditional love forgives all—it is ever hopeful and enduring.[1] This means forgiving students, of course, but it also implores educators to forgive themselves. A Buddhist point of view would direct educators to put themselves into their students' skin, and allow them into ours, to become one with them, creating a type of impartial perspective that enables understanding and love through forgiveness.[2]

It never ceases to be humbling and a bit scary when I allow myself to become vulnerable with my students. It is a tightrope walk allowing them into my skin while maintaining my professionalism, but I usually take the risk because the reciprocity that is an agape community requires my students to see me as much as I see them. The understanding that we build is mutual, as is the trust. So, I let them know when I am having a tough day, and that I have a personal and professional life that are not always easy to manage. I don't always feel well and am not always at my best. I'm angry sometimes and I hurt. I give them permission to see me at my worst and to respectfully address any hurt that I cause them. I allow them some access to my skin because it makes me authentically human and gives my students an opportunity to be human as well, or perhaps humane is the more appropriate word. It is humane to forgive.

Similarly, as described earlier, restorative justice is a democratic engagement based on community consensus.[3] Dialogue aids all parties: the accused, the injured, and the community that is affected by discord. It helps us to put on each other's skin and make sense of an injurious circumstance until healing and harmony are restored.[4] Africans who embrace Ubuntu teach their children to let go of hate, to communicate well, and to reconcile themselves to their offenders.[5] Spiritual and material interconnection does not allow one to hate or hold a grudge without visiting that same hate or bitterness upon oneself.[6] If we all share a common destiny and we wish that destiny to be love, we must forgive, and we must teach our students to forgive. Otherwise, again, according to Fromm, we fail to love altogether and across all contexts. Without forgiveness, we engage in a curriculum of anti-love and Ubuntu degrades to "I am [imbalanced] because we are [out of balance]."

One of my most devastating teaching moments occurred during my second year in the field and called for a mutual forgiveness between my students and me for the hurt we caused each other. An eighth grade young lady, Jasmine, walked over to my desk and slid a giant manilla envelope on top of my paperwork without a word. She just glared at me, seeking acknowledgment of the gift. I finally opened the envelope during my planning period to find several poems she had written. Jasmine was sharing a sacred space with me where her secret thoughts and her creativity were hidden from the rest of the world.

Several of the poems described intimate sexual encounters that an inexperienced person would have a difficult time expressing—notions and feelings that only someone sexually active would know. I became concerned that

Jasmine may be exploring her sexuality at such a young age without guidance or could be the victim of sexual abuse. Under the counsel of the guidance office, I hesitantly called her mother to arrange a meeting. My intention was not to tell on her but my hands were tied as an educator. I was bound by law to report any possible abuse of a child. Her mother refused to attend the meeting and sent her father instead. I was mortified but stuck at that point to honor the appointment. We talked, and I affirmed my gentle concern for Jasmine that she had support to help her process these types of thoughts without divulging my other concerns. It was a good meeting. Her father unemotionally professed his gratitude for my time and investment in his child.

The following day when my 8th grade class arrived, I was met with glaring eyes and angry faces. My whole class refused to speak to me. I became *shunned* by my students. I soon learned that when Jasmine arrived at home after school, her father asked her to produce her poems, which he promptly ripped up in front of her. He destroyed them all whether they contained the questionable themes or not. I attempted to apologize, but it was weeks of enduring the corporate anger of my students, loving on them one day at a time, until one student at a time came around to smiling and speaking to me again.

Finally, I think Jasmine could not bear the divide between the two of us. She walked over to my desk with several of her classmates during lunch and just stared at me. I apologized once again, explaining that I had called her mom out of worry for her well-being, and that I did not approve of the results of the meeting. Jasmine's classmates seemed satisfied and walked away. She plopped down in a chair next to me so we could continue to talk and heal our broken hearts together. Our class was back to our normal joyful, agape community the following day. Jasmine continued to send her poetry to me years after I had left the area. With some support and encouragement, she eventually submitted her poetry to a journal and won a poetry competition.

Years later, I had taken a field trip with my high school Spanish students to an annual dance production. This performance was specifically designed for young students and featured a historical, cultural perspective on dance throughout the Spanish speaking world. As always, I took all of my Spanish I students with several parent chaperones. To our shock, the year's performance was salacious. I was appalled and tried to figure out how to protect my students and honor their parents and the school in the middle of an active show. My students were restless in their seats, knowing the culture we had established in my classroom and uncertain as to how to react to what they were seeing. Students from other local schools cheered and whistled and inappropriately heckled the dancers. Rude as it was, the chaperones and I clustered about my seat to quickly discuss our plan. We decided that our only option was to stand the entire student body up mid-performance and exit.

It was an embarrassing spectacle in its own right to file that many students out of an active theater as the surrounding classes of students hissed and jeered at us. In my attempt to protect my students, I left them wide open to public ridicule and wasn't sure they would understand how I could abandon them to humiliation in that way. Thankfully, with the support of my chaperones and an explanation of my motives, my students easily forgave me. We had built enough trust over the months and years that they knew I was acting in their best interest, even if it felt momentarily terrible. The company director and choreographer ran out of the theater to meet us and were deeply apologetic once I explained our position. It did not take long for word to get through the school that we had taken a public stand against this dance company. My students could ultimately be proud of themselves and their spark of social activism.

Close to my retirement from K-12 education, I was the one who had to do the forgiving. I had a tenth grade Spanish class with several difficult students. It took a few weeks to shape our community into one that was conducive to learning and grounded in a curriculum of agape. Among my regular offenders were Allen and Zaira. Allen was rude beyond measure, hostile, and unproductive. Zaira was regularly tempted to lie. It was a real trial not to become angered by these two students, particularly when they were two of several students who needed regular redirection. I held my ground, continued to love on all of them, and we eventually settled into an effective village of hard workers.

About mid-year, I caught Allen cheating on a test, which was a major infraction for this particular school. I had forgiven Allen so many times for his behaviors, and in the process, our hearts became forged together. His realization that he had been caught in his dishonesty did not result in his typical rudeness. He and I were both saddened. I had maintained his privacy and dignity as a member of the class, but had to report the incident to the Administration. Allen was disenrolled from the school shortly after that, and I admit that I cried like a baby to lose him. I received a heartwarming email from his mother thanking me for loving her son and letting me know how much he would miss me.

Zaira, on the other hand, stayed all year, and around the springtime, had concocted the most outrageous lie. I was disappointed, and for the first time, she was as well. Zaira was disappointed in herself that she had broken my heart and, without prompting, brought a supportive friend with her to apologize to me. She was surprised to tears that I did not yell or punish her but had easily forgiven her indiscretion once again. In the cases of Allen and Zaira, it would have been easier and more instinctual to be angered by their behavior, even to the point of dislike. In forgiving them and continuing to trust and believe that they could do better, the sweet reward of our bonded hearts was worth the work.

These were not the only times I had to put in the work of forgiving my students. I had two classes in two distinct schools where the fallout from our American persistence to track our students produced an almost uninhabitable learning environment. Twice, I had all male classes who had been deemed academically immature for their math classes. The assignment to the appropriate math classes based on their readiness impacted the rest of their scheduled classes so that, regardless of their readiness for English, science or history, they were glued together and labeled by themselves and their peers as the "dumb group."

The dehumanizing experience of feeling "dumb" led my students to act the part. It was torturous to engage them or to motivate them to achieve their potential. I spent more time on classroom management than instruction, which speaks to the implications of a lack of harmony or balance as they are understood by African and Native American worldviews. The social and emotional interference that results from tracking incites an imbalance in which students lose the cognitive diversity, and in this case gender diversity, that is vital to student engagement and motivation.[7] I was struggling to forgive my students, struggling to like them, and let alone love them. The coups d'etat was when one of my wealthy White students yelled to a student who had fewer resources and was Puerto Rican, "You know your mom ought to be cleaning my floors!" This comment, although I addressed it, was personal to me. He might as well have said that to me. How was I to forgive such an outlandish display of racism?

Forgiveness does not mean a teacher takes no action. I worked hard to forgive this young man, as I did with my other young men in these classes, and I also began to collaborate with the coaches and my administrators. We agreed that I would be furnished with a whistle and, since most of them enjoyed the workouts in their sports programs, my guys would run stairs when their energy got the best of them. I was finally able to smile warmly at my students, with understanding and love, when they became unruly. I would gently ask them if they needed to unload some excess energy from the day, offering to stop class and run it out. A miraculous focus came over my two classes of young men.

Forgiving them for me was directly connected to attempting to reach them. When I accomplished one, I was able to accomplish the other.

Forgiving my students turns out to be considerably easier than forgiving myself. While I was still in my infancy as a pedagogue, I had three young men in my Spanish II class who were from a rural area of the country where students, especially Black students, were not expected to thrive. One of the young men was a regular visitor during our lunch bunch. He was a spark of life whenever he occupied an informal space, but during class, when the tone was academic, he produced no homework and rarely participated. Another young man was charismatic, popular, and full of humor. There wasn't a party he did not attend. I tried to encourage him to work as enthusiastically as he partied, but he refused. The last young man was so distant in the classroom that I would almost forget he was there. He was exceedingly mature, more so than any of his classmates. He had every physical sign of adult male maturity and behaved as if surrounded by children beneath his station. He would not give me enough conversation to encourage him to excel.

Mr. Charisma did attend a parent conference that I had requested in the hope of upward progress, but his mother sat before us both coddling him and crying from defeat. I was never able to connect with the parents of the other two young men. In my own immaturity, I allowed these three students to chart their own course for failure, and in that, I failed them. Forgiving myself for not pushing harder to know and understand these three remains a work that I am still processing today.

At the adult level, a student, Billy, in one of my Wounded Warrior Basic Course cohorts complained bitterly about being forced to read William Shakespeare's *Romeo and Juliet*. The literature cannon for the course always included a selection of Shakespeare's work because it forced the students to learn to decode, a necessary skill on standardized tests at that time. Billy, like many students before him, became excited by his growing ability to understand the details of the text and analyze it in a way that connected its themes to contemporary life experiences. The course timing did not allow us to read more than half of each play. To allow for closure and a full experience with the literature, every cohort was rewarded with a viewing of the play in its contemporary movie version. Twelve O'clock would come quickly and my students would beg me not to end class. "Please! Just ten more minutes!" We did have enough autonomy that I could allow them to run over a few minutes, so I allowed it.

As we neared the conclusion of the movie, what I did not realize, through my own fault, was that Billy had never read or seen *Romeo and Juliet* in secondary school. I had taken great pride in knowing my students, asking questions and paying attention to the types of signals that should have alerted me to the fact that Billy would not know how tragically the story would end. He began to yell at the characters, as if to warn them of a tragic end to their ruse, "DON'T DO IT! SHE'S JUST ASLEEP!!!" Billy stood up out of his seat, yelling at the screen with greater fervor, and at the death of Juliet, he brought both of his fists down onto the table in a furry, "F----!!!!" Billy blew out of my classroom door leaving the rest of us stunned and confused until one of his classmates said, "I don't think he's ever read this before."

The entire class was dismayed as to how it could have been possible for Billy to be unfamiliar with a ninth grade text, but I knew better. I had been teaching long enough to know the disparities between schooling experiences across the United States and that I should never assume a student's prior knowledge. I was sick to my stomach and quickly apologized to my students as I ran after Billy to comfort him and apologize. I found Billy and, after a lengthy conversation, he calmed down and accepted my apology. Billy forgave me, but I could never give back the joy and dignity that he lost in class that day, a failure on my part that I have had to live with, and for which I have needed to forgive myself.

Two of my Wounded Warrior students caused me to become ashamed of myself, although, thankfully, I can laugh about it at this point. They were both relatively quiet—relaxed in a way that was unsettling—and enormously tall and stalky. One of my students was White, and he kept a padlock on his backpack. The other was Apache. He kept the biggest knife I have ever seen at his hip. It was a relatively long walk between my classroom and the parking garage, one that took a circuitous short cut between buildings and kept me hidden from pedestrians and traffic. My two students, in all of their stillness, had a habit of catching up with me early in the trimester, persistent in wanting to walk with me to my car. Sometimes only one of them accompanied me; other times it was both of them.

My imaginations were creating all kinds of violent scenarios in which I was the victimized protagonist. I spent weeks half listening to their conversations while I scanned the route for any possible modes of escape should I become threatened. What I came to realize, eventually, was that these two students had taken it upon themselves to escort their teacher, whom they highly esteemed, safely to her car. They were PROTECTING ME. How embarrassing to think that my students were attempting to love me, and all I could imagine is that they might do me in. I had to forgive myself for my fear driven assumption. Had

I simply discussed my misgivings early on, I might have quickly understood their admirable intentions.

Thankfully, the aim of a curriculum of agape is not perfection. Love, like teaching, is an action that takes practice and endurance. The point of forgiveness and its indispensable tie to agape is to acknowledge that we are all learners in the never ending process of being and becoming. Bell Hooks captured the essence of this idea in stating, "forgiveness and compassion are always linked: how do we hold people accountable for wrongdoing and yet at the same time remain in touch with their humanity enough to believe in their capacity to be transformed?"[8] Forgiveness allows us to liberate our students from their imperfections while also liberating ourselves from our own. In my experience, forgiveness, as it is bound to unconditional love, maintains reciprocity with relationship, that key factor leading to student engagement and motivation.[9]

Explore, Think, Act

Chapter 10 explores the idea of forgiveness as a salient aspect of a curriculum of agape. It is theoretically impossible to love unconditionally without exercising forgiveness. Through my experiences loving my students unconditionally, it is evident that perfection is not the goal or expectation, for educators or for students. We are all diamonds in the rough and need forgiveness, if we are to achieve the potential for brilliance that is in all of us. Explore your own experiences with hurt and anger towards your students or yourself and where healing and restoration are needed.

(A) Think about your actions in the classroom and those of your students.
1. Is there anything within your curricular or pedagogical practice that might require forgiveness from your students? Is there an area where you need to restore your relationship with your students?
2. Have your students hurt or angered you in a way that you need to forgive? Is there an area where your students need to restore their relationship with you?
(B) Annotate your responses to part A and consider implementing a Talk Circle. Be certain that you are properly trained and prepared to facilitate a productive, healing circle. See the website below for guidance if you need help. An online search will easily provide resources to help if you are conducting a "virtual circle". Create a three stage set of Talk

Circles to open an honest dialogue that will heal and restore your classroom relationships.

1. Talk Circle 1-Testing the Waters: Give your students permission to speak freely and divulge any areas of hurt or anger that you have caused them. Listen, acknowledge them and accept responsibility for your actions, perceived or real.

2. Talk Circle 2-Taking them Deeper: Give your students permission to speak freely and divulge any areas of hurt or anger that they have caused one another. Guide your students to Listen, acknowledge the hurt and anger, and accept responsibility for their actions, perceived or real.

3. Talk Circle 3-All in: Ask your students for permission to speak freely and divulge any areas of hurt or anger that they have caused you. Remind them that you love them unconditionally, and you want to improve/restore your relationship with them. Guide your students to listen, acknowledge your hurt and anger, and accept responsibility for their actions, perceived or real.

4. Create a method as a class community of addressing moments of hurt and anger, and requesting future Talk Circles as needed.

For more information: https://www.heartland.edu/documents/idc/talkingcircleclassroom.pdf

Notes

Part IV

1 King, M. L. (2012). *A gift of love: Sermons from strength to love and other preachings* (p. 46). Beacon Press.

Chapter 10

1 Graybill, L. S. (2002). *Truth and reconciliation in South Africa:Miracle or model?*. Lynne Rienner Publishers.

    Mayaka, B., & Truell, R. (2021). Ubuntu and its potential impact on the international social work profession. *International Social Work, 64*(5), 649–662.

    Missler, C., & Missler, N. (2014). *The way of agape*. King's High Way Ministries.

    Robinson-Morris, D. W. (2018). *Ubuntu and Buddhism in higher education: An ontological (re) thinking*. Routledge.

    Talking Circles Overview. First Nations Pedagogy Online Project. (n.d.). Retrieved January 13, 2022, from https://firstnationspedagogy.ca/circletalks.html.

2 Nhat Hanh, T., & DeAntonis, J. (2014). *How to love*. USA: Parallax Press.

    Op. Cit., Robinson-Morris (2018).

3 Op. Cit., Graybill (2002).
  Op. Cit., Mayaka & Truell (2021).
  Op. Cit., Missler & Missler (2014).
  Op. Cit., Robinson-Morris (2018).
  Op. Cit., *Talking Circles*.
4 Ibid.
5 Op. Cit., Graybill (2002).
  Op. Cit., Mayaka & Truell (2021).
6 Ibid.
7 Gallardo, E. V. (1994). Hierarchy and discrimination: Tracking in public schools. *Chicano-Latino L. Rev.*, *15*, 74.
  Hunter, R. C., & Donahoo, S. (2002). Discrimination in tracking and specialized education programs. In *Challenges of urban education and efficacy of school reform*. Emerald Group Publishing Limited.
8 McLeod, M. (1998, January). *Angelou*. Shambhala Sun. Retrieved August 19, 2022, from http://www.hartford-hwp.com/archives/45a/249.html
9 Bluestein, J. (2008). *The win-win classroom: A fresh and positive look at classroom management*. Corwin Press.

CONCLUSION

With so many concerns within the field of teaching—teacher shortages, bureaucratic interference, poor student engagement and motivation—it can feel as if the entangled mess that is education reform in the most prosperous country on the globe cannot be undone.[1] If anything, education reforms seem to tighten the knot of an already burdened system of inequity that is stretched too thin.[2] Unlike the boy with his finger in the dike, realistically, patchwork seldom recovers pervasive structural damage, particularly when the damage is deeply rooted and the load on that structure is voluminous. Dr. Martin Luther King, Jr., said every person, in this case every educator and education policy maker, is obliged to decide whether he or she will "walk in the light of creative altruism or in the darkness of destructive selfishness." Based on Freire's premise that it is impossible to teach without the capacity to love, I do not believe that our educational system will ever repair the historical or contemporary damage it has caused students and teachers until its stakeholders—educators—address the loveless and imperialistic approach it has taken to teaching and learning, a commodification of minds and bodies that more accurately serves commercialism rather than a democratic society.[3]

Redefining love as it informs teaching and learning, healing its watered down misuse within the general lexicon, hopefully gives educators a reflective and reflexive pause to contemplate upon our current state as a manifestation of our past behaviors and then to act carefully and lovingly to recover our craft, our students, and ultimately our society towards wholeness and harmony.[4] Agape as a curricular and pedagogical practice is reflective, calling us to consider how our political, economic, and social experiences shape and redefine who we are as educators.[5] It is equally reflexive when we embrace a diverse spectrum of worldviews that challenge us as educators to come outside of ourselves and question the sources of our own identities—biased thoughts, attitudes, values, assumptions, and actions—that affect our relationships with our students and the learning environment we create for their benefit.[6]

In the context of the historical and contemporary development of U.S. education, particularly in light of current curricular and pedagogical reforms, a curriculum of agape beckons us to examine the ways in which our social and professional systems have limited our understandings of love and its impact on our behavior as pedagogues, as well as the learning outcomes of our students. It calls educators to question how social realities in teaching, born out of our Apprenticeships of Observation, formal training, and field experiences have shaped our professional onto-epistemologies towards a curriculum of anti-love, contradicting the type of supportive, socially driven learning environment that effectively develops the whole child as well as a healthy society.[7] As educators, we must recognize that we are actively responsible for shaping our surroundings via the classroom, surroundings that have a direct and multidimensional connection back to us as individuals.[8] When our students suffer, we suffer, and when all is well with our students, all is well with society and us.[9] It is essential to our collective well-being that educators critically assess the way we are experienced and perceived by our students and revise a more ethical, democratic, and humane way of being and relating to our classrooms through love.[10]

Notes

1 Buddin & Zimmer, R. (2005). Student achievement in charter schools: A complex picture. *Journal of Policy Analysis and Management*, 24(2), 351–371. https://doi.org/10.1002/pam.20093.

Cajete, G. (1994). *Look to the mountain: An ecology of indigenous education*. ERIC.

Dove, M. K. (2004). Teacher attrition: A critical American and international education issue. *Delta Kappa Gamma Bulletin*, 71(1).

Edelman, M. W. (2009). The cradle to prison pipeline: America's new apartheid. *Harvard Journal of African American Public Policy*, 15(Summer Issue), 67–68.

Flannery, M. E. (2019). *The epidemic of anxiety among today's students*. NEA. Retrieved November 11, 2021, from https://www.nea.org/nea-today/all-news-articles/epidemic-anxiety-among-todays-students.

Horowitz, J. M., & Graf, N. (2020, May 30). *Most U.S. teens see anxiety, depression as major problems*. Pew Research Center's Social & Demographic Trends Project. Retrieved November 11, 2021, from https://www.pewresearch.org/social-trends/2019/02/20/most-u-s-teens-see-anxiety-and-depression-as-a-major-problem-among-their-peers/.

Johnson, S. (2020). *Afrocentricity: Student voices on African American identity in multicultural education reform*. The University of Texas at San Antonio.

Ladson-Billings, G. (2006). From the achievement gap to the education debt: Understanding achievement in U.S. schools. *Educational Researcher, 35*(7), 3–12.

Pinar, W. (2004). *What is curriculum theory?*. Routledge.

Sass, D. A., Flores, B. B., Claeys, L., & Pérez, B. (2012). Identifying personal and contextual factors that contribute to attrition rates for Texas public school teachers. *Education Policy Analysis Archives/Archivos Analíticos de Políticas Educativas, 20*, 1–26.

2 Op. Cit., Buddin & Zimmer, R. (2005).

Op. Cit., Dove (2004).

Op. Cit., Edelman (2009).

Op. Cit., Ladson-Billings (2006).

Op. Cit., Pinar (2004).

Op. Cit., Sass et al. (2012).

3 Darder, A. (2011). Chapter 9: Teaching as an act of love: Reflections on Paulo Freire and his contributions to our lives and our work. *Counterpoints, 418*, 179–194.

Freire, P. (2005). *Teachers as cultural workers: Letters to those who dare teach with new commentary by Peter McLaren, Joe L. Kincheloe*. Westview Press.

Gordon, B. M. (1986). The use of emancipatory pedagogy in teacher education. *The Journal of Educational Thought (JET)/Revue de la Pensée Educative*, 59–66.

Nouri, A., & Sajjadi, S. M. (2014). Emancipatory pedagogy in practice: Aims, principles and curriculum orientation. *The International Journal of Critical Pedagogy, 5*(2).

4 Bolton, G. (2010). *Reflective practice: Writing and professional development*. Sage Publications.

Robinson-Morris, D. W. (2018). *Ubuntu and Buddhism in higher education: An ontological (re) thinking*. Routledge.

5 Op. Cit., Bolton (2010).

Freire, P. (1993). *Pedagogy of the oppressed* (New Rev 20th-Anniversary ed.): New York: Continuum.

6 Op. Cit., Bolton (2010).

Op. Cit., Robinson-Morris (2018).

7 Op. Cit., Bolton (2010).

Boyd, A., Gorham, J. J., Justice, J. E., & Anderson, J. L. (2013). Examining the apprenticeship of observation with preservice teachers: The practice of blogging to facilitate autobiographical reflection and critique. *Teacher Education Quarterly, 40*(3), 27–49.

Op. Cit., Freire (1993).

Fromm, E. (2000). *The art of loving: The centennial edition*. A&C Black.

8   Op. Cit., Bolton (2010).

   Forbes, J. D. (2001) Indigenous Americans: Spirituality and ecos. *Daedalus: Journal of the American Academy of Arts & Sciences*. Retrieved May 26, 2021, from www.amacad.org/publication/indigenous-americans-spirituality-and-ecos.

   Lipner, J. (1998). Capturing gods: The god of love and the love of god in Christian and Hindu tradition. *Boardman Lectureship in Christian Ethics, 3*. Retrieved May 26, 2021, from http://repository.upenn.edu/boardman/3.

   Op. Cit., Robinson-Morris (2018).

   Tshivhase, M. (2018). Love as the foundation of Ubuntu. *Synthesis Philosophica, 65*(1/2018), 197–208. https://doi.org/10.21464/sp33112.

9   Degruy-Leary, J. (2017). *Post-traumatic slave syndrome: America's legacy of enduring injury.* Portland, OR: Joy DeGruy Publications Inc.

   Op. Cit., Lipner (1998).

   Nhat Hanh, T., DeAntonis, J. (2014). *How to love.* United States: Parallax Press.

10 Op. Cit., Bolton (2010).

   Op. Cit., Freire (1993).

   Op. Cit., Fromm (2000).

GLOSSARY

Axiology—a philosophical study that justifies distinct value systems.

Banking—A concept coined by Paulo Freire to describe a pedagogy that assumes students come to us without prior knowledge, whose education upholds a prescribed sociocultural stratification.

Curriculum—The content that satisfies the scope and sequence of a course or set of courses. It encompasses the explicit, implicit and hidden knowledge and skills that a student should acquire along with the tools that measure the degree of mastery. Curriculum includes all materials, activities, lesson plans and benchmark standards.

Dialogue/Dialogical—referring or relating to a discussion.

Discursive—written or spoken discussion or debate around a topic.

Epistemology—a philosophical study that justifies knowledge and knowledge construction.

Instructional Design—the use of learning and instructional theories to develop an education program, inclusive of curriculum and pedagogy, that is based on the needs of learners.

Marginalized—a person or group rendered socially unimportant or disempowered.

Ontology—a philosophical study of the nature of being and becoming.

Pedagogy—All interactions between teachers and students that are intended to foster learning, including philosophies, approaches, methodologies and classroom design.

Praxis—an educator's ongoing ethical and moral practice of critical, self-reflective action related to curricular and pedagogical experiences.

Restorative—the process whereby interpersonal relationships are repaired and strengthened, most often in response to harm or an offense.

Sliding Signifier—a term in discourse analysis describing a referent with socially negotiable meaning.

Transformative—inspiring a deep and lasting, positive change in a person's perceptions, ideals or behaviors.

REFERENCES

2017–18 suspension rate. Suspension Rate—State (CA Dept of Education). (n.d.). Retrieved December 1, 2021, from https://data1.cde.ca.gov/dataquest/dqCensus/DisSuspRate.aspx-?year=2017-18&agglevel=State&cds=00.

A&E Television Networks. (n.d.). *The Hatfield & McCoy Feud.* History.com. Retrieved February 7, 2022, from https://www.history.com/shows/hatfields-and-mccoys/articles/the-hatfield-mccoy-feud

Aap-AACAP-Cha declaration of a national emergency in child and adolescent mental health. American Academy of Pediatrics. (2021, October 19). Retrieved January 5, 2022, from https://www.aap.org/en/advocacy/child-and-adolescent-healthy-mental-development/aap-aacap-cha-declaration-of-a-national-emergency-in-child-and-adolescent-mental-health/?campaign_id=9&emc=edit_nn_20220104&instance_id=49344&nl=the-morning®i_id=86340798&segment_id=78602&te=1&user_id=d88a92611aab0bb98a785ee5af35f796.

Abi-Raad, M. (2019). Western organizational theories: Middle Eastern style: How much do you know about the culture. *The Journal of Organizational Management Studies,* 2019, 1–16.

Abo-Zena, M. M., Sahli, B., & Tobias-Nahi, C. S. (2009). Testing the courage of their convictions: Muslim youth respond to stereotyping, hostility, and discrimination. In *Muslim voices in school* (pp. 1–26). Brill Sense.

Adams, C. (2020). *Not all Black people are African American: Here's the difference.* CBS News. Retrieved November 11, 2021, from https://www.cbsnews.com/news/not-all-black-people-are-african-american-what-is-the-difference/.

Ali, S. (2019). A second-class workforce: How neoliberal policies and reforms undermined the educational profession. *Journal of Curriculum and Teaching, 8*(3), 102–110.

Amaya, R. (2004). Mañana Yo me voy con Cristo. *Para ti lo mejor.* Berea Music.

Amidon, J. (2013). Teaching mathematics as agape: Responding to oppression with unconditional love. *Journal of urban mathematics education, 6*(1), 19–27.

Apple, M. W. (2004). *Ideology and curriculum* (3rd ed.). New York: RoutledgeFalmer.

Apple, M. W. (2017). *Cultural and economic reproduction in education: Essays on class, ideology and the state* (Vol. 53). Routledge.

Apple, M. W., & Beane, J. A. (2007). *Democratic schools: Lessons in powerful education.* Heinemann.

Arabic customs and traditions. Arab Academy. (2017, May 15). Retrieved February 9, 2022, from https://www.arabacademy.com/arabic-customs-traditions/

Armstrong, K., Rose, A., Peters, N., Long, J. A., McMurphy, S., & Shea, J. A. (2006). Distrust of the health care system and self-reported health in the United States. *Journal of General Internal Medicine, 21*(4), 292–297.

Armstrong, K., Ravenell, K. L., McMurphy, S., & Putt, M. (2007). Racial/ethnic differences in physician distrust in the United States. *American Journal of Public Health, 97*(7), 1283–1289.

Aronson, J. (2002). Stereotype threat: Contending and coping with unnerving expectations. In *Improving academic achievement* (pp. 279–301). Academic Press.

Aronson, J., Quinn, D. M., & Spencer, S. J. (1998). Stereotype threat and the academic underperformance of minorities and women. In *Prejudice* (pp. 83–103). Academic Press.

Arredondo, P., Gallardo-Cooper, M., Delgado-Romero, E. A., & Zapata, A. L. (2015). Latino worldviews and cultural values. *Culturally Responsive Counseling with Latinas/os,* 15–30. https://doi.org/10.1002/9781119221609.ch2

Au, W. (2017). When multicultural education is not enough. *Multicultural Perspectives, 19*(3), 147–150. https://doi.org/10.1080/15210960.2017.1331741.

Au, W., Brown, A. L., & Calderón, D. (2016). *Reclaiming the multicultural roots of US curriculum: Communities of color and official knowledge in education.* Teachers College Press.

Awad, G. H. (2010). The impact of acculturation and religious identification on perceived discrimination for Arab/Middle Eastern Americans. *Cultural Diversity and Ethnic Minority Psychology, 16*(1), 59.

Baker, M. (2012). Modernity/coloniality and Eurocentric education: Towards a post-Occidental self-understanding of the present. *Policy Futures in Education, 10*(1), 4–22. https://doi.org/10.2304/pfie.2012.10.1.4.

Balingit, M., & Dam, A. V. (2019). *U.S. students continue to lag behind peers in East Asia and Europe in reading, math and science, exams show.* The Washington Post. Retrieved November 11, 2021, from https://www.washingtonpost.com/local/education/us-students-continue-to-lag-behind-peers-in-east-asia-and-europe-in-reading-math-and-science-exams-show/2019/12/02/e9e3b37c-153d-11ea-9110-3b34ce1d92b1_story.html.

Beachum, & Gullo, G. L. (2020). School leadership: Implicit bias and social justice. In *Handbook on promoting social justice in education* (pp. 429–454). Springer International Publishing. https://doi.org/10.1007/978-3-030-14625-2_66

Beane, J. A. (2005). *A reason to teach: Creating classrooms of dignity and hope: The power of the democratic way.* Heinemann Educational Books.

Belgrave, F. Z., & Brevard, J. K. (2015). *African American boys: Identity, culture, and development* (2015 ed.). New York, NY: Springer.

Bergstrom, A., Cleary, L. M., & Peacock, T. D. (2003). *The seventh generation: Native students speak about finding the good path.* ERIC.

Berk, R. A. (2000). Does humor in course tests reduce anxiety and improve performance? *College Teaching, 48*(4), 151–158. https://doi.org/10.1080/87567550009595834

Beyer, L. E. (1996). *Creating democratic classrooms: The struggle to integrate theory and practice* (The practitioner inquiry series). ERIC.

Bluestein, J. (2008). *The win-win classroom: A fresh and positive look at classroom management.* Corwin Press.

Bolton, G. (2010). *Reflective practice: Writing and professional development.* Sage Publications.

Boyd, A., Gorham, J. J., Justice, J. E., & Anderson, J. L. (2013). Examining the apprenticeship of observation with preservice teachers: The practice of blogging to facilitate autobiographical reflection and critique. *Teacher Education Quarterly, 40*(3), 27–49.

Brayboy. (2005). Toward a tribal critical race theory in education. *The Urban Review, 37*(5), 425–446. https://doi.org/10.1007/s11256-005-0018-y

Brown, K. D. (2013). Trouble on my mind: Toward a framework of humanizing critical sociocultural knowledge for teaching and teacher education. *Race Ethnicity and Education, 16*(3), 316–338.

Brown, K. D., Brown, A. L., & Grant, C. A. (2015). *Black intellectual thought in education.* Routledge.

Buddin, & Zimmer, R. (2005). Student achievement in charter schools: A complex picture. *Journal of Policy Analysis and Management, 24*(2), 351–371. https://doi.org/10.1002/pam.20093

Cajete, G. (1994). *Look to the mountain: An ecology of indigenous education.* ERIC.

Centers for Disease Control and Prevention. (2021). *Facts about suicide.* Centers for Disease Control and Prevention. Retrieved November 10, 2021, from https://www.cdc.gov/suicide/facts/index.html.

Chapman, G. (2009). *The five love languages: How to express heartfelt commitment to your mate.* Moody Publishers.

Chapman, G. D. (2010). *The five love languages of teenagers: The secret to loving teens effectively.* Moody Publishers.

Chapman, G., & Campbell, R. (2008). *The five love languages of children.* Moody Publishers.

Chapter four: The African Ubuntu philosophy. (n.d.). Retrieved January 4, 2022, from https://repository.up.ac.za/bitstream/handle/2263/28706/04chapter4.pdf?sequence=5

Cheng, Y. C. (1996). Relation between teachers' professionalism and job attitudes, educational outcomes, and organizational factors. *The Journal of Educational Research, 89*(3), 163–171. https://doi.org/10.1080/00220671.1996.9941322.

Clark, C. (2002). Effective multicultural curriculum transformation across disciplines. *Multicultural Perspectives, 4*(3), 37–46.

Cleary, L. M., & Peacock, T. D. (1998). *Collected wisdom: American Indian education.* ERIC.

Contrera, J. (2018). *A boy tried to kill himself by jumping from a highway bridge: He killed someone else instead.* The Washington Post. Retrieved November 10, 2021, from https://www.was hingtonpost.com/news/local/wp/2018/12/13/feature/the-boy-on-the-bridge/.

Copple, C., & Bredekamp, S. (2009). *Developmentally appropriate practice in early childhood programs serving children from birth through age 8.* National Association for the Education of Young Children. 1313 L Street NW Suite 500, Washington, DC 22205-4101.

Corbin, J., & Strauss, A. (2008). *Basics of qualitative research (3rd ed.): Techniques and procedures for developing grounded theory.* Thousand Oaks: SAGE Publications, Inc.

Cowen-Fletcher, J., & Melia, J. (1994). *It takes a village.* New York, NY: Scholastic.

Cox, J. W., & Rich, S. (2022, January 2). *'please help me': Kids with guns fueled a record number of school shootings in 2021.* The Washington Post. Retrieved January 5, 2022, from https:// www.washingtonpost.com/dc-md-va/2021/12/31/2021-school-shootings-record/?campaign _id=9&emc=edit_nn_20220104&instance_id=49344&nl=the-morning®i_id=86340 798&segment_id=78602&te=1&user_id=d88a92611aab0bb98a785ee5af35f796

Crozier, W. R. (2004). Recollections of schoolteachers' nicknames. *Names, 52*(2), 83–99.

Cruickshank, D. R., Jenkins, D. B., & Metcalf, K. K. (1995). *The act of teaching.* New York: McGraw-Hill.

Curos, G. (n.d.). *What makes a master teacher.* George Couros. https://georgecouros.ca/blog/ archives/9978

Curtin S. C. (2020). State suicide rates among adolescents and young adults aged 10–24: United States, 2000–2018. *National Vital Statistics Reports, 69*(11). Hyattsville, MD: National Center for Health Statistics. 2020.

Darder, A. (2011). Chapter 9: Teaching as an act of love: Reflections on Paulo Freire and his contributions to our lives and our work. *Counterpoints, 418,* 179–194.

Darder, A. (2015). *Culture and power in the classroom: Educational foundations for the schooling of bicultural students.* Routledge.

Darder, A. (2017). *Reinventing Paulo Freire: A pedagogy of love.* Taylor & Francis.

Darder, A. (2019). *Decolonizing interpretive research: A subaltern methodology for social change* (1st ed.). Routledge.

Dee, T. S. (2004). Teachers, race, and student achievement in a randomized experiment. *The Review of Economics and Statistics, 86*(1), 195–210. https://doi.org/10.1162/00346530432 3023750.

Degruy-Leary, J. (2017). *Post-traumatic Slave Syndrome: America's legacy of enduring injury.* Portland, OR: Joy DeGruy Publications Inc.

De Klerk, V., & Bosch, B. (1999). *Nicknames as evidence of verbal playfulness.* Multilingua, 18(1), 1–16. https://doi.org/10.1515/mult.1999.18.1.1

Deloria, V., Deloria Jr, V., & Wildcat, D. (2001). *Power and place: Indian education in America.* Fulcrum Publishing.

Delpit, L. (1995). *Other people's children: Cultural conflict in the classroom.* New York: New Press.

Delpit, L. (2013). *"Multiplication Is for White people": Raising expectations for other people's children.* New York, USA: The New Press.

De Mente, B. L. (2016). *Etiquette guide to China: Know the rules that make the difference!.* Tuttle Publishing.

DeSilver, D. (2020). *U.S. academic achievement lags that of many other countries.* Pew Research Center. Retrieved November 11, 2021, from https://www.pewresearch.org/fact-tank/2017/02/15/u-s-students-internationally-math-science/.

Di Marco, M., Venter, O., Possingham, H. P., & Watson, J. E. (2018). Changes in human footprint drive changes in species extinction risk. *Nature communications, 9*(1), 1–9.

Donnelly, D. F., McGarr, O., & O'Reilly, J. (2014). 'Just Be Quiet and Listen to Exactly What He's Saying': Conceptualising power relations in inquiry-oriented classrooms. *International Journal of Science Education, 36*(12), 2029–2054.

Dorn, E., Hancock, B., Sarakatsannis, J., & Viruleg, E. (2020). COVID-19 and student learning in the United States: The hurt could last a lifetime. *McKinsey & Company, 1,* 1–9.

Dove, M. K. (2004). Teacher attrition: A critical American and international education issue. *Delta Kappa Gamma Bulletin, 71*(1), 8–30.

Du Bois, W. E. B. (2009). *Souls of Black folk.* MobileReference.com.

Dustova, G., & Cotton, S. (2015). Classroom management strategies. *The CTE Journal, 3*(2), 32.

Dutton, J. (2021, June 11). Critical race theory is banned in these states. Newsweek. Retrieved January 12, 2022, from https://www.newsweek.com/critical-race-theory-banned-these-states-1599712

Edelman, M. W. (2009). The cradle to prison pipeline: America's new apartheid. *Harvard Journal of African American Public Policy, 15*(Summer Issue), 67–68.

Faircloth, S. C., & Tippeconnic, J. W. (2009). *The dropout/graduation crisis among American Indian and Alaska native students: Failure to respond places the future of native peoples at risk.* Civil Rights Project/Proyecto Derechos Civiles. Retrieved December 1, 2021, from https://eric.ed.gov/?ff1=eduHigh%2BSchools&q=source%3A%22civil%22%2B-source%3A%22center%22%2B-source%3A%22perspective%22%2B-source%3A%22arts%22&id=ED511323.

Fisher, M. H., & Crawford, B. (2020). "From School of Crisis to Distinguished": Using Maslow's hierarchy in a rural underperforming school. *The Rural Educator (Fort Collins, Colo.), 41*(1), 8–19.

Flannery, M. E. (2019). *The epidemic of anxiety among today's students.* NEA. Retrieved November 11, 2021, from https://www.nea.org/nea-today/all-news-articles/epidemic-anxiety-among-todays-students.

Flinders, D., & Thornton, S. (2013). *The curriculum studies reader* (4th ed.). New York: Routledge.

Forbes, J. D. (2001). Indigenous Americans: Spirituality and ecos. *Daedalus: Journal of the American Academy of Arts & Sciences.* Retrieved May 26, 2021, from www.amacad.org/publication/indigenous-americans-spirituality-and-ecos.

Freire, P. (1993). *Pedagogy of the oppressed* (New Rev 20th-Anniversary ed.): New York: Continuum.

Freire, P. (2005). *Teachers as cultural workers: Letters to those who dare teach with new commentary by Peter McLaren, Joe L. Kincheloe.* Westview Press.

Fromm, E. (2000). *The art of loving: The centennial edition.* A&C Black.

Gallardo, E. V. (1994). Hierarchy and discrimination: Tracking in public schools. *Chicano-Latino L. Rev., 15,* 74.

García, E., & Weiss, E. (2019). *U.S. schools struggle to hire and retain teachers: The second report in 'The perfect storm in the teacher labor market' series.* Economic Policy Institute. Retrieved November 10, 2021, from https://www.epi.org/publication/u-s-schools-struggle-to-hire-and-retain-teachers-the-second-report-in-the-perfect-storm-in-the-teacher-labor-market-series/.

Gatto, J. T. (2010). *Weapons of mass instruction: A schoolteacher's journey through the dark world of compulsory schooling.* New Society Publishers.

Gatto, J. T. (2017). *Dumbing us down: The hidden curriculum of compulsory schooling.* New Society Publishers.

Gay, G. (2018). *Culturally responsive teaching: Theory, research, and practice.* Teachers College Press.

Ghaljaie, F., Naderifar, M., & Goli, H. (2017). Snowball sampling: A purposeful method of sampling in qualitative research. *Strides in Development of Medical Education* (online), *14*(3). https://doi.org/10.5812/sdme.67670

Gill, J. H. (2002). *Native American worldviews an introduction.* By Jerry H. Gill. Amherst, NewYork: Humanity Books, 2002.

Giroux, H. A. (2004). Critical pedagogy and the postmodern/modern divide: Towards a pedagogy of democratization. *Teacher Education Quarterly, 31*(1), 31–47.

Giroux, H. A., & Giroux, S. S. (2006). Challenging neoliberalism's new world order: The promise of critical pedagogy. *Cultural Studies ↔ Critical Methodologies, 6*(1), 21–32. https://doi.org/10.1177/1532708605282810.

Goldberg, J. (2016, July 30). *It takes a village to determine the origins of an African proverb.* Goats and Soda. Retrieved November 11, 2021, from https://www.npr.org/sections/goatsandsoda/2016/07/30/487925796/it-takes-a-village-to-determine-the-origins-of-an-african-proverb.

Gordon, B. M. (1986). The use of emancipatory pedagogy in teacher education. *The Journal of Educational Thought (JET)/Revue de la Pensée Educative,* 59–66.

Graybill, L. S. (2002). *Truth and reconciliation in South Africa: Miracle or model?.* Lynne Rienner Publishers.

Gregory, A., Skiba, R. J., & Mediratta, K. (2017). Eliminating disparities in school discipline: A framework for intervention. *Review of Research in Education, 41*(1), 253–278.

Grossman, P. L., Smagorinsky, P., & Valencia, S. (1999). Appropriating tools for teaching English: A theoretical framework for research on learning to teach. *American Journal of Education, 108*(1), 1–29.

Grubin, D. (2010). *Death & legacy, part 2 | The Buddha.* PBS. Retrieved May 27, 2021, from https://www.youtube.com/watch?v=XW_JmF7OF-Y.

Guru purnima (2021). *Date, history, importance and significance.* The Indian Express. (2021, July 23). Retrieved January 4, 2022, from https://indianexpress.com/article/lifestyle/life-style/guru-purnima-2021-date-history-importance-and-significance-7393152/

Guy-Evans, O. (2020). *Bronfenbrenner's ecological systems theory.* Bronfenbrenner's Ecological Systems Theory | Simply Psychology. Retrieved November 10, 2021, from https://www.simplypsychology.org/Bronfenbrenner.html.

Hale, J. E. (1982). *Black children, their roots, culture, and learning styles.* Provo, Utah: Brigham Young University Press.

Hall, S. (2017). *The fateful triangle: Race*, ethnicity, nation. Harvard University Press.

Hall, S. (2018). *Essential essays, volume 1: Foundations of cultural studies*. Duke University Press.

Hammond, Z. (2014). *Culturally responsive teaching and the brain: Promoting authentic engagement and rigor among culturally and linguistically diverse students*. Corwin Press.

Haynes, N. M., Emmons, C., & Ben-Avie, M. (1997). School climate as a factor in student adjustment and achievement. *Journal of Educational and Psychological Consultation, 8*(3), 321–329.

Healey, J. (1998). *It takes a whole village to raise a child*. African Proverb of the Month. Retrieved 2021, from https://afriprov.org/.

Helfenbein, R. J. (2021). *Critical geographies of education: Space, place, and curriculum inquiry*. Routledge.

Hernandez, F., McPhetres, J., & Hughes, J. (2021). *Using adolescent perceptions of misconduct to help educational leaders identify and respond to sexual misconduct*. SAGE Open, 57(4). https://doi.org/10.1177/2158244021997419.

Horowitz, J. M., & Graf, N. (2020, May 30). *Most U.S. teens see anxiety, depression as major problems*. Pew Research Center's Social & Demographic Trends Project. Retrieved November 11, 2021, from https://www.pewresearch.org/social-trends/2019/02/20/most-u-s-teens-see-anxiety-and-depression-as-a-major-problem-among-their-peers/.

Hunter, R. C., & Donahoo, S. (2002). Discrimination in tracking and specialized education programs. In *Challenges of urban education and efficacy of school reform*. Emerald Group Publishing Limited.

Hurst, M. (2021). *'my baby told me he was tired': First-grader who killed himself may have been bullied to death, parents say*. kens5.com. Retrieved November 11, 2021, from https://www.kens5.com/article/news/community/first-grader-death/273-bf2203fa-e368-4bfe-8f84-c2770fc49a9d.

Huynh, V. W. (2012). Ethnic microaggressions and the depressive and somatic symptoms of Latino and Asian American adolescents. *Journal of youth and adolescence, 41*(7), 831–846.

Ingersoll, R. M., & Smith, T. M. (2003). The wrong solution to the teacher shortage. *Educational Leadership, 60*(8), 30.

Irvine, J. J. (2003). *Educating teachers for diversity: Seeing with a cultural eye*. New York: Teachers College Press.

Jaffe, P., Straatman, A., Harris, B., Georges, A., Vink, K., & Reif, K. (2013). Emerging trends in teacher sexual misconduct in Ontario 2007–2012. *Education & Law Journal, 23*(1), 19–39.

Jelinek, L., Jacobsen, D., Kellner, M., Larbig, F., Biesold, K. H., Barre, K., & Moritz, S. (2006). Verbal and nonverbal memory functioning in posttraumatic stress disorder (PTSD). *Journal of Clinical and Experimental Neuropsychology, 28*(6), 940–948.

Johnson, S. C. (2019). U.S. education and the persistence of slavery. *Journal of Curriculum and Pedagogy*, 1–20. https://doi.org/10.1080/15505170.2019.1618757.

Johnson, S. (2020). *Afrocentricity: Student voices on African American identity in multicultural education reform*. The University of Texas at San Antonio.

Johnson, K., & Williams, L. (2015). *When treating all the kids the same is the real problem*. SAGE Publications, Ltd., https://dx.doi.org/10.4135/9781452286914

Johnston-Parsons, M., Wilson, M., & The Teachers at Park Street Elementary (2007). *Success stories from failing school: Teachers living under the shadow of NCLB*. Charlotte, NC: Information Age.

Joselowsky, F. (2007). Youth engagement, high school reform, and improved learning outcomes: Building systemic approaches for youth engagement. *NASSP Bulletin, 91*(3), 257–276. https://doi.org/10.1177/0192636507306133.

Kayi-Aydar. (2018). Teaching and learning styles in Middle-Eastern cultures. In *The TESOL Encyclopedia of English language teaching* (pp. 1–5). John Wiley & Sons, Inc. https://doi.org/10.1002/9781118784235.eelt0800

Khanna, N. (2010). "If you're half Black, you're just Black": Reflected appraisals and the persistence of the one-drop rule. *The Sociological Quarterly, 51*(1), 96–121.

Kilenyi, E. (2001). *Pregúntale A Las Estrellas*. Hal Leonard Corporation (Original work published 1917).

King, J. E. (1991). Dysconscious racism: Ideology, identity, and the miseducation of teachers. *The Journal of Negro Education, 60*(2), 133–146. https://doi.org/10.2307/2295605

King, J. E., & Swartz, E. E. (2015). *The Afrocentric praxis of teaching for freedom: Connecting culture to learning*. Routledge.

King, M. L. (2012). *A gift of love: Sermons from strength to love and other preachings*. Beacon Press.

Kleinfeld, J. (1975). Effective teachers of Eskimo and Indian students. *The School Review, 83*(2), 301–344.

Kline, T. (n.d.). *Applying Maslow's hierarchy of needs in our classrooms*. ChangeKidsLives. Retrieved November 11, 2021, from http://www.changekidslives.org/actions-4.

Kohli, R., & Solórzano, D. G. (2012). Teachers, please learn our names!: Racial microaggressions and the K-12 classroom. *Race Ethnicity and Education, 15*(4), 441–462.

Kridel, C. (2010). Currere. In *Encyclopedia of curriculum studies* (Vol. 1, pp. 178–178). SAGE Publications, Inc., https://www.doi.org/10.4135/9781412958806.n102

Ladson-Billings, G. (1995). But that's just good teaching! The case for culturally relevant pedagogy. *Theory Into Practice, 34*(3), 159–165. https://doi.org/10.1080/00405849509543675.

Ladson-Billings, G. (2006). From the achievement gap to the education debt: Understanding achievement in U.S. schools. *Educational Researcher, 35*(7), 3–12.

Ladson-Billings, G. (2009). *The dreamkeepers: Successful teachers of African American children*. Somerset, USA: Wiley.

Ladson-Billings, G. (2014). Culturally relevant pedagogy 2.0: aka the remix. *Harvard Educational Review, 84*(1), 74–84.

Larson, C. L., & Ovando, C. J. (2001). *The color of bureaucracy: The politics of equity in multicultural school communities*. Taylor and Francis Group, 7625 Empire Dr., Florence, KY 41042.

Lave, J., & Wenger, E. (1991). *Situated learning: Legitimate peripheral participation*. Cambridge, UK: Cambridge University Press. Reading Chapters 1 and 2.

Leavy, A. M., McSorley, F. A., & Boté, L. A. (2007). An examination of what metaphor construction reveals about the evolution of preservice teachers' beliefs about teaching and learning. *Teaching and Teacher Education, 23*(7), 1217–1233.

Lee, C. D., & Smagorinsky, P. (2000). *Vygotskian perspectives on literacy research: Constructing meaning through collaborative inquiry*. New York: Cambridge University Press.

Lengel, T., & Kuczala, M. (2010). *The kinesthetic classroom: Teaching and learning through movement.* Corwin Press.

Leslie, P. L., & Skipper, J. K. (1990). Toward a theory of nicknames: A case for socio-onomastics. *Names, 38*(4), 273–282.

Li, G. (2005). Other people's success: Impact of the "model minority" myth on underachieving Asian students in North America. *KEDI Journal of Educational Policy, 2*(1) 69–86.

Lipner, J. (1998). Capturing gods: The god of love and the love of god in Christian and Hindu tradition. *Boardman Lectureship in Christian Ethics, 3.* Retrieved May 26, 2021, from http://repository.upenn.edu/boardman/3

Liskin-Gasparro, J. E. (1984). *The ACTFL proficiency guidelines: A historical perspective.*

Logan, J., & Burdick-Will, J. (2016). School segregation, charter schools, and access to quality education. *Journal of Urban Affairs, 38*(3), 323–343. https://doi.org/10.1111/juaf.12246

Lopez, B. (September, 19, 2022). *Texas has banned more books than any other state, new report shows.* Texastrubnue.org, https://www.texastribune.org/2022/09/19/texas-book-bans/ accessed January 28, 2023.

Losen, D. J., Hodson, C. L., Keith II, M. A., Morrison, K., & Belway, S. (2015). *Are we closing the school discipline gap?* University of California. Los Angeles.

Malott, C. (2007). *A call to action: An introduction to education, philosophy, and Native North America* (Vol. 324): Peter Lang.

Manke, M. (1997). *Classroom power relations: Understanding student-teacher interaction.* Routledge.

Martin, A. J., & Collie, R. J. (2019). Teacher–student relationships and students' engagement in high school: Does the number of negative and positive relationships with teachers matter?. *Journal of Educational Psychology, 111*(5), 861.

Marvel, J., Lyter, D. M., Peltola, P., Strizek, G. A., Morton, B. A., & Rowland, R. (2007). *Teacher attrition and mobility: Results from the 2004–05 teacher follow-up survey. NCES 2007–307.* National Center for Education Statistics.

May, S., & Sleeter, C. E. (2010). *Critical multiculturalism: Theory and praxis.* Routledge.

Mayaka, B., & Truell, R. (2021). Ubuntu and its potential impact on the international social work profession. *International Social Work, 64*(5), 649–662.

McCarter, S. (2017). The school-to-prison pipeline: A primer for social workers. *Social Work, 62*(1), 53–61. https://doi.org/10.1093/sw/sww078.

McGowan, P. J. (2016). Mapping the terrestrial human footprint. *Nature, 537*(7619), 172–173.

Mcleod, S. (2016). *Albert Bandura's social learning theory.* Albert Bandura's Social Learning Theory | Simply Psychology. Retrieved November 10, 2021, from https://www.simplypsychology.org/bandura.html.

Meiners, E. R. (2010). *Right to be hostile: Schools, prisons, and the making of public enemies.* Routledge.

Merry, M., & New, W. (2008). Constructing an authentic self: The challenges and promise of African centered pedagogy. *American Journal of Education, 115*(1), 35–64. https://doi.org/10.1086/590675.

Miron, G., & Applegate, B. (2007). *Teacher attrition in charter schools.* East Lansing, MI: Great Lakes Center for Education Research and Practice.

Missler, C., & Missler, N. (2014). *The way of agape*. King's High Way Ministries.

Montero-Sieburth, M., & Villaruel, F. (2003). *Making invisible Latino adolescents visible: A critical approach to Latino diversity*. Routledge.

Montuoro, P., & Lewis, R. (2014). Student perceptions of misbehavior and classroom management. In *Handbook of classroom management* (pp. 354–372). Routledge.

Moradi, A. R., Doost, H. T. N., Taghavi, M. R., Yule, W., & Dalgleish, T. (1999). Everyday memory deficits in children and adolescents with PTSD: Performance on the Rivermead Behavioural Memory Test. *The Journal of Child Psychology and Psychiatry and Allied Disciplines, 40*(3), 357–361.

Morris, Z. A. (2015). Contemporary professional boundaries and their relationship with teacher and student well-being. In *Routledge international handbook of social psychology of the classroom* (pp. 400–410). Routledge.

Murrell Jr, P. C. (2002). *African-centered pedagogy: Developing schools of achievement for African American children*. SUNY Press.

Nanticoke Lenni-Lenape Tribal Nation. (2019). *Native American naming ceremonies. We are still here!* Retrieved November 11, 2021, from https://nlltribe.com/native-american-naming-ceremonies/.

Nasir, N. S. (2019). *"We dare say love": Supporting achievement in the educational life of Black boys*. New York, NY: Teachers College Press.

National Dropout Prevention Center. (2018). *Economic impacts of dropouts*. Retrieved from https://dropoutprevention.org/resources/statistics/quick-facts/economic-impacts-of-dropouts/

NCES-National Center for Education Statistics (2021). *Analyzing teacher mobility and retention: Guidance and considerations report 1–2*. Retrieved May 28, 2021, from https://nces.ed.gov/pubsearch/index.asp?HasSearched=1&searchcat2=subjectindex&L1=49&L2=19

Ndimande, B. S. (2018). The struggles against Fundamental Pedagogics in South Africa: Toward the pedagogy of common good. In N. Hobbel & B. Bales (Eds.), *Navigating the common good in teacher education policy: Critical and international perspectives* (pp. 128–145). New York: Routledge.

Neason, A. (2020). *Where have all the black and brown teachers gone?* The Hechinger Report. Retrieved November 23, 2021, from https://hechingerreport.org/black-brown-teachers-gone/.

Neill, A. S. (1960). *Summerhill; a radical approach to child rearing*. New York: Hart.

Nelson, B. (2013). *Elevating student voice: How to enhance student participation, citizenship and leadership*. Taylor and Francis.

New international version of the bible. (2021). NIV Bible Online. www.biblehub.com

Nhat Hanh, T., & DeAntonis, J. (2014). *How to love*. Berkeley, CA: Parallax Press.

Nieto, S. (2013). *Finding joy in teaching students of diverse backgrounds: Culturally responsive and socially just practices in U.S. classrooms*. Heinemann.

Noel, J. (2002). Education toward cultural shame: A century of Native American education. *The Journal of Educational Foundations, 16*(1), 19.

Noltemeyer, A., Bush, K., Patton, J., & Bergen, D. (2012). The relationship among deficiency needs and growth needs: An empirical investigation of Maslow's theory. *Children and Youth Services Review, 34*(9), 1862–1867. https://doi.org/10.1016/j.childyouth.2012.05.021

Nouri, A., & Sajjadi, S. M. (2014). Emancipatory pedagogy in practice: Aims, principles and curriculum orientation. *The International Journal of Critical Pedagogy, 5*(2), 76–87.

Ogbu, J. U. (1978). *Minority education and caste:The American system in cross-cultural perspective.* New York: Academic Press.

Owen, P. M., & Gillentine, J. (2011). Please touch the children: Appropriate touch in the primary classroom. *Early Child Development and Care, 181*(6), 857–868.

Patton, M. Q. (2002). *Qualitative research and evaluation methods.* Thousand Oakes, CA: Sage.

Payne, K. E., Philyaw, Z., Rabow, J., & Yazdanfar, S. (2018). Names: A new dimension of transformation. *Race Ethnicity and Education, 21*(4), 564–571.

Pinar, W. (2004). *What is curriculum theory?*: Routledge.

Pinar, W., Reynolds, W., Slattery, P., & Taubman, P. (2008). *Understanding curriculum: An introduction to the study of historical and contemporary curriculum discourses* (Vol. 17). Peter Lang.

Pines, A., & Gal, R. (2006). The effect of food on test anxiety. *Journal of Applied Social Psychology, 7*, 348–358. https://doi.org/10.1111/j.1559-1816.1977.tb00759.x.

Platt, T., Wagner, L., & Ruch, W. (2016). The association between class clown dimensions, school experiences and accomplishment. *Learning and Individual Differences, 51*, 327–332.

Polanin, M., & Vera, E. (2013). Bullying prevention and social justice. *Theory into Practice, 52*(4), 303–310.

Price, J. M. (2007). Democracy: A critical red ideal. *Journal of Thought, 42*(1/2), 9–25.

Price, M., Kallam, M., & Love, J. (2009). The learning styles of Native American students and implications for classroom practice. In *Eighth Native American symposium and film festival: Images, imaginations, and beyond.* Southeastern Oklahoma State University, pp 36–45. Retrieved from https://www.youthinarts.org/wp-content/uploads/2019/04/Native-Learning-Styles.pdf

Public Broadcasting Service. (n.d.). *PBS online: Only a teacher: Schoolhouse pioneers.* PBS. Retrieved November 10, 2021, from https://www.pbs.org/onlyateacher/john.html.

Racial/Ethnic enrollment in public schools. Coe—racial/ethnic enrollment in public schools. (2021). Retrieved December 1, 2021, from https://nces.ed.gov/programs/coe/indicator/cge.

Ragosta, J. (2014). *Virginia statute for establishing religious freedom* (1786). Retrieved from http://www.EncyclopediaVirginia.org/Virginia_Statute_for_Establishing_Religious_Freedom_1786.

Ramose, M. B. (2014). Ubuntu. In *Degrowth* (pp. 240–242). Routledge.

Red Shirt, D. (2015). *The Lakota children are called wakanyeja 'little sacred ones'.* Native American Times. Retrieved November 11, 2021, from https://nativetimes.com/index.php/life/commentary/11125-the-lakota-children-are-called-wakanyeja-little-sacred-ones.

Robinson-Morris, D. W. (2018). *Ubuntu and Buddhism in higher education: An ontological (re) thinking.* Routledge.

Rojas, L., & Liou, D. D. (2017). Social justice teaching through the sympathetic touch of caring and high expectations for students of color. *Journal of Teacher Education, 68*(1), 28–40.

Safi, O. (Ed.). (2018). *Radical love: Teachings from the Islamic mystical tradition*. Yale University Press.

Safi, O. (2020). *"God commands you to justice and Love": Islamic spirituality* . ⸺IIIT. Retrieved June 6, 2022, from https://iiit.org/wp-content/uploads/Omid-Safi-Final.pdf

Saldaña, J. (2016). *The coding manual for qualitative researchers* (3rd ed.). Los Angeles: SAGE.

Sass, D. A., Flores, B. B., Claeys, L., & Pérez, B. (2012). Identifying personal and contextual factors that contribute to attrition rates for Texas public school teachers. *Education Policy Analysis Archives/Archivos Analíticos de Políticas Educativas, 20*, 1–26.

Schwegler, A. (2007). Black ritual insulting in the Americas: On the art of "VociferaR" (Colombia), "Vacilar" (Ecuador) and "Snapping", "Sounding" or "Playing the Dozens" (USA). *Indiana, 24*, 107–155.

Seeman, M. (1976). The psychopathology of everyday names. *Psychology and Psychotherapy: Theory Research and Practice, 49*, 89–95. https://doi.org/10.1111/j.2044-8341.1976.tb02356.x.

Sexual abuse by teachers is on the rise—The Children's Center for Psychiatry, Delray Beach, FL. The Children's Center for Psychiatry, Psychology, & Related Services. (2021, August 23). Retrieved November 10, 2021, from https://childrenstreatmentcenter.com/sexual-abuse-teachers/.

Shakeshaft, C. (2013). *Know the warning signs of educator sexual misconduct*. Phi Delta Kappan. *2013; 94*(5), 8–13. https://doi.org/10.1177/003172171309400503.

Shaw, B. (1922). *Man and superman: A comedy and a philosophy*. Brentano's.

Smith-Maddox, R. (1999). The social networks and resources of African American eighth graders: Evidence from the National Education Longitudinal Study of 1988. *Adolescence, 34*(133), 169–170.

Stainton, R. J. (1998). Quantifier phrases, meaningfulness "in isolation", and ellipsis. *Linguistics and Philosophy, 21*(3), 311–340.

Stajkovic, A. D., & Luthans, F. (1998). Social cognitive theory and self-efficacy: Goin beyond traditional motivational and behavioral approaches. *Organizational Dynamics, 26*(4), 62–74.

Stephens, J. M., Rubie-Davies, C. M., & Watson, P. (2015). The role of meaning systems in the development of motivation. In *Routledge international handbook of social psychology of the classroom* (pp. 95–108). Routledge.

Stop Educator Sexual Abuse Misconduct and Exploitation [SESAME]. (n.d.). Retrieved November 10, 2021, from https://www.sesamenet.org/.

Strategies to reduce test anxiety. LSU Health New Orleans. (2021). Retrieved November 11, 2021, from https://nursing.lsuhsc.edu/AcademicSuccessProgram/StrategiesTestAnxiety.aspx#:~:text=Integrating%20relaxation%20techniques%20into%20your,Maintain%20a%20realistic%20viewpoint.

Talking circles overview. First Nations Pedagogy Online Project. (n.d.). Retrieved January 13, 2022, from https://firstnationspedagogy.ca/circletalks.html

Taylor, K. B., & Reynolds, D. J. (2019). Dissonance. In rethinking college student development theory using critical frameworks. *Journal of College and Character, 21*(3), 234–236.

Templeton, J. (1999). *Agape love: A tradition found in eight world religions.* Templeton Foundation Press.

Thapa, A., Cohen, J., Guffey, S., & Higgins-D'Alessandro, A. (2013). A review of school climate research. *Review of educational research, 83*(3), 357–385.

The social wolf. Living with Wolves. (2021, August 2). Retrieved January 22, 2022, from https://www.livingwithwolves.org/about-wolves/social-wolf/.

The state of Mental Health in America. Mental Health America. (2022). Retrieved January 22, 2022, from https://www.mhanational.org/issues/state-mental-health-america

Torres-Mackie, N. (2019). *Understanding name-based microaggressions.* Psychology Today. Retrieved November 11, 2021, from https://www.psychologytoday.com/intl/blog/underdog-psychology/201909/understanding-name-based-microaggressions.

Trojan, P., & Przemysław, T. (1984). *Ecosystem homeostasis.* Springer Science & Business Media.

Tshivhase, M. (2018). Love as the foundation of Ubuntu. *Synthesis Philosophica, 65*(1/2018), 197–208. https://doi.org/10.21464/sp33112.

United Tribes says every child sacred. Tribal College Journal of American Indian Higher Education. (2012, March 26). Retrieved November 11, 2021, from https://tribalcollegejournal.org/united-tribes-child-sacred/.

Vars, G. F. (1981). To touch or not to touch? That is the question!. *Middle School Journal, 12*(3), 14–17.

Vygotsky, L. (1997). Interaction between learning and development. In N. Gauvain & M. Cole (Eds.), *Readings on the development of children* (pp. 29–36). New York, NY: W.H. Freeman and Company.

Vygotsky, L. S., & Cole, M. (1978). *Mind in society: The development of higher psychological processes.* Cambridge: Harvard Univ. Press.

Walton, G. M., & Cohen, G. L. (2007). A question of belonging: Race, social fit, and achievement. *Journal of personality and social psychology, 92*(1), 82.

Ware, F. (2006). Warm demander pedagogy: Culturally responsive teaching that supports a culture of achievement for African American students. *Urban Education, 41*(4), 427–456.

Weissberg, R. P., Durlak, J. A., Domitrovich, C. E., & Gullotta, T. P. (2015). Social and emotional learning: Past, present, and future. In J. A. Durlak, C. E. Domitrovich, R. P. Weissberg, & T. P. Gullotta (Eds.), *Handbook of social and emotional learning: Research and practice* (pp. 3–19). The Guilford Press.

Westheimer, J. (2015). *What kind of a citizen: Educating our children for the common good.* New York: Teachers College.

Williams, C. S. (2011). *Combating teacher burnout—THE* Journal. Retrieved from https://thejournal.com/articles/2011/11/03/teacher-burnout.aspx

Willis, D. E., Andersen, J. A., Bryant-Moore, K., Selig, J. P., Long, C. R., Felix, H. C., ... & McElfish, P. A. (2021). COVID-19 vaccine hesitancy: Race/ethnicity, trust, and fear. *Clinical and Translational Science, 14*(6), 2200–2207.

Willis, J. (2010). The current impact of neuroscience on teaching and learning. In Sousa, D. A. (Ed.), *Mind, brain and education: Neuroscience implications for the classroom* (pp. 45–68). Solution Tree Press.

Wivestad, S. M. (2008). The educational challenges of agape and phronesis. *Journal of Philosophy of Education, 42*(2), 307–324. https://doi.org/10.1111/j.1467-9752.2008.00626.x.

Woodson, C. G. (1933). *The mis-education of the Negro.* Washington, D.C.: Associated Publishers.

Yard, E. (2021, June 17). *Emergency department visits for suspected suicide attempts among persons aged 12–25 years before and during the COVID-19 pandemic—United States, January 2019–May 2021.* Centers for Disease Control and Prevention. Retrieved January 5, 2022, from https://www.cdc.gov/mmwr/volumes/70/wr/mm7024e1.htm?campaign_id=9&emc=edit_nn_20220104&instance_id=49344&nl=the-morning®i_id=86340798&segment_id=78602&te=1&user_id=d88a92611aab0bb98a785ee5af35f796

Yeager, D. S., & Dweck, C. S. (2020). What can be learned from growth mindset controversies?. *American Psychologist, 75*(9), 1269.

Zehr, H. (2015). *The little book of restorative justice: Revised and updated.* Simon and Schuster.

Zirkel, P. A. (2000). Don't touch!. *NASSP Bulletin, 84*(614), 84–87.

Zou, I. (2021). *Texas Senate bill seeks to strip required lessons on people of color and women from "Critical race theory" law.* The Texas Tribune. Retrieved November 11, 2021, from https://www.texastribune.org/2021/07/09/texas-critical-race-theory-schools-legislation/.

NOTES ON CONTRIBUTORS

Special Contribution

Lauren Dones is a Master's student at Georgetown University, pursuing a degree in physiology. Her passions for educational justice and healthcare reform direct her work with children of color in economically disadvantaged communities, as well as the development of strategies for overcoming the hurdles that poorly impact access to our U.S. health system. She is a Bluford Health Leadership Institute Scholar and served as a research assistant to Dr. Stacy Johnson, investigating issues of curricular and pedagogical equity, diversity and inclusivity in education.

INDEX

www.ingramcontent.com/pod-product-compliance
Lightning Source LLC
Chambersburg PA
CBHW071243050326
40690CB00011B/2248